RAAF Base Uranquinty

(Judie Trotter)

EMPIRE AIRMEN STRIKE BACK

THE EMPIRE AIR TRAINING SCHEME AND 5SFTS, URANQUINTY

Peter Ilbery

Foreword & Dedication

Uranquinty is a small village in central New South Wales between Wagga Wagga and The Rock. During World War II, it was the nearest township to No. 5 Service Flying Training School or "Bar 20" as it was affectionately known to thousands of airmen and airwomen.

The appellation of "Bar 20" now seems obscure but it was a place returned to from leave, if not exactly with a feeling of pleasure, then, with a sense that a worthwhile job was being done there. Everyone was in some way contributing to keeping the kites[1] in the air which led at the end of each month to the highly visible output of 40 to 50 pilots for the war effort.

Some years ago on returning to Uranquinty, I was surprised and saddened to find no sign of a once bustling air force station. Enquiry at the village store revealed that at least once a week others, seeking something with which to empathise, would come in asking directions to the aerodrome. It would appear that there has long been a need to create a tangible focus for the pilots who earned their wings at 5SFTS, the instructors who trained them and the station personnel who supported this part of the Empire Air Training Scheme.

Going out along the Yarragunly road and turning towards the landmark of The Rock, the landscape begins to look familiar, reinforced some kilometres further on by recognition of the peeling white-painted station gates. Beyond, instead of a Royal Australian Air Force base, stretches a large empty paddock. Despite its return to farmland, in the imagination a straight road stretches beyond and the mind's eye fills in the once familiar details to left and right, and follows the road, going off before the parade ground, leading up a slight incline to the hangars and flights.

Turning around from this deserted village as if to leave through the main gates is to think of all those who had done so during 1941-45 and particularly those pilots who went out to fight and died. Each month beginning with 17 Course of the Empire Air Training Scheme in November 1941, trainee pilots came in from their elementary flying training schools and three months later, reduced in number and having received their wings, went out on postings. This book opens windows on where some of them went.

An appeal for a memorial has been answered by Wagga Council with the support of local bodies, former personnel of the base, the Royal Australian Air Force, and the Returned and Services League of Australia, together with a grant from the Local Commemorative Activities Fund (LCAF). Council agreed to the naming of a rest area opposite the Uranquinty store as Wirraway Park and for the erection there of permanent displays flanking a mark of respect to provide a focal point for the air base's history, otherwise being rapidly lost. At last a nostalgic visit will be rewarded with the feeling that all has not been forgotten.

In regard to the aerodrome itself, as with all visits to disused and dismantled aerodromes, one feels the need to do something but little of substance is possible. At "Bar 20" restoration of the main gates will symbolise those who went out and who did not survive.

This book is dedicated to the memory of 5SFTS, Uranquinty and especially to those of its pilots who served in the Royal Air Force and Royal Australian Air Force during the Second World War for whom, as is the nature of war in the air, there is no known grave:

Roll of Honour - Missing Memorials

18 Course
Atwell GJ, 411673; (27), P/O, 614 Sqn RAF, off Italy, 20- 4-44. Malta Missing Memorial.
Bell MH, 405995; (21), P/O, 19 Sqn RAF, Holland, 9- 9-44. Runnymede Missing Memorial.
Bull DWW, 409023; (21), F/S, 56 OTU RAF, Scotland, 27- 4-43. Runnymede Missing Memorial.
Markwell IA, 414054; (24), F/O, 452 Sqn RAAF, Netherlands East Indies, 24-12-44. Ambon Missing Memorial.
McRoberts BOK, 412563; (21), Sgt, 53 OTU RAF, United Kingdom, 3-11-42. Runnymede Missing Memorial.
Woodey JE, 411625; (24), W/O, 131 Sqn RAF, France, 7- 6-44. Runnymede Missing Memorial.

19 Course
Carter JW, 412912; (22), P/O, 137 Sqn RAF, United Kingdom, 1- 4-44. Runnymede Missing Memorial.
Dripps DC, 409392; (27), P/O, 550 Sqn RAF, Germany, 24-12-43. Runnymede Missing Memorial.
Fleming RC, 413113; (26), F/L, 101 Sqn RAF, Germany, 9- 7-43. Runnymede Missing Memorial.
Gilbert RD, 413188; (22), W/O, 181 Sqn RAF, France, 19- 8-44. Runnymede Missing Memorial.
Mason DW, 413220: (25), P/O, 198 Sqn RAF, France, 18- 6-44, Runnymede Missing Memorial.
Myers NL, 413088; (22), F/L, 242 Sqn RAF, off French Coast, 13- 8-44. Malta Missing Memorial.
Pearsall AL, 408266; (28), F/O, 16 Sqn RAF, English Channel, 8- 3-44. Runnymede Missing Memorial.

20 Course
Baetz HL, 414379; (20), F/S, 184 Sqn RAF, Atlantic, 12- 3-43. Runnymede Missing Memorial.
Ball E, 405991; (24), P/O, 4 Sqn IAF, Indian Area, 14- 8-44. Singapore Missing Memorial.
Bartlett SW, 405994; (19), F/S, 58 OTU RAF, Scotland, 5- 5-43. Runnymede Missing Memorial.
Coward CTG, 414003; (22), F/O, 42 Sqn RAF, India, 22-12-43. Singapore Missing Memorial.
Kewish WK, 414409; (21), W/O, 215 Sqn RAF, India, 3- 3-44. Singapore Missing Memorial.
Negus BL, 414072; (26), P/O, 207 Sqn RAF, Germany, 18-10-43. Runnymede Missing Memorial.
Steel TJ, 405701; (21), F/O, RAAF Survey Flight, off Queensland Coast, 23- 7-45. Sydney Missing Memorial.

21 Course
Boyce RF, 413520; (21), F/O, 78 Sqn RAF, off Dutch New Guinea Coast, 29-10-44. Lae Missing Memorial.

22 Course
Goodwin AG, 413985; (24), F/O, 2 Aircraft Depot RAAF, Morotai, 21- 9-45. Ambon Missing Memorial.

23 Course
Munro HC, 10941; (25), F/O, 4 Sqn RAAF, off New Guinea, 26-11-43. Lae Missing Memorial.
Pratten ME, 416994; (26), P/O, 463 Sqn RAAF, North West Europe, 22- 5-44. Runnymede Missing Memorial.
Wilson RE, 409624; (26), W/O, 450 Sqn RAAF, Yugoslavia, 23- 2-44. Malta Missing Memorial.

24 Course
Gilmore WE, 8685; (27), W/O, 78 Sqn RAAF, off Kai Is, 14-10-44. Ambon Missing Memorial.
Webb NE, 420726; (27), F/O, 463 Sqn RAAF, France, 4- 7-44. Runnymede Missing Memorial.

26 Course
Cowley JD, 421188; (23), F/O, 31 Sqn RAAF, North Borneo, 11- 6-45. Labuan Missing Memorial.
Hatcher IC, 417183; (20), F/O, 86 Sqn RAAF, off Merauke, 8- 9-43. Port Moresby Missing Memorial.
Keyes RJ, 420571; (21), W/O, 76 Sqn RAAF, New Guinea Area, 28- 1-45. Lae Missing Memorial.
Salter AJ, 414841; (22), F/S, 4 Sqn RAAF, New Guinea, 26-11-43. Lae Missing Memorial.
Saywell GW, 414962; (22), F/L, 2 AD RAAF, Kyushu, Japan, 18- 3-46. Labuan Missing Memorial.

27 Course
Balcombe GR, 420825; (22), F/O, 100 Sqn RAF, Germany, 15- 2-44. Runnymede Missing Memorial.
McDonald FG, 418154; (21), F/S, 23 Sqn RAAF, New Guinea, 31- 1-44, Lae Missing Memorial.

Walsh HJ, 421479; (20), F/S, 84 Sqn RAAF, Gulf of Carpentaria, 10- 3-44, Sydney Missing Memorial.

28 Course

Roantree N, 422300; (20), F/S, 76 Sqn RAAF, New Britain, 23- 9-43. Rabaul Missing Memorial.

29 Course

Armstrong BA, 423581; (22), P/O, 85 Sqn RAAF, off West Australian Coast, 3-10-43. Sydney Missing Memorial.

Heath LD, 423305; (21), P/O, 166 Sqn RAF, Baltic Sea, 30- 8-44. Runnymede Missing Memorial.

Richards JJ, 418466; (20), F/S, 21 Sqn RAAF, New Guinea, 5- 3-44. Lae Missing Memorial.

30 Course

Devine EN, 426556; (21), P/O, 622 Sqn RAF, Germany, 12- 2-44. Runnymede Missing Memorial.

31 Course

Wallace DJ, 429418; (20), P/O, 80 Sqn RAAF, New Guinea, 24- 8-44. Lae Missing Memorial.

32 Course

Mitchell WD, 422968; (21), P/O, 455 Sqn RAAF, North Sea, 8- 3-45. Runnymede Missing Memorial.

Regan LJA, 424798; (22), F/O, 80 Sqn RAAF, New Britain, 5- 4-44. Rabaul Missing Memorial.

33 Course

Klingner ACF, 425945; (26), P/O, 260 Sqn RAF, Adriatic Sea, 29- 4-45. Malta Missing Memorial.

Leamon FN, 425861; (21), W/O, 332 Sqn RAF, Germany, 25- 3-45. Runnymede Missing Memorial.

Parry RW, 434265; (20), F/S, 80 Sqn RAAF, New Guinea Area, 13- 1-45. Ambon Missing Memorial.

34 Course

Edmonds CJ, 419802; (21), F/S, 84 Sqn RAAF, Northern Territory Area, 23- 3-44. Sydney Missing Memorial.

Pitt AF, 432259; (22), W/O, 5 OTU RAAF, off Williamtown, 21- 9-45. Sydney Missing Memorial.

35 Course

Caddy PO, 432340: (20), F/S, 19 OTU RAF, United Kingdom Coast, 28- 8-44. Runnymede Missing Memorial.

37 Course

Brown RPS, 434615; (20), F/S, 78 Sqn RAAF, New Guinea Area, 10- 8-44. Lae Missing Memorial.

39 Course

Thornley NL, 34772; (22), F/S, 80 Sqn RAAF, Halmaheras, 14- 1-45. Ambon Missing Memorial.

Wedd CW, 35027; (23), F/S, 1654 Conversion Unit RAF, United Kingdom Coast, 12- 4-45. Runnymede Missing Memorial.

44 Course

Brown LE, 435439; (24), Sgt, 77 Sqn RAAF, Dutch New Guinea, 6-12-44. Lae Missing Memorial.

Eddison ED, 563; (24), F/L, 30 Sqn RAAF, New Guinea, 27-5-43, Lae Missing Memorial.

No gravestone in yew-dark churchyard
Shall mark their resting place;
Their bones lie in the forgotten corners
Of earth and sea.

Inscription on Runnymede Memorial
By Paul Scott

BANNER BOOKS

cknowledgements

The need for a mark of respect at Uranquinty has been clearly expressed by all those contacted and who have contacted me with a special interest in its history. I have been conscious of the importance attached by them to the preservation of the spirit of those times from the material entrusted to me and of my own frailty in attempting to encapsulate it in a book. Unhappily, the stories of those who passed through the gates of 5 Service Flying Training School in the early years have been few, and indeed more recent telling has been interrupted by age and illness. However we can all be grateful to those former personnel whose spoken and written words, garnered in the following pages, have given us some memories of 5SFTS and windows on where they went after 'Quinty. Those providing interviews and letters are listed under References.

Over a lengthy period, unstinted aid has been received from David Wilson, Janet Beck, Molly Angel and Richard Bain in researching the material held in the RAAF Historical Unit, Canberra. Although RAAF copyright applies to this material, permission has been given for its reproduction.

Group Captain Alan MacGregor, Air Adviser, British High Commission, Canberra obtained the aid of Mr Clive Richards of the United Kingdom Ministry of Defence (MOD) Air Historical Branch in locating and recalling from the United Kingdom Public Record Office, Kew, the agreements between the United Kingdom, Canada, Australia and New Zealand concerning the Empire Air Training Scheme. They are reproduced with the kind permission of the MOD United Kingdom. The MOD Copyright Administrator waived the usual fees in view of the book being published to accompany the launching of a memorial to 5SFTS, Uranquinty. British Crown Copyright/MOD applies to excerpts from **Flying Training** which are reproduced with permission of the Controller of Her Britannic Majesty's Stationery Office.

David and Jenny Duprez compiled the illustrations and David has rephotographed and put all the visual material onto CD. The photographs were scanned in colour and adjustments made, including removal of yellowing, before changing to grey scale. Cropping followed, together with retouching of the worst areas of deterioration occurring over the more than half century since they were taken.

Lex McAulay has enthusiastically supported the book from its concept to its publication in time for the unveiling of the memorial.

My wife, Marianne, has given me the seclusion needed to ponder and write over a long period together with editorial aid and proof reading while the book was in preparation. Our elder son, Peter, has helped me through the pains of word processing and younger son, James, with encouragement, and proof reading, as have many friends.

First Published in 1999 by Banner Books
122 Walker Street, MARYBOROUGH
Queensland 4650
Australia

Design & Production by McTaggarts The Printers
63 Torquay Rd. HERVEY BAY
Queensland 4655.
Email: mcprint@mctaggart.com.au

Cataloguing In Publication information

Ilbery, Peter, 1923-

Empire airmen strike back : the Empire Training Scheme and 5 SFTS, Uranquinty.

Bibliography,
Includes index.
ISBN 1 875593 20 9

C ontents

		Page
Introduction		
Chapter 1	The Empire Air Training Scheme	1
Chapter 2	Training Aircraft	9
Chapter 3	RAAF Station Uranquinty - Formation	13
Chapter 4	RAAF Station Uranquinty – 1941-45	21
Chapter 5	From Call-up to Elementary Flying Training School	27
Chapter 6	Instructors	35
Chapter 7	Trainees – Intermediate Training Squadron	43
Chapter 8	Avoidable Accidents	53
Chapter 9	Trainees – Advanced Training Squadron	57
Chapter 10	Overseas	65
Chapter 11	England	73
Chapter 12	Windows on Where They Went - Singles	79
Chapter 13	Windows on Where They Went – Multies	91
Chapter 14	Windows on Where They Went – SWPA	99
Chapter 15	Memorials and Return and Epilogue	111
Lists		
1.	Roll of Uranquinty Graduates and	125
	Key to Cemeteries Designation	157
2.	Major Casualties by Course among Graduates of 5SFTS, Uranquinty	160
3.	List of Fatal Training Accidents	161
Appendix 1	Memorandum United Kingdom/Canada/Australia/ New Zealand - 1939	162
Appendix 2	Memorandum United Kingdom/Australia - 1939	175
Appendix 3	Memorandum United Kingdom/Australia - 1941	178
Endnotes		180
References		192
Abbreviations		194
Index		196

I ntroduction

The British, Canadian, Australian and New Zealand Governments have agreed to combine in the training of the skilled personnel of a vast air force on a scale which is literally without precedent. Statement and Broadcast by the Prime Minister, The Rt Hon. R.G.Menzies, K.C., M.P, 11 October, 1939.[1]

As events of the thirties unfolded it became increasingly obvious to the Royal Air Force that the challenge provided by the expansion of the German Air Force would have to be met. To match and eventually overcome the many years' lead of German rearmament, the RAF would need to expand from its ill-prepared, small but quality nucleus into hundreds of squadrons. The production of thousands of aircraft was envisaged. Britain, with manpower already committed in so many ways to the prosecution of the looming war, would require aircrew in greater numbers than she could muster, and to meet the threat would require the assistance of the Dominions. However it was not until the commencement of hostilities that the Empire Air Training Scheme Agreement (EATS)[2] was hurriedly cobbled together. Late in 1939 the United Kingdom, Canada, Australia and New Zealand agreed to train aircrews for the planned acceleration of aircraft production in British and Commonwealth factories. So imperative was the need that the first intake of trainees (No. 1 Course EATS) took place simultaneously in these countries and in Southern Rhodesia in April 1940.

The opening of the first training schools in the Dominions coincided with the great German offensive of April and May 1940. To the British the contrast must have appeared ironic but to the Nazis it must have been ludicrous. Here was a nation beginning a long term plan at the end of the war – or almost the end ! At this time, the Dominions offered to send every available aircrew and machine to Great Britain. Britain refused: she had faith in her ability to hold on until the scheme began pouring out its thousands of trained aircrew.

It was a close call when, during the summer of 1940, troop-laden German barges awaited the clearance of the RAF from the Channel sky to attempt the invasion of England. At first the German Air Force attacked English airfields, installations and communications but in September concentrated on mass daylight raids on London, believing that the RAF would be destroyed in its defence. The culminating day of the Battle of Britain, taken as 15th September, saw Mr Winston Churchill at Fighter Command's bomb-proof Operations Room fifty feet below ground at Uxbridge. Wave after wave of enemy aircraft were plotted by radar converging on London and all Britain's available squadrons were put into the air. Strained to the last reserves the RAF had just enough Hurricanes and Spitfires and determined pilots to prevent the Luftwaffe achieving air supremacy over the daylight skies of England. The Prime Minister addressed a crowded House of Commons and in referring to the Battle of Britain concluded with the immortal passage: "The gratitude of every home

in our island, in our Empire and indeed throughout the world, except in the abodes of the guilty, goes out to the British airmen, who, undaunted by odds, unwearied in their constant challenge and mortal danger, are turning the tide of world war by their prowess and devotion. Never in the field of human conflict was so much owed by so many to so few."[3]

Failing to defeat the RAF in daylight, Germany resorted to night raids in the attempt to weaken the English people's will. For weeks on end one or two hundred bombers attacked London every night. The King and Queen continued to live in the capital and daily moved among the people where destruction was severest. Stoicism displayed was exemplary and the blitz only strengthened the nation's resolve. Around the world, and especially in the British Dominions, there was admiration for the nation resisting a fulminating dictatorship which had until then carried all before it. The mood became one of giving it back, which later was to become a reality as our air power grew through the EATS to match and then exceed the many years' lead of German rearmament.

In 1940 there had been about a score of Australian pilots available to fight in the Battle of Britain.[4,5] A squadron of Short "Sunderland" flying boats ordered in England by Australia was to remain there and at the end of 1939, manned by 200 fully trained Royal Australian Air Force personnel, it became, as 10Sqn, the first Australian squadron on active service. In August 1940, 3Sqn was the first RAAF squadron to arrive in the Middle East.

With conversion of the peaceful nation of Australia into war mode, tens of thousands of its young men were to train as airmen under the EATS and form RAAF overseas squadrons to take up the offensive in the battle from Britain and swell aircrew numbers in RAF squadrons. 452Sqn, formed in Lincolnshire in April 1941, was the first Australian EATS squadron in RAF Fighter Command. 455Sqn, formed in Williamtown, was the first Australian EATS squadron in RAF Bomber Command, where it commenced operations in October 1941 from Swinderby in Lincolnshire.

Under the EATS agreement, Australia was originally to supply 36% of the 28,000 aircrew to be trained over the next three years. But the scheme was quickly a success and the numbers rapidly escalated. Despite the subsequent demands imposed on the RAAF with the Japanese entry into the war, Australia was able to fulfil its commitments to the EATS with RAAF aircrews continuing to be posted to squadrons in Britain, while extra EATS airmen were trained for squadrons in the South West Pacific Area (SWPA) .

The EATS required a massive support structure. Suitable sites for aerodromes were selected by the respective air forces in Australia, Canada, New Zealand, Rhodesia, South Africa and the United Kingdom. Land for the many airfields was resumed and in far-off New South Wales at Uranquinty the Lewington family was obliged to sell their farm. As a consequence of war, they had to vacate in six weeks the family property developed over two generations, although cropping was allowed for one year. The task began of changing a farm into an air force station[6] to receive eager if apprehensive young men for pilot training. This beautiful piece of country in tranquil New South Wales was changed drastically with the pulling out of trees and the appearance of large areas of concrete and bitumen and an array of functional buildings. Other sites in Australia, and hundreds more in England, Scotland and the other Dominions, became ground training schools in which recruits learnt their ABC as servicemen; elementary flying training schools; service flying training schools; air observer schools; bombing and gunnery schools; wireless operators schools; and air navigation schools. Their construction in itself was a major effort.

The school at Uranquinty, No. 5 Service Flying Training School, was set up to train pilots in advanced flying on Wirraways as part of the Empire Air Training Scheme.

C hapter 1   The Empire Air Training Scheme

Looking back to the pressures of 1939-40 one can only admire those planning air supremacy in the long term when the short term was the struggle to survive.

RAAF pilot training before the EATS

Following the formation of the Royal Australian Air Force (RAAF) in 1921 a Flying Training School (FTS) was established at Point Cook, Victoria, for the training of pilots. Those selected to go to the FTS from Duntroon, where all officer training was carried out, on graduation served a four-year period in the RAAF on a short term commission after which they reverted to the army. To be viable the school at Point Cook ran courses for between 30 and 40 trainees every six months but only a very few of the graduands would be required by the RAAF so that the bulk of the graduates went to Britain. There had been an arrangement from 1923 between the United Kingdom and Australia that pilots trained at Point Cook would be commissioned into the Royal Air Force (RAF).

In 1937 the position was reversed. Air Commodore Garrisson[1] recalls that from the course graduating in June that year 36 went to the RAF and four remained in Australia, while from his own course graduating in December only four went to the RAF with the remainder, including himself, staying in Australia.

The RAAF was embarking on its expansion. Before the out break of World War II the RAAF numbered less than 4,000. At the conclusion of hostilities it had 180,000 personnel and had become the fifth largest air force in the world. It was achieved within the framework of the remarkable Empire Air Training Scheme.

Accepted as an Air Cadet in July 1939 Pilot Officer Vern Polley graduated in March 1940 from the last intake for Short Service Commissions, No. 26. In July 1940 he was a staff pilot for the EATS at Cootamundra making his way through the Central Flying School (CFS) at Camden to become an instructor of EATS pupil pilots at Uranquinty in October 1941.[2]

Pilot training under the EATS

The United Kingdom enlisted the aid of her Dominions at an Empire Air Training Conference held at Ottawa in October 1939. Australia was represented by the Minister for Air (Hon. J.V. Fairbairn), the Assistant Chief of Air Staff (Wing Commander G. Jones) and Messrs Elford and Kellaway.[3]

Empire Air Training Conference, held at Ottawa in 1939.

Third Row (L to R): J.R. Smyth, United Kingdom; F.R. Howard (United Kingdom); C.V. Kellway (Australia); A/C E.W. Stedman (Canada); G/C A Gray (United Kingdom); Lt-Col K.S. MacLachlan D/M National Defence, Canada); G/C J.M. Robb (United Kingdom); A.D Heeney (Canada); G/C L.N. Hollinghurst (United Kingdom); R.E. Elford (Australia); W.L. Middlemass (New Zealand). Second Row: J.B. Abraham (United Kingdom); Dr O.D. Skelton (Under Secretary of State for External Affairs, Canada); T.A. Barrow (Air Secretary, New Zealand); Sir Gerald Campbell (High Commissioner for the United Kingdom); Hon. I. Mackenzie (Minister of Pensions and National Health, Canada); W/C G. Jones (Asst CAS, Australia); Hon. C.D. Howe (Minister of Transport, Canada); Dr W.C. Clark (Dep. Minister of Finance, Canada); A/V/M G.M. Croil (CAS, Canada). Front Row: A/C/M Sir R. Brooke-Popham (United Kingdom); Col. the Hon. J.L. Ralston (Minister of Finance, Canada); G/C H.W.L. Saunders (CAS, New Zealand); Hon. Senator R. Dandurand (Canada); Rt. Hon. Lord Riverdale (United Kingdom); Rt. Hon. W.L. Mackenzie King (Prime Minister of Canada); Hon. J.V. Fairbairn (Minister for Air, Australia); Rt. Hon. E. Lapointe (Minister of Justice, Canada); Rt. Hon. H.H. Balfour (Under Secretary of State for Air, United Kingdom); Hon. N.M. Rogers (Minister of National Defence, Canada); A/M Sir C. Courtney, United Kingdom). (Courtesy Wings, 25 April 1944 p. 11.)

Australia agreed to train aircrew for service with the RAF. A Memorandum of Agreement between the United Kingdom and Australia concerning the Empire Air Training Scheme was signed on 27 November respectively by Lord Riverdale and Mr Fairbairn.[4] The original document held at the Public Record Office (PRO), Kew, lends insight into the urgency of the matter, as retyping of the document (to add written alterations, amend faulty format and include the omission of the heading for Article 9) was not awaited before the signatures were added. It dealt with matters relating to the training of pilots and aircraft crews in Australia, and their subsequent service with the RAF, and the provision of pupils from Australia for training in Canada as pilots and aircraft crews. The United Kingdom concluded a similar agreement with New Zealand at the same time which allowed for a contribution relative to its size and the nature and extent of the program. Group Captain H.W.L. Saunders RAF, then Chief of the New Zealand Air Staff, signed for New Zealand and again Lord Riverdale for the United Kingdom.[5]

In December the overall EATS was hurriedly stitched together by the governments of the United Kingdom, Canada, Australia and New Zealand. The air training plan put forward by the United Kingdom was an annual requirement of 50,000 aircrew (20,000 pilots and 30,000 observers and air gunners). Britain's commitment would be 4/9 of this number while the remainder would be allocated on a population basis of 56% to Canada, 36% to Australia, and 8% to New Zealand. Canada, cushioned by distance from hostilities, was to be the centre of the massive EATS, the machine efficiently ticking away to ultimately provide air superiority for the RAF.

The four party Memorandum of Agreement was signed in Ottawa on 17 December 1939 by Lord Riverdale, Mr Mackenzie King for Canada, Mr S.M. Bruce for Australia and Mr Jordan for New Zealand.[6] The EATS objective was to ensure that sufficient aircrews would be available from the United Kingdom and the Dominions to fly the aircraft flowing at an accelerating rate from British factories. Agreement to the fundamental principles of the scheme was never in doubt. However the vastness of the scheme and its ramifications within the material and financial resources of the partners required negotiation. Forthrightness in discussion by the Commonwealth governments in reaching this remarkable agreement has been misinterpreted as divisiveness by some recent commentators, when in fact there was underlying unity in the face of ruthless dictatorship. Such comment, from the safety of another time and place, misrepresents the spirit of those perilous times so as to be historically incorrect and fails to appreciate the need for short cuts (carrying a risk of bungles)

Done in quintuplicate, at Ottawa, this 17th day of December, 1939.

On behalf of the Government of the United Kingdom

On behalf of the Government of Canada

On behalf of the Government of Australia

On behalf of the Government of New Zealand

Signatures to the Empire Air Training Scheme, Ottawa, 17th December, 1939. Lord Riverdale (United Kingdom), Mr Mackenzie King (Canada), Mr Bruce (Australia), and Mr Jordan (New Zealand)

(Courtesy Public Record Office, Kew.)

necessary to achieve rapid results. While the Union of South Africa was not a party to this EATS agreement, it offered facilities for the training of pilots for the RAF in South Africa. The British colony of Southern Rhodesia was invited to join in the EATS and formed the Rhodesian Air Training Group.[7]

Under the agreements, the Government of Australia was to arrange as speedily as possible facilities to allow for acceptance into advanced pilot training of 336 pupils in Australia and 80 in Canada every four weeks (see Appendix 2, Articles 3 and 4). The intake figures had to allow for about one third reduction in the output, due to wastage, i.e. failure or `scrubbing´ of pilots during training (Appendix 1, Table "A"). Also every four weeks there was to be an intake of 320 wireless operator-air gunners and 84 observers, of which 72 and 42 respectively would go to Canada after initial training. Australia agreed to send to Southern Rhodesia each month 40 men for training as pilots, having completed initial training in Australia (10 drafts were sent but with the entry of Japan into the war the last was sent in November 1941).[7] The agreements were to become operative immediately they were ratified and to remain in force until 31 March 1943 unless following agreement it was decided otherwise.

For the pilot training program there were to be 13 elementary flying training schools (EFTS) and 16 service flying training schools (SFTS) for the scheme in Canada. The discrepancy between the numbers of the flying training schools was because two SFTSs were required for Australians and one for New Zealanders, their EFTS courses having been done in their own countries.[8] For the program in Australia there were to be eight SFTSs.

Air Marshal Sir Charles Burnett, who had commanded RAF Training Command from 1936 to 1939, was seconded to the RAAF as Chief of Air Staff, charged with responsibility for organising Australian planning for the EATS. In a remarkably short time for such an immense undertaking, sufficient facilities were in place to allow the scheme to commence. Number 1 Course started training simultaneously within Initial Training Schools (ITS) in the United Kingdom, Canada, Australia, New Zealand and Southern Rhodesia on 29 April 1940. After that date all aircrew training in the Dominion was to be carried out under the EATS.[9] The first intake into Australian ITSs was 293 airmen; the first draft for Canada, following ITS instruction, left in September. The scheme was planned to become fully operative in two years.

Enough cannot be said to emphasise the importance of the EATS to the entire war effort. It was loyally and precisely carried out, in spite of the great distances separating the four partners and the many dislocations and impediments which their plans suffered through the changing fortunes of war.[10]

The first RAAF draft of fully trained aircrew reached Britain from Canada within 12 months of the opening of the ITSs, and two months later the first draft of aircrew entirely trained in Australia. With the entry of Japan into the war in December 1941, Australia's part in the scheme was reviewed by Cabinet. While the flow of EATS graduates continued to Australia's biggest air front in Britain, the sailings of EATS recruits to Canada ceased for four months, but were then made up. Within two years the scheme had become fully operative and Australia had a training system that handled one thousand EATS aircrew recruits a month, and, in addition, outside the EATS quota, was training aircrews needed for the RAAF at home.

Personnel sent overseas, although placed at the disposal of the United Kingdom,[11] remained members of the RAAF throughout their service.[12] Under Article 12 of the agreement of 27 November (Appendix 2) and Article 15 of the agreement of 23 December (Appendix 1), the United Kingdom Government undertook that pupils of Canada, Australia and New Zealand would be identified, after completion of training, with their respective Dominions, either by the method of organizing Dominion units and formations or in some other way, such methods to be agreed upon with the respective Dominion Governments. Under Article 1 of the agreement of 17 April 1941, eighteen RAAF squadrons were to be formed for service outside Australia and these squadrons of the RAAF were to be additional to those RAAF squadrons already serving in the United Kingdom, the Middle East and the Far East, as described in the Memorandum attached to the Air Board Minute of 31 March 1941.[13] The rate of formation of these new squadrons depended on how the projected air force expansion could be achieved but nevertheless the aim was to form these eighteen squadrons within the next eighteen months in accordance with the following schedule[14]

By March, 1941 ... ... 2 squadrons to be formed.
By June, 1941 ... ... 6 squadrons to be formed.
By September, 1941 ... ... 9 squadrons to be formed.
By December, 1941 ... ... 12 squadrons to be formed.
By March, 1942 ... ... 15 squadrons to be formed.
By April or May, 1942 ... ... 18 squadrons to be formed.

These new squadrons formed under the EATS were, by the agreement of 23 December 1940 (Appendix V), squadrons of the RAAF.[15]

While the cost of the five RAAF squadrons already serving was being met by Australia, the cost of the eighteen new RAAF squadrons was to be borne by the United Kingdom.[16] All EATS aircrew were to retain their identity by wearing RAAF uniform. In the UK this dark blue uniform, or best blues, was only worn on special occasions or on leave, following the issue of the sensible, serviceable RAF blue/grey battledress. Battledress was worn on most occasions and universally by all nationalities, including those from occupied Europe like the Poles, with distinguishing country of origin shoulder flashes. Later as sufficient dark blue cloth became available RAAF battledress was issued progressively from Australia House.

At the request of the United Kingdom Government, the RAAF concentrated largely on the EATS in Australia.[17] To complement the aircrew program an increased output of tradesmen for ground crew was needed from technical schools. The demand for them in the huge expansion of the training program in Australia was such that they were not sufficient to accompany their counterparts in the air in commensurate numbers into the RAF squadrons, where most Australian aircrew were going, let alone into the eighteen overseas squadrons scheduled under Article 1 of the agreement of 17 April 1941. These latter squadrons, with mostly Australian aircrew, were to a varying extent supported by RAF ground crews. It was the intention that the RAF ground personnel should gradually be exchanged for RAAF personnel, but it was not achieved.

Before the first course to graduate from 5SFTS Uranquinty (17 Course) became operational, the product of the earlier courses, at the four SFTSs which had commenced training before Uranquinty started, were flying with the RAAF squadrons formed to that time and with the RAF in the UK, Middle East and Far East. The trickle was beginning to become a flood.

In June 1942, once again at Ottawa, the EATS due to expire in March 1943 was extended to 31 March 1945. Australia was retaining aircrew surplus to RAF needs for service in the Pacific. In February 1944, the Air Ministry in London asked that the despatch of fully trained aircrew for the United Kingdom for March and April be delayed as a large surplus had accumulated. In June 1944, the Air Ministry requested the cessation of all overseas drafts. Deceleration of the EATS followed with the return of Australian aircrew training in Canada and the possibility of the return of aircrew from the United Kingdom in increasing numbers. Steps were taken to plan for the gradual closing of training schools, maintaining only those necessary to supply the RAAF in the SWPA.[18] The EATS had enabled air superiority to be achieved and enough reserves had been accumulated to meet any eventuality after the invasion of Europe. Indeed after D-Day aircraft were painted with prominent zebra markings making them readily identifiable so that, with so many in the air compared to the Germans, the likelihood of them being shot at by friendly forces was reduced.

Zebra markings;
Beaufighters of 455Sqn wearing the universal Allied D-Day livery of black and white stripes.

The Minister for Air announced the expiration of the EATS in March 1945:[19] no longer was there need for aircrew reinforcements either for the European or Pacific theatres. To the end of March 1945, 10,351 aircrew trainees had gone to Canada (of whom 4,760 were categorised as pilots), several hundred had been trained in Rhodesia, and in Australia the total number of graduates of the EATS was 27,387 (10,882 pilots, 6,071 navigators, and 10,434 air gunners). In all the total enlistments had amounted to 51,114 and the number of Australians trained under the EATS amounted to 37,538.[20]

Table 1.

Number of Australians trained under the EATS: 37,538

in:	Australia	Canada	Rhodesia
Pilots	10,882	4,069	514
Navigators	6,071	2,399	61
Air gunners	10,434	3,100	8
Total trained	27,387	9,568	583

From DPR Publication – "Victory Roll".

Among the 37,538 Empire Air Trainees who had graduated, 11,219 were killed in air operations or accidents[22] representing a major casualty rate of 30%. The rate is reflected in the earlier courses at Uranquinty (see Major Casualties by Course among Graduates of 5SFTS, Uranquinty). However 5SFTS started at 17 Course; in the earlier courses still of the EATS elsewhere, the losses were greater. In the high risk squadrons like the strategic bombers and the strike fighters, it was the norm to have less than a 50% chance of completing a tour of operations. "Remarkably, almost 30% of all Australians killed in action or missing presumed dead during World War 2 – that is the total for all services and all theatres – were members of the RAAF serving in the air war against Germany and Italy."[22,23]

The EATS in Australia had operated twelve EFTSs[24] and eight SFTSs[25] in graduating its pilots. No. 5SFTS, Uranquinty had graduated over 1,500 of them.

Seventeen of the projected 18 EATS squadrons had been formed; five in the Middle East and 12 in the United Kingdom of which one served later in the Middle East and two went to Australia in 1942.

In messages exchanged at the end of the war between the Secretary of State for Air (Sir Archibald Sinclair) and the Minister for Air (Mr Drakeford), the EATS was referred to as "a major factor in winning the war." In Mr Drakeford's message, he said that a magnificent chapter of history had ended with the closing down of the EATS, and that probably no other single factor had had a greater bearing on our present victorious position.[26]

Chapter 2   Training Aircraft

The Government of Australia will endeavour to manufacture all the aircraft including engines and spare parts required for single engine training at the Service Flying Training Schools – these aircraft being of the Wirraway or similar type.
EATS Agreement between the United Kingdom and Australia, Article 8(g).[1]

Under the EATS agreement between H.M. Government in the United Kingdom and H.M. Government in Australia of 27 November 1939, the share of the cost of the scheme in Australia to be borne by the Government of the United Kingdom is shown at Article 8 (see Appendix 2). The contributions included[2]

- engines for Tiger Moth airframes manufactured in Australia up to a maximum of 50% of the total number of aircraft required for the initial equipment and immediate reserve establishments for the full training capacity of the elementary flying schools.
- All the Anson aircraft (without wings) that may be required for the initial equipment and immediate reserve establishments for the full training capacity of the Service Flying Training Schools, the Air Observers Schools and the Air Navigation Schools.
- All the Battle aircraft that may be required for the initial equipment and immediate reserve establishments for the full training capacity of the Bombing and Gunnery Schools and the Air Armament School.
- the first 233 of the airframes and first 291 of the engines for the Wirraway, together with an appropriate stock of spare parts, for single engine training at the Service Flying Training Schools.

Under the EATS, the Air Ministry undertook to supply intermediate and advanced trainers. These consisted of 792 Ansons and 432 Battles, to be provided in kind, and the Wirraways at an estimated cost[3] in December 1939 of 12,000 pounds each, when the first order was placed with the Commonwealth Aircraft Corporation (CAC).

De Havilland manufactured the Tiger Moth and propellers for the Wirraway, No.1 Aircraft Park at Geelong assembled the Battle, and 2 Aircraft Park at Bankstown the Anson. Under 8(h) of the Memorandum of Agreement of 27 November 1939, Australia was to make arrangements as speedily as possible to manufacture wings for Anson aircraft in Australia although the United Kingdom undertook to supply wings until wings manufactured in Australia became available.[4]

Because of the difficulty of transporting the fuselages imported from Britain after disembarkation from the ship, it was desirable that the place of erection should not be far from the port. Since it was proposed that Clyde Engineering at Granville would manufacture the wings, the erection centre should be nearby. Accordingly an Air Board Minute of 19 April 1940 recommended the preparation of an aerodrome at Bankstown at an estimated cost of 60,000 pounds to provide an erection centre for Avro Ansons.[5]

For the service flying training under the EATS of pilots on multi-engine aircraft, the British Airspeed Oxford was chosen, and on single-engine aircraft the North American Harvard was selected, not least because large numbers could be readily available from the United States. In Australia the Harvard Mark 1 was manufactured under licence with Wackett modifications.

Resurgent Germany had been the reason for an overseas mission in 1936 led by Wing Commander Lawrence Wackett in search of an aircraft which could be manufactured by the newly formed CAC, should Australia find itself without supplies from England. CAC, the initiative of Broken Hill P/L, Broken Hill Associated Smelters P/L and General Motors-Holden Ltd, included the Orient Steam Navigation Company Ltd, Imperial Chemical Industries of Australia and New Zealand Ltd, and the Electrolytic Zinc Company of Australasia Ltd.[6]

Touring the United Kingdom, Europe and the United States, Wackett, who had once commanded the RAAF Experimental Section at Randwick, was accompanied by two RAAF officers, one being the chief workshop officer. Their brief was self-sufficiency; to select an aircraft which, including its engine, could be manufactured in Australia with Australian material.

Considering the state of the fledgling aircraft industry, whatever was chosen would present enormous difficulties for manufacture in Australia. An aboriginal word for challenge, for it was certainly that, was the apt name of Wirraway given to the choice of North American Aviation's NA-16.[7]

NA-16, the fixed undercarriage forerunner of the Wirraway
(J. Millard)

On arrival in Australia in 1937, the NA-16 was test flown by the man who was to become the Chief of Air Staff 1957-61, Air Chief Marshal Sir Frederick Scherger. The retractable undercarriage version, the NA-33, while not too complicated, also had toe-operated hydraulic wheel brakes on the rudder bars, and a variable pitch three-bladed propeller. The latter was to be made locally by De Havilland (Australia), the maker of the ubiquitous Tiger Moth.

The NA-33 arrived in Australia in April 1938 for manufacture under licence, and, by agreement with North American Aviation, CAC could modify the design to RAAF requirements. The wings and tail were strengthened for dive bombing and it was given two forward-firing 0.303 Vickers machine guns. The first Wirraway was taken on strength by the RAAF in July 1939 just two months prior to the outbreak of war. In all, 755 were to be built.

Although the airframe production was expanding, there was only a trickle of engines. Australia, not having made motor engines before the war, now had to turn out aero engines. The manufacture under licence of the Pratt & Whitney Wasp power plant provided many problems, from seizing of bearings to failure of spark plugs. At first the Wirraways were equipped with imported engines.

The nine cylinder air-cooled radial engine developed 600hp for the Wirraway's take-off weight of two and a half tons. It gave a cruising speed of 180 mph for training purposes.[8]
The following description of a Wirraway applies to the one held by the Australian War Memorial currently displayed at Treloar C.[9] As A20-103 it had been a training aircraft at 5SFTS Uranquinty and an operational aircraft with 4Sqn (See Chapter 8).

CA – 5 Wirraway Mk II

Performance:

Maximum speed	220mph at 8,600ft
Operating speed	177mph at sea level (2,100rpm and 28" boost)
Range	640 miles at operating speed
Endurance	3 hours at operating speed
Ceiling	23,000ft

Dimensions:

Span	43ft
Length	27.83ft
Height	8.73ft

Weight:

Empty	3,992lbs, maximum gross weight 6,450lbs.

Power Plant:
600hp Pratt & Whitney R-1340-S1H1-G Wasp 9-cylinder air cooled radial engine (built at CAC). Rated power of engine at take off – 650hp at 2,300rpm.

Armament:
Two forward firing 0.303 inch Vickers Mk V machine guns and one Vickers Mk 1.

Wirraway A20-719
Jack Curtis (39 Course)

Wirraway 458, VH-WRX (A20-719) is owned by a syndicate. Coordinator of the syndicate is Rob Greinert of Classic Aviation, and members are former Qantas Captain and Wirraway instructor Ray Saever, former TAA Captain Owen O'Malley, former Qantas Captain Ian McLeay, current serving Qantas Captain Doug Haywood and Jack Curtis, Chief Pilot and Check Captain for Dakota National Air and former Wirraway pilot at Uranquinty on 39 Course. This aircraft was to have overflown the RAAF Memorial at Uranquinty during it's unveiling on 19 September 1999, but was destroyed prior to the ceremony in a flying accident at Nowra in which sadly Captain O'Malley and his passenger lost their lives.

Wirraway cockpit
(John McDonald)

C hapter 3   RAAF Station Uranquinty - Formation

Riverina Site Chosen For New RAAF Service Flying Training School[1]

Under the EATS, eight service flying training schools were to be established in Australia. Point Cook, Wagga, Amberley and Geraldton were already operating, when, at the end of 1940, other aerodrome sites were being assessed for additional service flying training schools. In New South Wales, Scone was not selected owing to the presence of low hills within two miles and Mudgee's approaches were also unsatisfactory. Junee was rather small and considerable surface preparation was necessary. Corowa had a large portion occupied by mounds and depressions of gilgai and Condobolin could be too dusty.[2]

On 20 February 1941, at the same time as Mallala, South Australia, was selected as the site for 6SFTS, Uranquinty, about 14½ miles south-west of 2SFTS Wagga, and 1½ miles west of the village of Uranquinty, was chosen for the fifth flying school for intermediate and advanced training of Empire Air Trainees in Australia. It was the second SFTS in New South Wales.[3] The announcement by the Department of Air read[1]

> Necessary buildings and services for aircraft and personnel are being planned, and training is scheduled to begin in November. Before then a small advance party will occupy the school in order to complete preliminary arrangements for the intake of trainees.... The opening of new schools like the one to be formed at Uranquinty means the output of the Empire Air Scheme will be increased according to plan and schedule.

From the air, the Riverina, with its thousands of acres composed of extensive waving wheat fields and sheep grazing into wind, took on the appearance of one large landing field. The site chosen for 5SFTS was on the Sydney-Melbourne railway line and comprised lands owned by Mr A. Lewington of approximately 1002 acres[4] presided over by the massive shape of The Rock. The estimated cost of acquisition was 11,900 pounds.[5] To secure immediate occupation and enable commencement of constructional works, possession was taken under National Security (General) Regulations, Regulation 54. The estimated expenditure on constructional work, buildings and engineering services was over 200,000 pounds. Ministerial approval of the proposals and expenditure, subject to scrutiny by the Board of Business Administration, was given by Mr McEwen on 19 May 1941.[6]

The contract for the construction of the buildings at a cost of 100,000 pounds was awarded to Messrs J. Stubbs of Sydney. The firm commenced work in September 1941, employing local men from Uranquinty and Wagga Wagga, the latter being transported to the site each day by Fearnes buses of Wagga.[5]

As tenure under the regulations was restricted to the duration of the war and six months thereafter only, it was considered that the assets accruing upon completion of the project would not be secured until title was secured by the Commonwealth.[7] Further areas were taken over under the regulations for a relief landing ground at "Yarragundry" and armament ranges at East Bullenbung.[8]

The RAAF Directorate of Works and Buildings already had plans[9] drawn up in April so that by the time the Advance Party arrived much of the following construction had taken place.

> To allow a clear angle of approach of 1 in 30 to all aerodrome boundaries, surrounding timber was felled or lopped with the owners' permission and carried out in accordance with their reasonable requirements. Trees were allowed to remain around the homestead on the north and camp buildings on the south. In the area to be used by aircraft the requirement was that the surface should be firm and smooth allowing a car to be driven over it at 35 mph without discomfort. All areas even enough for aircraft operation were not disturbed, it being essential that as much as possible of the existing herbage be allowed to remain. Undulations and mounds were graded and dams pumped out and filled. Cropped and fallow paddocks were smoothed by harrowing and rolling with an 8-ton roller. Internal fencing was removed, post holes filled, trees grubbed out and low spots covered with three inches of good red loam and consolidated. The whole of the aerodrome area was fertilized and seeded to ensure establishment of a good mat of grass. The boundary fence was rabbit and sheep proofed and at the main entrance opening of 20 feet double gates were installed.

Service Flying Training School, Uranquinty from the air in 1943.
(H. Frost).

These white painted gates are still there today so that it is possible for the mind's eye to travel along the vestige of the main road stretching ahead and to create on either side a picture of the base as it once was. To the left were the quarters for the station staff, gymnasium/cinema and hospital. There were ablutions, kitchens and messes for officers, sergeants, and airmen, and canteens, laundries, boilers and all the appurtenances of a self-contained functioning unit that went with so many camps hurriedly put up for the war effort, including the post office with its connection to the outside world. To the right a road went off between the guardhouse and the parade ground and wound around between the flight huts and the School of Instruction to the trainees quarters.

Aerial view of the former 5SFTS in 1987.
(Jenny Lewington).

A sketchy outline of the growth of the station is available in the Personal Occurrence Reports (PORs) held at RAAF History Section, Canberra.[10] They provide a day to day account of personnel administrative matters. On 13 October 1941 the Advance Party under F/L W.R. Armstrong, of three officers and 63 airmen, entered the base, followed by the adjutant, F/L V.S. Vincent on the eighteenth, and on 20 October the Nucleus Party of five officers and 67 airmen under the Commanding Officer, G/C U. Ewart. These first officers were S/L J. Black RAF, F/O J. Bradley and P/O S. Rosenfeld (engineering), S/L V. Knight (medical)[11], S/L C. Tobin and P/O S. Barry (administration), F/L F. Johnson (accounting) and F/O A. Robinson (equipment). S/L Black is remembered by the early ground staff for his pleasant and encouraging presence and most active and important role in the establishment of the station as well as sporting the RAF moustache of the time.

The first airmen were from the widely dispersed air force organisations at Amberley, Ascot Vale, Bankstown, Benalla, Bradfield Park, Camden, Canberra, Darwin, Deniliquin, Essendon, Geraldton, Narrandera, Narromine, North Shore, Parkes, Point Cook, Port Pirie, Rathmines, Richmond, Somers, Tamworth, Temora, Waterloo, Williamtown and Woolloomooloo. Their groups and trades reflect the early and orderly development of the air force station from scratch. The categories were; in Group 1, blacksmith, coppersmith, fitter, instrument maker, welder; Group 2, carpenter, electrician, fabric worker, painter, wireless mechanic; Group 3, caterer, cook, orderly, shoemaker, storekeeper, tailor; Group 4, clerk; Group 5, aircrafthand, guard, labourer, mess steward, service police, telephone operator. Others included armourer, drill instructor, dental mechanic, engineer, flight mechanic/rigger and photographer.

Among these first airmen were Russell Marriott, 18849, an aircraft electrician from 4 Sqn Canberra, who recalled "being one of a handful of pioneers with few facilities and no aircraft"[12] and "Chum" Day 35902, in equipment, "whose huts were surrounded by wheat crops."[13] It was harvest time on Mr Lewington's property and Aircraftsman Boorn[14] remembered being enlisted, in view of the shortage of labour, to stook the wheat. October 22 saw the arrival of F/L Eric Cook, F/O Frank Gardner and F/O Verdun Polley, the first three pilots. Vern Polley also wrote to the same effect that, "we three were the first instructors with no aeroplanes and the place was only a third built."[15] However, within four days they were on a train to 1 Aircraft Depot Laverton in order to commence ferrying aircraft to the school.

On 26 October S/L I. Williams (RAF) 34188, the Chief Ground Instructor, arrived. Under the EATS the syllabus of instruction throughout the UK, Canada, Australia, New Zealand and Southern Rhodesia was to be in accordance with that laid down for each similar course of training as taught in the RAF.[16] Having initiated the training program he moved on to do the same at 8SFTS Bundaberg on 4 January 1942, and F/L F.G. Huxley became CGI.

On 28 October the first three Wirraways were flown in - A20-378 (F/L Cook), A20-385 (P/O Gardiner) and A20-376 (F/O Polley).[17]

Pilot Log Book of F/O V.H. Polley for October 1941

On 29 October the three ferry pilots again departed for Laverton and the following day brought in three more Wirraways. On 31 October joined by another future instructor, F/L Brand, the ferry pilots brought in another four.

On 3 November S/L C.F. King (RAF) arrived to be O.C. Intermediate Training Squadron and Chief Flying Instructor (CFI). F/L S. Middlemiss, who arrived on 10 November, was flight commander.[18] On the same day, joined by F/O Kerville and P/O McCulloch, the instructors come ferry pilots, flew in six Wirraways.

Ross Leek joined the ground staff during November "as one of those who kept them flying" describing himself as one of the "grease monkeys" - fitter 2Es and flight mechanics.[19]

> They were responsible for and kept the motors always serviceable. As a fitter I was a higher mustering and higher paid than a flight mechanic and supposed to be a better tradesman. I found a lot of flight mechs were practically just as, or more, efficient. Fitters 2A or "paper hangers" were responsible for maintaining all the aircraft from the bulk head/fire wall aft and all the hydraulics and all the airframe, hence the "A". The aircraft hand general was called upon to do all the "unsung" jobs – stand in for or help any trade – see all aircraft fuelled and with engine oil. The electricians or "sparks" were responsible for all electrical gear and also self explanatory were the musterings for instrument makers and armourers.

Ground staff on the job.
(D. Gardner RAAF Museum).

Group in front of CO's Anson on Quinty tarmac.
Sgt Deaths, Fitter 2E; LAC Brookes, Flight Mechanic; LAC McGregor, 2E;
ACW Mayo, Flight Rigger; F/L Sephton, pilot; LAC Hooper, 2E;
LAC Grace, Fitter 2A; LAC Scott, 2E; Sgt Wilson, 2A.
(G. Grace, F. Hall, A. Hooper)

Wirraway being steam-cleaned during routine maintenance at 5SFTS.
(Australian War Memorial negative number P0448/212/066).

From Uranquinty Ross Leek was posted to 114 Mobile Oxygen Unit. The unit was attached to 10RSU Milne Bay and ended the war at Noemfoor.[20]

> We made it (oxygen) in an incredibly antiquated double trailer powered by a 1927 Crossley motor (totally reliable). Air was pumped to 3,000psi and then expanded to form liquid air which then went through a cracking tower and filters. If you served in the Pacific, i.e. PNG to Borneo, you may well have inhaled some of "our" oxygen. In the end the Yanks were producing three times the volume in a quarter of the time but our stuff was the "bestest".

Names on Page 138

Trainees in summer, winter and flying garb.

On 16 November a new sight at 5SFTS Uranquinty was airmen wearing a white flash as a cockade in the peak of their forage caps. They were the first of the Empire Air Trainees. Derek Beaurepaire, after completing elementary flying training school at Narromine on 17 Course, remembers

we missed out on an overseas posting and went off to what we believed was Wagga. On arrival we were loaded into trucks and found ourselves in the paddocks of Uranquinty. At this stage there were a few Wirraways, half built hangars, lecture huts with no roofing and no windows and the sleeping accommodation was fully air conditioned with one vast open roof to the stars! There was one mess with the officers who had silver, tablecloths, etc. and sergeants who had a bit less, and on the other side of the hut the aircrew trainee leading aircraftsmen with knife, fork, plate and spoon – very convivial with everyone watching each other's manners![21]

On 17 November, 17 Course started flying with 50 trainees. Each instructor had a number of pupils and LAC Beaurepaire was one of F/L Cook's. F/O Polley's were LACs Davies, Donellan, Marsh and Nelson. Flying meant work for the tankers and refuelling crews. Bill Boorn recalled

there were two tankers. The old Albion with gate gears was in excellent condition mechanically but so slow when laden with 90 octane fuel. The other was a fairly modern International with six forward gears. All fuel was pumped by hand. There were four men plus a driver to each vehicle and all were exhausted at the end of the day.[22]

By the end of November, the effective strength of the station was 31 officers, 492 airmen and 50 air crew, and with the arrival of further Wirraways, there were 28 on charge.[23]

Aircraft maintenance was well in place with "daily inspections", the state of the aircraft being noted in its own record, the EE77. Those aircraft found unserviceable were worked on by the ground staff – carburettor, generator, gas analyser – or whatever engine, airframe or hydraulics problem which could be repaired relatively easily. The flight duties commenced with "starting up" and carried through to "night shift". Each morning a crew "untied" the aircraft and removed the canvas engine cover preparatory to starting and warming up the contrary Wasp engine of the Wirraway. At cessation of flying, "night shift" commenced at 1600hrs and it was not until all aircraft were again serviceable that work finished, be it the small hours of the morning. Subsequently all aircraft had 40, 80 and 240 hourly inspections over and above the daily. Ross Leek elaborated

the 240 hourly inspection was a thorough overhaul with every aspect of the aircraft checked. Finally repainted it went on the flying line again as new. A stint in the 240 hangar was not as good as "outside" duties which were much more interesting and where you had a chance to watch the flying or be sent out to one of the satellite 'dromes where lots was happening. Perhaps a back seat ride would be going.[24]

Nothing illustrates so well the importance of what the ground staff were doing in maintaining the serviceability of the aircraft and the safety of the aircrew, as the consequence when something was not done[25]

Flight mechanic awarded penal forfeiture of 14 days pay in that he failed to fill the engine oil tank to correct level on Wirraway Aircraft A20/111 as was his duty to do, thereby causing damage to the said Aircraft (A20/111 engine No. 385) to the extent of approximately 1000 pounds.

LAC awarded 14 days C.B. in that he after having removed an F24 Camera from Wirraway Aircraft A20-188 negligently left a wire lead in the aircraft in such a manner as to foul the flying control cables, an act likely to cause damage to the aircraft or personnel flying it. "An Act to the prejudice of good order and Air Force discipline" A.F.A. Section 40.

LAC awarded seven days field punishment being guilty of neglect likely to cause damage to His Majesty's Aircraft in that he at 5SFTS whilst carrying out a 240 hourly inspection on Wirraway A20-606 neglected to split pin Fuel Cock Control causing the said aircraft to force land.

In December, with the arrival of P/O W. Stuart. simulated flight on instruments under the Link Trainer hood commenced.[26] The trainee was now able to view plotted on paper the accuracy of prescribed navigation courses which he had flown blind on instruments alone.

PORs record visits from some names destined to become very well known in the annals of the RAAF - Air Commodore Jones on 7 November 1941 flying in a Vega-Gull; Air Commodore D, Wilson 27 December; Air Vice Marshal Wrigley on 22 March 1942; Group Captain Scherger on 12 June and Air Commodore Wackett on 20 August.[27]

Intermediate Training Squadron

Tarmac, hangers and flight huts of Advanced Training Squadron

School of Instruction, trainees' quarters, parade ground, gym, hospital and The Rock.

Administration and guardhouse, sergeants', airmens' and WAAAF's quarters.

Anson and service hangers

Transport, main gate and officers' quarters.

(G.Grace, F.Hall, A.Hooper)

C hapter 4   RAAF Station Uranquinty 1941-45

The total strength of the 5SFTS Uranquinty rose to about 1500 until the EATS terminated in February 1945.[1] At its height there had been 133 aircraft on the base; 128 Wirraways, two De Havilland Dragons, two Moth Minors and one Wackett Trainer.

On 14 December 1941, 48 trainees arrived for the second course at Uranquinty, which was 18 Course EATS.[2] It and the next few courses were augmented by trainees from 2SFTS Wagga, at Forest Hill, which from July 1940 had been training pilots to "wings" standard on Wirraways and Avro Ansons. At this juncture the station assumed a role change to become 5 Aircraft Depot. With service flying about to close at Forest Hill, F/O R. Paxton came across to Uranquinty for flying duties and other instructors followed; Bill Newton, later to be awarded the Victoria Cross, was one.[3]

On 15 December 1941, 17 Course finished ITS, and F/Os Cook and Polley progressed with them into ATS becoming respectively O.C.s of X and Y Flights ATS.[2] At this stage the few trainees who were scrubbed became Duty Pilots or Link Trainer Instructors.

Later in the month F/O R. Susans arrived from 4SFTS for flying duties, having been a flying instructor at Point Cook and Geraldton after completing No. 2 Instructors Course at Camden. He had joined the RAAF towards the end of 1939 and finished his flying training as a cadet at Point Cook on 28 Cadet Course in June 1940.[4]

In February 1942 Vern Polley and Eric Cook became OCs of X and Y Flights respectively of ATS. The popular CFI, S/L John King RAF, returned to England in April having been temporarily in command of the unit.[2] After he left there was no actual CFI, S/L Tim O'Connell being OC of ATS and F/L Middlemiss OC ITS.

During March, S/L Phil Ford from Air Board, F/O Polley and five flight sergeants ferried seven new Wirraways for 12Sqn from Uranquinty to Darwin via Mildura, Parafield, Pirie, Marree, Oodnadatta, Alice Springs, Tennants Creek and Daly Waters. There was an air raid alarm at Batchelor on 12 March before they set out the next day to return with the seven old, exchanged Wirraways. One over-shot at Tennants Creek – the pilot stayed there for six months installed in the pub and became known as "the king of Tennants Creek". Vern Polley lost his tail wheel at Alice Springs and taxied with the tail up all the way home.[5]

On 27 March 1942, wings were presented to the 40 pilots who graduated from Course 17. Eleven were posted to 2 Communication Flight at Kingsford Smith Aerodrome, Mascot whose duties were travel flights and the ferrying of aircraft to units. Seven went to the CFS Camden to undergo 17 Elementary Instructors Course. Other postings were to 3AD, Archerfield, 3WAGS, Maryborough and the remainder to embarkation depots.[6]

18 Course graduated on 18 May and from then on 5SFTS produced a batch of pilots every month with two exceptions

- there was a gap between the graduations of 20 Course on 22 July and 21 Course on 16 September, and 22 and 23 Courses graduated together on 13 October. Courses 20 to 25 also graduated fewer pupils than average. The perturbations can be explained by the interference with the flying training program caused by the flurry of activity surrounding 64 and 65 Reserve Squadrons and the consequent unavailability of instructors and Wirraways. Bill Merrett recalled that 'on 22 Course, after only one week at Uranquity, 13 pupils were shipped off to Canada to do SFTS',[7] and this may have happened to other courses.
- there was a gap between 50 and 57 Courses from January to June 1945, and, although the graduations had continued monthly through to 50 Course, there was no 49 Course. The gap in numbering is explained by the glut of pilots finally produced by the EATS as it was coming to an end with the holding back of 49 Course which resumed as 57 Course six months later. In between 50 and the final 57 Course, refresher courses were conducted at Uranquinty for pilots currently surplus to demands.

Originally at 5SFTS accommodation was to be provided for 70 Officers, 97 sergeants, 200 trainees, 805 airmen totalling 1,172. By February 1942 the effective strength was 61 officers, 93 trainees and 681 airmen totalling 835. In March the total had risen to 962 comprising 66 officers, four nurses, 132 trainees, 758 airmen and two airwomen.[6]

"Saturday leave, Wagga, October 1944"
48 Course: Left to right; Keith Holland, "Slim" Littlewood, Eric Wills, John Fullerton-Smith,
Keith Graham, Ken Hall, Greg Morrison, Bill Williams and Dudley Fulton.
(R. Davies)

Uranquinty worked a six-day week with Saturday off. The army at Kapooka, between Uranquinty and Wagga Wagga, had Sunday off. Saturday provided for most the chance to catch up with chores and letter writing, and for the trainees to learn the week's lessons against examination day. Local leave after a few aimless outings tended not be taken, except for those with friends or relatives in the district, and many did not bother to leave the base. Instead the station stood down several times a year and there were special trains to the big cities of Sydney and Melbourne from which most hailed. PORs contain pages and pages of lists of those granted allowances for the four to five-days leave. The ranks and numbers are also given, providing a comprehensive register of those currently on the station. Key personnel were left on the base and took leave at another time, sometimes combining two leaves in one, especially if they were from distant areas.

On 16 April 1942, a Station Ground Defence Exercise was held in which one Company from 21st Reconnaissance Battalion at Wagga Wagga, with 22 Bren carriers and armoured cars, assisted personnel of 5SFTS in defence of station against attack by three Companies of the A.M.F. Unit. RAAF personnel dispersed to slit trenches, and Vickers and Lewis gun posts and first aid posts were manned according to the Station Defence Scheme.[6]

In mid 1942 the war outlook was grim – the Japs were advancing in New Guinea and our troops were in the Middle East. PORs contain list after list of station personnel attending bayonet training courses and gas courses. The best of the Wirraways were formed into two reserve squadrons.

Reservists were at this stage being called up into temporary positions while awaiting admission to aircrew training and some were classified as aircrew guards. Some were posted to Uranquinty to augment the guards set at night over the aircraft in the hangars and on the tarmac and the precious fuel resources. Provision was made originally for four 10,000 gallon underground petrol tanks in line with the policy of their installation away from the vulnerable seaboard.[8] There were three 1000 gallon oil tanks and another 500 gallon petrol tank in motor transport. There were also dumps where petrol was stored in drums and flammable stores requiring vigilance. Some AC2 aircrew guards spent several months at Uranquinty where they received instruction in ground subjects by day. Denny Kingsbury remembers some miserable winter months at 5SFTS as an aircrew guard in 1942. He had volunteered for aircrew from the army and the RAAF transferred him and other "reserves" out of the army while it was able to do so.

> We were woken to mount guard with 303 rifles on the bleak tarmac among the parked Wirraways. The winter wind and the monotony of four hours on the interminable "graveyard" shift from midnight to 0400hrs had to be suffered to be believed. There was the temptation for shivering "desperates" to seek the shelter of a Wirraway's cockpit despite the possibility of discovery by the duty officer and being put on charge.[9]

PORs do not reveal a guard being placed on charge but they do present, through recording misdemeanours of a variety of personnel, an interesting sideshow of the life and times relating to Uranquinty[10]

> LAC awarded seven days CB by O.C. Intermediate Training Squadron for absenting himself without leave for one day and three hours and forfeits two days pay.
> A flight rigger wrote and forwarded a letter through the post containing Service information, contrary to AFOs. Automatically forfeits seven days pay.
> An airman awarded two days detention for walking in Wagga Wagga with his cap off and not wearing his identity discs.
> LAC awarded 14 days field punishment on 1st charge and fined 5/- on 2nd charge in that he at Uranquinty Hotel acted in an unairman like manner by using insubordinate language and in that he was drunk **A.F.A. Section 40** "conduct to the prejudice of good order and air force

discipline" and **A.F.A. Section 19** "Drunkeness".
An airman awarded 15 days detention in that he had a camera in his possession contrary to SSOs (possession of a camera is an offence against the National Security Regulations).

F/O Jim Dive was posted to 5SFTS in July 1942 to teach navigation and acquired quite a practice as Defending Officer at Court Martials, having the advantage that as a lawyer he knew more about the law than the average RAAF officer and from his job more about flying than the usual legal officer. One case recalled was that of a staff Sergeant Pilot charged with flying at less than 500 feet over the neighbouring army establishment at Kapooka which was separated from Uranquinty by a range of low hills. In cross-examination of the rather unpopular squadron leader who had laid the charge he was asked to plot from an Ordinance Survey map the heights of Kapooka, the intervening hills and his position of observation from the tarmac. It was clearly demonstrated that the lowest point over Kapooka visible from the tarmac was about 1,200 feet. The Charge was dismissed, with adverse comments about the prosecution, and Jim Dive was lavishly entertained by a very gratified Sergeant's Mess.[11]

F/L Eddison leads a wings parade past the saluting base on Churchill Square
in front of the gymnasium / cinema.
(1942 photograph from F/L Eddison's sisters Pamela Yonge and Marion Douglas)

The gym allowed Keith Doyle on 36 Course to sharpen his boxing ability and win the right to box as a welterweight for Uranquinty against the Army at Kapooka
   On the night, I received a thump between the shoulder blades and turned to meet a soldier shaped like a beer barrel who said he was their welterweight. I saw no point in aggravating him in advance by saying 'how long ago.' Round 1- RAAF throws straight left. Army's head goes back. Army throws straight left and it stops two inches short. RAAF realises there is a reach advantage and takes the round. Half way through round two, Army's second, who looked as though he had had more fights than feeds, shouted 'get him, Freddy.' Army rushed at RAAF, wrapped one arm around his back and proceed to pummel from close range. Not according to the Marquis of Queensberry but result a draw.[12]

Scrubbed as a pilot, there was a wait of some weeks before Keith was remustered to navigator/ bomb aimer
   The WO(D) sent for me 'you can't do nothing, I had better find a job for you.' He elaborated you can sell the stuff in the canteen especially the french letters as the WAAAFs cannot be

asked to do that. Stupidly I told the hut of my 'promotion' to part-time condom salesman. That evening they all arrived and formed a long queue buying one each – giggling WAAAFs and an embarrassed LAC. However never let it be said that I don't carry great memories of Uranquinty.

George Clissold remembered one exciting activity at "Bar 20" when the Bishop of Riverina sought partners for the girls from The Rock at the debutantes ball. Course 22 who provided the escorts had a hilarious time practising the waltz with one another in their hut.[13]

Women's Auxiliary Australian Air Force

In July 1942 the effective strength had grown to 66 officers, one WAAAF officer, four nurses, 239 trainees, 832 airmen and 123 airwomen totalling 1275. During May, 24 airwomen had been posted from 2RD Bradfield Park in the categories of Messwoman, Clerk Stores, Sick Quarters Attendant, Storeshand, Fabric Worker and Tailoress. By August there were 131 airwomen.[14] The growth in the number of airwomen is reflected in this newspaper snippet from the memorabilia kept by Olive Jardine (WAAAF Cpl McNeil)[15]

> A visiting journalist watching night flying reported a confusion of sounds as plane after plane, engines revving, taxied, turned into wind and left onlookers choking in the gritty swirl of their slipstreams.
>
> With the exception of the pilots, a few aircraft mechanics and two airmen controlling signalling Aldis[16] lights, WAAAFs had charge of operations. They were driving flyers to the taxi point where they picked up their aircraft. They were standing by the emergency ambulance and fire tender, WAAAF telephonists were on duty in the control room and most important of all WAAAF cooks and messing staff were getting ready meals and drinks for the boys coming off flying. WAAAF timekeepers were out in the field working in the glare of the Chance light like a miniature lighthouse which flooded the field for returning flyers ....

The third birthday party of the formation of the WAAAF,[17] which eventually numbered 27,200, was marked with a parade before the Commanding Officer, G/C Curnow,[18] on 15 March 1944.

WAAAF group at Birthday Parade, Uranquinty, 15 March 1944
Front rank (L to R): Bronwyn Gell, Pat Orman, Nancy King,
June Fawcett, Evelyn Jenkins, Inez Stevens, and Mary Brownlee.
(Joan Sullivan).

WAAAFs worked with or replaced airmen as flight riggers doing the inspections on airframes, and as fitters or flight mechanics on engines. When ACWs Del Leys and Nancy Wilson reported for duty at No.1 Tarmac at Uranquinty

"The poor flight sergeant in charge nearly had a heart attack but we soon proved we could do the work and got along fine with the ground crew. We were the first two WAAAFs to do the flight riggers' course at Ascot Vale."

Sheila Van Emden was a flight mechanic in the major inspection hangar[19]
"In May 1944, 14 WAAAFs took the place of 12 airmen who were posted north. We worked 7 days straight if things were tough. We were a mixed lot and helped each other, tears and laughter. We had Monday night dances and put on concerts in the gym."

Joan Sullivan (nee Symons) 106211 was a clerk general in Station HQ from October 1942 to June 1944 and worked for the SAO, CO and Adjutant. As she typed PORs and DROs, much of the data gathered for this book about 5SFTS from these sources can

W/C Curnow addressing the WAAAF Birthday Parade
(Joan Sullivan)

be ascribed to her typewriter. She did her "rookie" training at Robertson, NSW and became accustomed to the complete loss of privacy which attended life in a hut with 30 or 40 other girls.[20] In Hut 81, Edna Hillier (nee James) 109938 said there was a little fur coat, its true ownership unknown, which was used by all its inhabitants on those occasions when stepping out in civvies.[21] Like most former personnel they have fond memories of Uranquinty although it was recounted with some wryness that, when the outside girls came to station dances in their pretty dresses, the WAAAFs were in uniform, most often drabs.[22]

Concert We're Away performed in the gym
(AWM PO56/64/28)

C hapter 5

From Call-up to
Elementary Flying Training School

Recruiting brochures did not need to paint a glowing picture of the conditions of service, as school leavers were queuing up to join the RAAF. So many young men wanted to fly, though first they had to turn 18 and obtain parental or guardian consent before application to join the RAAF would be accepted.   Advertising rates of pay for aircrew, which were superior to the army, was almost irrelevant, although the promise of a King's commission for one third of graduating pilots was icing on the cake.

"They all want to be fighter pilots when they grow up nowadays."

(Daily Express or Daily Mail, 1944.)

Because of the queue, there was then a wait before volunteers for aircrew could be interviewed and undergo the rigorous medical and aptitude testing at the recruitment centre.[1] Physical fitness for flight training, for example exclusion of colour blindness, was needed. Only selected were those educated to a level high enough for them to be able to cope with the mathematics and science required for aircrew training in ground subjects like navigation and meteorology. The Air Training Corps was a valuable source of young recruits as they had already received some of the desired background and they were ready to start aircrew training immediately on reaching 18.

R.A.A.F. Publication No. 93.
(June, 1940.)

COMMONWEALTH OF AUSTRALIA.

—————

ROYAL AUSTRALIAN AIR FORCE.

—————

MANUAL

FOR

AIR CREW RESERVISTS.

—————

✓

Photo-lithographed by Authority:
L. F. JOHNSTON, COMMONWEALTH GOVERNMENT PRINTER, CANBERRA.
3709.   (Printed in Australia.)

Cover of RAAF Publication No. 93 (June 1940).

The RAAF, having selected the recruits it wanted and applied the Oath of Allegiance, guarded its future property zealously by issuing reserve badges for those it was unable to absorb at once. An issue was made of a superb instructional book, the RAAF **Manual for Aircrew Reservists** compiled from the RAF Publications No. 129 Flying Training Manual, Part 1, Land Planes and No. 1234 Manual of Air Navigation, Vol. 1.[2] On the fly was "Air crew reservists should find the publication of interest and of value if it is read and studied intelligently during the period they are awaiting call up." In potted form it contained much of the material that was to be inculcated during later training

> Elementary navigation
> Meteorology
> The theory of flight
> Engines
> Airframes

On reading a portion of the airframes section recently, more attention than would have been given by a reservist at that time was focused on the following passage

The elevator is hinged to the rear spar of the tail plane, and can be moved through an arc about its hinge.

The reason is seen in the accompanying triptych showing, after a belly landing back at base, how near loss of control had been following passage of Flak within an ace of the elevator hinge.

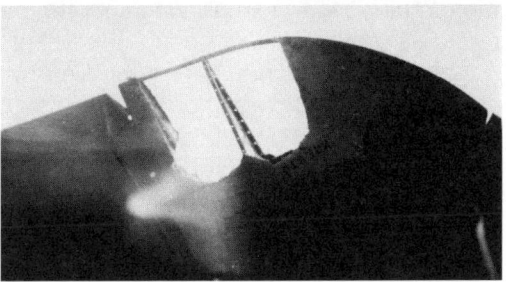

T for Tommie after an anti-shipping strike by the RAF Dallachy Strike Wing
in Fede Fjord on 11 April 1945

Most recruits wanted to be pilots and a "pilot only" category from the result of testing at the recruiting centre left the reservist with a degree of euphoria. There was then a seemingly interminable delay tempered by the observation that at least the waiting list was shortening. As the manpower shortage worsened and with the army vying for recruits, the air force made sure of retaining its rights over those it had screened and wanted by calling up its reservists in temporary positions such as aircrew guards or clerks.

Dick McKenzie 432851[2] (36 Course) was with a group of some sixty recruits told to report with a cut lunch to Woolloomooloo. Transferred in buses, the memory of that day was reinforced by the cat calls of "You'll be sorry" which greeted their arrival at Initial Training School, Bradfield Park.

Initial Training School

Every month, commencing simultaneously in the United Kingdom and the Dominions with 1 Course in April 1940, a new batch of aircrew trainees entered the Initial Training Schools (ITSs). Many aircrew trainees had just left school and few were out of their early twenties. Many in a different generation would have been on motor bikes. All were driven by the zeal to fly.

The initial training school in New South Wales was 2ITS Bradfield Park. Others were located at Somers in Victoria, Sandgate in Queensland, Victor Harbour in South Australia, and Clontarf in Western Australia.

Recategorisation might take place on call-up to the ITS in an attempt to segregate pilots from other aircrew categories by the result of aptitude tests, like the one for visual ability which required placing lions in cages on 3-D screens. It was important to try and foretell success or failure at the next stage of training at the elementary flying training school. The wastage to the war effort, in having failures later in training after expenditure of valuable resources, continued to be addressed by development of special tests. One of these was the co-ordination test which involved following a circle of light on a large screen with another circle of light controlled by the aspiring pilot with a joystick. Those who had obtained some experience on the Link Trainer,while waiting in temporary RAAF posts, were at an advantage and were able to achieve excellent but spurious scores for co-ordination. Other tests were evolved in attempts to lower the wastage or scrub rate.

Bob Davies (48 Course) had always wanted to fly after Kingsford Smith took him up as a five-year old, when a barn-storming flight organised by his father at Wagga was not full. He entered the RAAF at Bradfield park two weeks after turning 18 in November 1943, and after testing was graded PNBW (pilot, navigator, bomber, wireless).[3]

The difference in ages of the recruits, though small, was important at this time of life, and there were differences in background as well as temperament. These enforced acquaintances took a little while to shake down. Kitted, named and numbered[2] the aircrew trainees entered the service as aircraftsmen second class (AC2), ranked lower than an "erk",[4] sometimes used mischievously to describe all those entering at the bottom of other branches of the air force who were aircraftsman first class. Among the lowest echelon in the airforce there quickly developed a commonality of feeling of "us and them", especially in response to early meeting with air force discipline in the form of drill instructors.

Derek de Beaurepaire, born in England in 1922, and with his course set for Sandhurst from Rossall School, changed direction on being shown an Avro biplane which had just flown over Mount Everest. Moving to Australia with his parents to join the Australian side of the family, he became one of the 'drongos' in 'goon skins'[5] on 17 Course. Drill instructors became tongue tied with his name and they barely got past the 'de' before he said "present, Sir".

Discipline meant tedious drill sessions, inspection of clothing and personal appearance, and tidiness in the huts. As new members of the RAAF, there had to be instruction in and insistence on airforce law, Air Force Orders and King's Regulations. Who could forget "conduct prejudicial to good air force order and discipline" ?

The sense of unity became stronger over the ensuing weeks of meeting the hard physical challenge of training in the gym and of obstacle courses together with the mental one of seemingly endless lessons and the need to go over and learn them at the end of the tiring day. The emphasis placed on ground instruction would be continued all the way through training and beyond final graduation as aircrew. Struan Robertson (36 Course) recalled that the weekly round of mathematics and science as preamble to applied airforce subjects was broken on Tuesday nights by a live ABC concert, in the series of "Take it from here" by Jimmy Edwards and cast.[6]

Many new firm friendships were made only to have these bonds broken at the completion of ITS by being drafted into one of three streams, depending on assessment and categorisation, as either pilot, observer or wireless operator air gunner. Further, at this stage under the agreements of the EATS, every four weeks 42 observers and 72 wireless operator-air gunners from the output of the Australian ITSs went to continue their training in Canada, filling 1/10 of the places in the EATS schools.[7,8]

From 28 Course at 2ITS, John Wood was one of those sent to train as an air observer in Canada. The contingent went by train to Brisbane in August 1942 to embark on the *SS Klipfontein*.

> It was a terrible old rust bucket which had been taken over by the US Forces and was crewed by Americans including a lot of their servicemen being sent home for disciplinary reasons. They were supposed to cook for us but fortunately we had a baker and a butcher among our group and we managed to cross the Pacific reasonably satisfactorily, although all the bunks were in an unventilated hold below water level making conditions pretty terrible.
>
> It was then by train over the Rockies to a manning depot in Edmonton, Alberta where, meeting New Zealanders and snow, a new experience for most of us, we played some very unscientific ice hockey.[9]

In late November he was one of 26 Australians and four Canadians on No. 63 Course[10] of the Air Observer's School at Edmonton. At its completion in March 1943 he was one of three who had topped the course and was posted to Dorval, just outside Montreal, to join what was then called RAF Ferry Command.[11]

Postings

Dating from call-up came the realisation of the omnipotence and finality of Air Board directives. Friends who had joined up together were separated on being placed in groups according to alphabetical listing of names and subsequent posting to different establishments.

Whereas in the army groups of soldiers were kept banded together, in the air force airmen were dispersed following innumerable postings hither and thither by Air Board. The inevitable scattering had to be accepted with resignation. It might have been construed in the dry words of Ira Bensley as if it was done according to the principle "so that they wouldn't gang up on you".[12]

Recent companions became lost to view, some so effectively that they were not seen or heard of again. In following chapters there are accounts taken at random of the paths taken by some Empire Air Trainees. In these windows may be found some information regarding many of the activities in which others engaged during their unfolding air force careers, sometimes only vaguely known and even totally incomprehensible to those who followed other paths.

Under the EATS, Australia undertook the training of all its aircrew at its own ITSs. Having split off a proportion of the observer and wireless operator-air gunner streams to Canada, the remainder of aircrew trainees from ITS continued their training in Australia. The trainees on dispersion to elementary flying training, air observer, and wireless operator-air gunnery schools were assessed for their suitability to continue.

Elementary Flying Training School

The Country does not train or pay an airman to get killed – but to stay alive and kill his country's enemies.
>   (RAAF handout on going to elementary flying training school.)

There were 12 elementary flying training schools (EFTSs). One of these in NSW was 8EFTS Narrandera. Jim Banyard (21 Course), newly promoted from AC2 to LAC, arrived there at the time the Japanese entered the war. He recalled:
> It was summer and for some weeks instead of flying we were digging slit trenches around the aerodrome in temperatures of 100F. It was a very dry time and every morning the dust storms would blow up. Because of the hot winds and thermal currents we took off in the Tiger Moths very early in the morning. Reveille was at 0400 and we started flying at 0500 and finished about 0830. Then we had a break and did our technical and theoretical training in ground subjects during the afternoon.[13]

Ground subjects, previously the province of the classroom, now began to be applied. Beginning with the basic theory of flight, there commenced the transition to what was actually happening in and around the cockpit during flying, to do with controls and engines. Movements, at first jerky, became smoother as reflexes began to turn into flying habits, rather like learning to ride a bike. Dating from this time, Stephen Aboud developed the unusual habit of wearing his watch back to front to prevent it catching on the left side of the Tiger's cockpit where the throttle is hard up against the fuselage. He had his first bout of alcohol at Narrandera.
> We had a fellow on course who was pretty old, probably about twenty, who had transferred from the army and he urged the lads not to hang about the camp but to come to town and have a few beers. After a lot of badgering I went into Narrandera one Saturday afternoon and after repairing to the Greek café for the mandatory steak and eggs to bolster the RAAF diet I sat down at the bar of the hotel. I had three or four beers and didn't like it and said this isn't doing anything for me and the barmaid said have a rum with it. In my innocence I had about two rums and beer chasers and somebody took me out and put me on the bus and I didn't fly for 24 hours. However my subsequent dislike of beer soon wore off.[14]

George Clissold (21 Course) first soloed in February 1942 at 6EFTS Tamworth. Tamworth was in the process of being changed to an instructors' school and some of the course were chosen to fly their Tiger Moths to the new site for the EFTS at Narromine. Landing at Coonabarabran they received a right royal welcome, as the President of the CWA there was the mother of a fellow pupil pilot, Alan Chappell, and they flew on loaded with cake and fruit.[15]

At 11EFTS Benalla, where David Yates was doing his elementary flying at the end of 1941, half of his 28 Course was conducted on Tigers and half on Wackett Trainers. He had joined the RAAF after two years in engineering at the University of Sydney, which had to be kept quiet as otherwise he would not have been allowed to volunteer for aircrew.[16]

Keith Pollard (34 Course at Narrandera), on a cross country exercise, observed from 3,000ft the Tiger Moth supposed to be spaced out three minutes ahead of him low flying. Dropping down to be companionable he saw it skimming the treetops which whiplashed as he went past, and then appear to sideslip. Keith decided it would be best to see no more and politic to resume station at 3,000ft and continue the exercise. The pupil pilot of the other aircraft on reaching base explained the rent in his wingtip as being due to hitting an oil drum while taxying. Keith said

> He was charged and I escorted him to the subsequent hearing where he was more or less exonerated. However, as we left the room I heard the flight commander say "that's the first time I've known an oil drum smell like a gum tree." [17]

During EFTS one in three might be rejected during flying instruction. EFTS could also have its dangers. "As forgiving as was the much loved Tiger Moth, five trainees and two instructors were killed," wrote Denny Kingsbury of his 33 Course.[18] He continued

> At the end of EFTS a decision was made which had a profound effect on the chance of survival. Were we to be directed to "multis", aircraft with two or more engines, or to "singles" for further training? Many trainees posted to multis were to fill the ranks of Bomber Command, being drastically thinned in the RAF's strategic bombing campaign over Germany. As more bomber pilots were required, many single engine or SE pilots on arrival in England underwent conversion to multis. Another decision made by "the man at Air Board" was whether training would be continued in Australia or Canada.

Thus, there were more partings of the ways by the provision under the EATS for 80 of those successfully completing the elementary flying training courses every four weeks in Australia[19] to go to Canadian service flying training schools filling 1/8 of the EATS places.[20] In May 1943, Denny Kingsbury was one of the trainee pilots who embarked for Canada on the Liberty ship *President Munroe* which was in the same waters as the hospital ship *Centaur* when sunk by a Japanese submarine. Gaining his wings at No. 37 SFTS Calgary in Western Canada, he considered himself fortunate enough to be posted to No. 1 OTU at Bagotville, north of Montreal in Eastern Canada to fly Hurricanes. Again he considered himself lucky when, after crossing the Atlantic on the *Aquitania* in January 1944, he was posted to 57OTU where "his and most other pilots' ambition to fly a 'Spitty' was realised."[18]

From EFTS most trainee pilots went on to SFTS in Australia and from 17 Course onwards their destination included the newly opened 5SFTS Uranquinty.

Instruction in physical fitness, wireless (Morse), gunnery and instrument flying (Link Trainer)
(Wings)

THE ART OF INSTRUCTING

TEE EMM showing the TEE EMM heading with P/O Prune, the message from Portal and the heading THE ART OF INSTRUCTING[1]

hapter 6   Instructors

At the outbreak of war there was one flying training school and just sixteen instructors.

The training to be given shall be in accordance with the syllabus of instruction laid down for each similar course of training in the United Kingdom.[2]

Although steps were taken to implement the EATS agreement as soon as it was signed in November 1939, time was needed to open schools and train instructors and it was not until 29 April 1940 that the first pupils entered ITS. All aircrew training in Australia, the other Dominions and the United Kingdom would now be according to the EATS.[3]

No.1 Flying Training School at Point Cook had been graduating twenty or so pilots every six months from year long courses and when the EATS was signed Australia had facilities for training only 100 pilots a year. Commitment to the agreement entailed graduating hundreds of pilots every month which demanded the creation of a previously unthought of number of flying schools.[4] Australia not only undertook to provide facilities for the training of thousands of aircrew, she had to find instructors on the ground and in the air.

While a technical training program turned out technicians, some of whom became ground instructors, flying instruction was augmented from civilian sources with the aero clubs in each State and a number of schools being approved as contractors for flying training for the RAAF.[5] In NSW these were Airflite Ltd, Kingsford-Smith Air Service Ltd, Newcastle Aero Club, and NSW Aero Club.

At the end of 1939, a Flying Instructors' School had just been established at Point Cook with a training capacity of 46 every eight weeks. By retaining some of the best pupils graduating, the capacity was to be lifted to 50 but filling this capacity was dependent on a supply of trained pilots coming forward for entry. Apart from serving pilots with the RAAF, pupil flying instructors had to come from the Civil Air Reserve. At that time there were only 78 with more than 100 flying hours. There were several hundred, if over 50 hours was accepted, although some would not pass the medical examination and others would prefer to serve in the Field Force. Those enlisting were all in need of further flying experience at the civil flying schools before commencing an instructor's course. It was estimated that it would cost 30,000 pounds to give 150 pilots 75 hours at two pounds twelve shillings and sixpence an hour.[6] They would be paid eight shillings a day for an average period of ten weeks. Through the implementation of these measures, the few pre-war instructors were rapidly outnumbered by recently graduated instructors.

Earl Vonarx[7] started on the second course of the EATS one month after it commenced in April 1940. His flying instruction was by aero club pilots on Tiger Moths at 4EFTS Mascot. A bout of German measles put him back to 4 Course which was on Avro Ansons at 2SFTS Forest Hill. A burst eardrum delayed him further. He graduated on Avro Ansons in April 1941 on 6 Course, which was the first batch from which not all were sent overseas, each alternate graduate only, by name, going to "the disposal of the RAF".

Retained to become an instructor he was posted to 2BAGS Port Pirie to fly Fairey Battles which he considered a cut above the Wirraways with their cruising speed of 160 mph. At 100 feet after take off, the pitch control of the two speed propeller was pushed from 'fine' into 'coarse' giving a pronounced 'thunk' as the Battle went into a good rate of climb.

In October he went to Camden[8], where the Central Flying School had been formed, for an instructor's course of three weeks comprising 70 hours dual in Avro Trainers A6. These aircraft required to be flown very smoothly and were ideal for knocking off any roughness in the pilot's flying. He was introduced to the patter of instructors but at his next posting, 11 EFTS Benalla, developed some language and methods of his own as he in turn taught trainees. His pupils had one month on the Tiger Moth and then another on the Wackett (phased out over time as too difficult for trainees).

In the air the intense concentration of the pupil on the task at hand had to be understood by the instructor. If he said for example, while the pupil was fully engaged in making the final descending turn to line up on the runway, "don't hold off bank in a gliding turn", the correction was as if it had never been heard. The pupil did exactly the same thing next time. The job required patience and it was exacting to get a pupil up to the stage where confidence in his ability to go solo was not misplaced. A few pupils possessed aptitude, while others needed coaxing along to pass the solo test deadline of between eight and ten hours of dual flying time, and some, about one third at this time, were scrubbed. Some instructors, recognising the potential of a pupil making slow but steady progress, were rewarded when the trainee made it after some extra lessons which were not recorded in the flight book.

F/L Eric Cook, F/O Vern Polley and P/O Frank Gardner were the first three instructors at 5SFTS Uranquinty in October 1941. Initially employed in flying the new school's aircraft in from Laverton, they were soon joined in ferrying the Wirraways by F/L Brand, F/Os Kerville and Paxton and P/O McCulloch and by the end of November 1941 there were 28 aircraft on charge and flying instruction had started.[9]

Instructors might be separated by only a few months training from those they trained. As with master and pupil at the schools from which they had just left, where there was a match between the temperament of instructor and trainee progress was enhanced. If not, it could be an unhappy experience. Within the range of the jovial to the taciturn, after the same mistake had been made frequently, instructors could become more than impatient. Some in their exasperation could become "screamers" and use a taut phrase like "You'll kill me!".

The Song of 37 Course went to the tune of *Ivan Stravinsky*
>Our training made progress
>But we all must confess
>Our hopes of our wings we belied,
>For as we turned onto track,
>There's a scream from the back,
>"You'll spin and kill me",
>>An instructor cried.

The unfairness of the postings lottery, in being lumbered with teaching trainees instead of going to operational squadrons, was prone to rankle and eat away at instructors over the months and years, as their pupils sprouted wings and went overseas.

Following Singapore and Pearl Harbour, Reserve Squadrons were formed urgently at Uranquinty on 10 December 1941. Personnel and Wirraways were allotted and instructions given to make the aircraft operationally serviceable and prepare all equipment. There was some interference to the training program as instructors themselves were required to train for this role. Further the best of the Wirraways had to be modified for dive bombing, equipped with wireless and a rear gun, necessitating ferrying them to Sydney for fitment.[10] On 29 December the squadrons were numbered 64 and 65 (G.P.) Reserve Squadrons. On 28 January 1942, No.64 (G.P.) Squadron carried out a 3-day trial move to Corowa with ground personnel comprising 40% of total squadron ground personnel, the convoy arriving at Corowa at 1400. The squadron of 18 Wirraways (three flights of six) proceeded to Corowa via Deniliquin with operational training over three days from Thursday 29 January. Other exercises can be traced in PORs as in March 1942, when Wirraway A20-182 ground looped at Tennants Creek and another bounced and ground looped at Maree S.A..[12] Jim Dive, who taught Navigation to the trainees, became squadron navigator to S/L Nigel Pilcher OC ATS who commanded 65Sqn (Reserve). S/L Pilcher was later killed in New Guinea.

F/L Susans continued instructing until 1942 when he was posted to 3Sqn for service in the Western Desert, Malta, Sicily and Italy and was awarded the DFC and mentioned in despatches. In 1943 he was appointed to command 79Sqn in the Pacific and at the end of the war he was Wing Leader in the Spitfire Wing and again mentioned in despatches.[12]

Ira Bensley, who did his wireless training at 2WAGS, Parkes, on Wackett Trainers and his air gunnery at 2BAGS, Port Pirie, on Fairey Battles, was one of the Sergeant WAGS attached to the reserve squadrons at Uranquinty from 18 August 1942 to 3 February 1943.[13] He managed a gas operated Vickers machine gun from the position behind the pilot instructor. The squadrons did dive bombing and formation flying. On 25 November they flew over Sydney in support of the 100,000,000 pounds Austerity Loan when more that 100,000 people saw 5,000 RAAF men, nurses, WAAAFs and Air Training Corps cadets march through the city.

Flight of Wirraway Reserve Squadrons piloted by instructors over Martin Place.
From a crumpled Daily Telegraph of 26 November 1942.
(Ira Bensley)

WAGS at Christmas dinner in the Sergeant's mess, 1943.
(Ira Bensley)

In October 1942 Earl Vonarx returned for one month to CFS, which by now had moved to Tamworth,[8] in order to convert to Wirraways so as to be able to instruct at 5SFTS Uranquinty. From the mature pupils of his early days of instructing, the trainees were now younger, more in fear of being scrubbed and often too deferential to instructors. The flight commander made the most immature and nervous sit each day on the floor of the instructors' room and repeat several times "bugger all instructors" until the imprecation changed from a whisper to a confident note.[14]

Intermediate Training Squadron, 5SFTS in 1942. (Group of instructors)
(Australian War Memorial negative number P02-28.019)

The problem with instructing was that the pupil had to be allowed as much rope as possible before being corrected. Any number of situations required nice judgement as to whether the instructor should take over or, as in the case of a high bounce on landing, let the pupil continue to attempt to put the aircraft down when he might lose control. Derek Beaurepaire, a 17 Course pupil who had become an instructor, told his pupil after ballooning to go round again

> Whereat he rammed the throttle on so fast that he stalled the engine leaving me the task of being unable to do anything. I got the blame and a stamp in my log book – carelessness.[15]

In any number of situations there was little room left for manoeuvre and, while intervention too soon was stifling, lack of intervention might turn out to be very expensive as indicated in this entry in a POR of June 1944 when a flight sergeant instructor was severely reprimanded by his CO

> In that he when Instructor in Charge of His Majesty's Aircraft A20-564 with an LAC pupil failed to supervise the control exercised by the said LAC over the said aircraft whereby the said aircraft came into collision with aircraft A20-612 causing damage to both aircraft to the extent of approximately 20,000 pounds.[16]

By 1944 the monotony of instructing had got to a lot of instructors. On Stephen Aboud's first flight in a Tiger Moth the instructor said, how do you feel, and on his replying fine, he said, "Do you mind if we invert the aeroplane, you'll be hanging in your straps, but the instructors are having a competition to see who can fly the longest or furthest upside down." He thought the request was rather strange but the instructor was a good sort of chap. His hobby was duck shooting of which he was very fond. One day after he had given Stephen a few hours instruction, "he came out armed with a shot gun saying there are a lot of ducks on the farm over at Leeton. Having waved to his father, he said we'll go down the river and you take over and we'll see if we can shoot some ducks. Fortunately nothing got up as it is not hard to imagine some part of the aeroplane being blasted off. He was a funny fellow, a sergeant and it can be assumed he stayed one for the rest of his career, a lovely man."[17]

Incidents of maladroitness could be exasperating if funny afterwards. Earl Vonarx recalls coming in to land and not being able to get the undercart down.[18] He wrestled with the u/c handle but it would not budge and finally broke with his exertion. In preparing for a wheels-up landing he called to his pupil to tighten his straps which necessitated first unhooking them. In doing so the trainee found that he had done up the strap so that it had wrapped around his front u/c lever preventing the instructor's rear handle working.   The wheels then came down.

In 1944 Earl managed to obtain a special duties posting to the UK although pilots with more than 500 hours were not supposed to leave Australia. In September, although with a wealth of hours on SE aircraft, it was too late to expect a posting to fighters. He could never emulate those he referred to in the RAF jest:

> Why do fighter pilots wear their top button undone ? They don't live long enough to do it up.

Instead he was directed to the hazardous bomber stream to commence multi training at 20AFU Kidlington on Airspeed Oxfords. He then went through 27OTU at Church Broughton on Wellingtons and 1667HCU at Sandtoft on Lancasters, to be posted with over 2000 flying hours experience to 110 Sqn RAF, but not in time to become operational.

Ralph Oberg was flying instructor to Bill Merrett[19] who said of him – "a very steady and unflappable type. He was locked in to instructing at 'Quinty for some years but eventually got a little time on Boomerangs and survived the war."

F/L "Grumpy" Eddison, OC of Advanced Training Squadron, got away earlier from instructing at 5SFTS, but lost his life over New Guinea in 1943 on Beaufighters with 30 Sqn, beccoming one of those without known graves.

Finally Derek Beaurepaire got a posting away from instructing to do operational training at 2OTU Mildura. He found that the rules forbidding instructors from flying violent manoeuvres left him unprepared for the antics of the young who had just finished the flying course.[20]

> I had to do some awfully swift rethinking and my landings, night flying and instrument flying made up for my caution while others wrote themselves off. Red Walker who was on the same OTU course and had been Chief Instructor at Deniliquin selected me to be one of the pilots of the new 78 Kittyhawk Squadron to be formed at Camden.

Those who had done a tour of operations took their turn at instructing. From the Kittyhawks of 78Sqn David Yates[21] found himself posted in April 1944 to 32 Elementary Instructors Course at Parkes on Tigers. Subsequently he became "brassed off" instructing on Tigers at Temora. Then after another instructors course on Wirraways at Deniliquin, he was rewarded in January 1945 with a posting to the OTU at Parkes on Spitfires. Moving between the Kittyhawk and the Spitfire meant remembering in the latter to touch the brakes as the wheels retracted. Otherwise there was a bang as the wheels came to rest against the walls of the bay with the likelihood of a burst tire to contend with on landing. In March 1945 he went back to the South West Pacific with 457Sqn at Morotai.

The last word about instructors must come from a trainee experiencing a personality clash. Keith Pollard (34 Course) recalled a particularly bad day with the instructor ear-bashing him all the way round a low-level cross country exercise. When they landed at the satellite, Belfrayden, with the instructor still carrying on about all his mistakes, he was in such a nervous state and not capable of logical thinking that he exploded throwing all caution to the winds

> I called him all the filthy names I could think of. He said "you can't talk to me like that," to which I replied, "What do you mean I can't – I am talking to you like that, are you going so & so deaf, you so & so fool." I think I invented a few new swear words. "I'll have you on a charge – insubordination to a flying instructor and a commissioned officer." "Of course you will", I replied "You haven't any option you so & so idiot." "Well, take the aircraft solo", he said. Stunned silence but I was too far gone to let up, "It's no good me going solo in my present state, it would be waste of public money, you so & so fool." In retrospect it wasn't a bad answer for a distressed 18 year-old. "Are you yellow?", he said which set me off again. Quickly the thought went through my head, if I am going to spend the rest of the war in a military prison I may as well make it worthwhile. I said, "Well, get out." Before he got both feet on the ground I opened the throttle full bore and he must have gone to ground to let the tail plane pass over him. I loved side slipping in for a landing – circuits and side slips, full throttle again from take-off, round and round with the cylinder head temperature going up and down too. I finally cooled off, parked the aircraft, put my parachute on the rack and went into the flight office. Not a word was said. He must have told the flight commander "I have pushed this kid to the limit – if he doesn't kill himself – I won't press charges." His name appears a lot in my log book – he wasn't a bad bloke after all.[22]

Chapter 7 Trainees – Intermediate Training Squadron

You can tell a trainee pilot but you cannot tell him much
(Adage)

By the time trainees arrived all was in place for flying training to commence, and all thoughts were for getting airborne, and not one spared for the groundwork which had gone into the provision of accommodation and facilities. Power and light and water were taken for granted and only came to notice in the form of the obstruction lights and wind indicators atop the water tower. The construction of the basics, like the sewerage plant, never impinged on the minds of those using the latrines (except for the rumour (correct) that the officers' W.C.s had doors).

Uranquinty control tower and fire tender.

(Jenny Lewington).

What was seen were the Wirraway aircraft outside the Bellman hangars, and in the background the control tower with attendant fire tender and ambulance. But before joining the throng of ground staff on the tarmac, and the instructors and pupils emerging from the crew rooms, there were more lessons on the ground. The lessons carried on from those at ITS and EFTS. The emphasis on ground training is evident from an Air Board item listing expenditure of 6,852 pounds on furniture for these rooms as "necessary for the efficient training of Empire Air Training Scheme personnel, and, therefore, essential for the defence of Australia".[1]

Jim Dive was posted to 5SFTS in July 1942 as Navigation Officer, having completed the six month's specialist navigation course at 1GRS Cressy. He taught in the School of Instruction from 22 Course to 43 Course. Now in his eighties, he was asked to recall the program of ground instruction given in wartime 50 years ago. He describes it as appearing simple, but it was complicated by things like night flying and operating from satellite aerodromes, so that co-operation with the flying instructors was essential Each course was divided into two flights, each flight in charge of a senior pupil whose job it was to get the flight to the right place at the right time. Two four-hourly programs had to be prepared for each day and the lecturers were F/Ls Len Chapman, George McInerney, Bill Thomson and myself, and Sgt Geoff Ward ran the Morse. The subjects included armaments, aircraft and ship recognition, airframes, engines, meteorology, signals and navigation. Although navigation was usually allocated five hours a week and the principles instilled, it finally reduced to what a single engine pilot could manage with a calculator and navigation pad strapped to a knee and some maps.[2]

There was a technical library whose most avidly read books were the volumes of the Training Manual (TEE EMM).[3] A monthly publication of the RAF (and forerunner of Air Clues), its arrival was anticipated and read from cover to cover because of its light-hearted yet instructive approach, cleverly illustrated, to training problems. Some of the escapades of the main cartoon character P/O Prune, with his loveable yet foolish face, are reproduced.[4]

There was a separate Morse hut and another building housed the Link Trainers, where flight was simulated with instruments. Some trainees became addicted to the challenge provided by precision flying under the hood but others found these half-hour sessions a chore.

IT MAKES YOU THINK ! ! !
Hark to the Story of Christopher Spink
(TEE EMM)

Hark to the story of Christopher Spink,
A young Sergeant Pilot (from Sydney we think),
Who never from danger or hazard did shrink,
But suffered from one most unfortunate kink –
He just wouldn't practise I.F. in the Link.

One day, while returning to base o'er the drink,
The weather clamped down with a sky black as ink
And twenty-tenths cloud showing never a chink.
What happened that day caused a terrible stink;
For Christopher's flying just went on the blink
And the capers he cut would make anyone think
That he'd rammed in his finger right up to the brink.

    To cut short our story and save H.M.'s ink,

Our unhappy Chris finished up in the drink.
The kite was a write-off, and as you might think,
The poor duty pilot, in fear that he'd sink,
Until he was rescued , slept never a wink.

At the Court of Enquiry the Acting Chief Gink
Examined C.'s Log Book for times in the Link.
When he found sweet F.A. he raised such a stink
That C. was court-martialled and landed in clink
With practically nothing to do there but think.

But he thought to some purpose, and ironed out his kink,
And now Flying Officer Christopher Spink,
(D.F.C. and two bars), a most popular gink,
Makes a habit of standing sprog pilots a drink.
And to aid their refreshment he tips them the wink
That the way to keep out of the drink and the clink
Is by taking small regular doses of Link.

W.HOOPER

But all thoughts were of flying and what was impatiently anticipated was allocation to instructors and getting airborne. The issue of a parachute was a step in the right direction, but the first issue of equipment was from the barracks' blankets and straw stores. While the rest of the station slept on beds, life was made a little tougher for trainees as they discovered when their first job on arrival was to stuff straw into hessian bags to make the palliasses[5] on which they were to sleep on the floor.

A 37 Course song to the tune of *Charlotte* went like this
> One day when we entered this camp we adore,
> It was only to find that we slept on the floor,
> For the trainees don't matter in places like these
> Since in summer you sweat and in winter you freeze.

"Bar 20" is universally recalled with affection, but it does not take long before ex-trainees recall the dust storms of summer or the frosty winter nights on the NSW plain. The wooden huts did not prevent penetration of the dust through the walls nor the cold through the floors on which the trainees slept coccooned in palliasses. These same ungainly straw-stuffed hessian bags had to be somehow fashioned neatly into three equal folded layers, blankets folded squarely on top and the few possessions stored in kit-bags beneath uniforms draped tidily on nails on the wall, ready for daily hut inspections.

Being a local was very handy for Bob Davies, because he got home regularly at weekends, slept on a proper bed, and enjoyed his mother's cooking.[6] The problem was getting back to the 'drome on Sunday nights as there was no transport. However a goods train ran from Wagga Wagga to a little siding called Bon Accord, and after a trip standing between the wheat trucks on the buffers it was then only a short walk across a paddock. Somehow, he managed to avoid the fate of one airman after another charged under **'A.F.A. Section 11** – neglecting to obey SSOs in that he failed to enter by the main Gate as laid down in S.S.O. 1/F10.'[7]

Uranquinty received its trainees from 1EFTS, 5EFTS Narromine, 8EFTS Narrandera, 10 EFTS Temora and 11EFTS Benalla. They were the survivors of the high `scrub´ rates at these elementary flying training schools. Each month a new group arrived by train with about 60 hours flying experience on Tiger Moths.

At 'Quinty flying did not start so early in the morning because, unlike the light aircraft at EFTS, the Wirraways were not so susceptible to the updrafts and wind created by the sun as the day progressed. One group of trainees flew in the morning, doing lessons in the afternoon and the other group did vice versa.

LAC F.E. Taylor, put back with 14 others from 16 to 17 Course at Narromine because of a mumps outbreak, was on the first course at Uranquinty, and he was the first trainee to fly solo at 5SFTS.[8] However like other Tiger Moth pilots used to a wooden propeller and fabric covered wings and fuselage, he found the Wirraway at first an awesome metal machine complicated by its retractable undercarriage (u/c), flaps, variable pitch propeller and cruising speed twice that of the Tiger. Keith Doyle (36 Course) compared arrival at SFTS from EFTS with the transition from High School to University

> At first glimpse the Wirraway was quite a mark-up from the Tiger Moth and, not withstanding above average rating for aerobatics in Tigers, one's confidence was further somewhat shaken in conversation with the course ahead. They took satisfaction in advising us that an aircraft with high wing-loading like the Wirraway was inclined to drop a wing when held off at 6ft for landing unlike the Tiger which would gently come to ground if stalled at 20ft.[9]

At last airborne in a Wirraway
(K. Sly).

'Quinty was a big disappointment for Bill Merrett at first, because Course 22 didn't start flying for three weeks (as a consequence the small 22 and 23 Courses were to graduate on the same day).[10] At that time with the Japanese advancing and few aircraft of any significance available, some of the 5SFTS training aircraft were formed into reserve squadrons at Uranquinty for the defence of Sydney. A lot of close formation flying was practised, both as squadrons and as pairs which was detrimental to the training programme as it reduced the number of available aircraft and the instructors' time. The accompanying shortage of ground crew, caused by their allocation to the reserve squadrons, meant that trainees did a lot of their own basic servicing, and Bill developed a rash on his hands due to chemical dermatitis. But the delights of flying the Wirraway as the course unfolded then crowd the memory as he recalled the defined aerobatic area near The Rock where student pilots might let their enthusiasm run riot with spins, barrel rolls and flying in and out and under and over magnificent cumulus clouds.

H.T.B. Taylor 421770 ("Perky") came in to 5SFTS from 10EFTS Temora on 27 Course. Menigitis at ITS had required his course to be quarantined. He had a personal history of airsickness flying with an instructor and some pills for it from the MO had allowed him to pass a scrub test
  At 'Quinty I drew an instructor known to some as "screaming skull". The more he yelled the more I ignored him. Despite everything he got out one day and said "take it and go kill yourself." That was the day I was not sick and I never was again. Looking back on it I wonder was it fear of flying, nervous tension, or just fear of failure, that my first 50 hours of flying caused me airsickness most of the time.[11]

As the pupils' flying training at 'Quinty extended over four months, at any one time there were four courses on the station with two in the Intermediate Training Squadron (ITS) and two in the Advanced Training Squadron (ATS).

Intermediate Training Squadron

The Wirraway had dual controls, with the trainee seated in front of the instructor. Dual instruction of pupil pilots accounted for two thirds of the 50 hours of flying training given up to the wing's test. The test provided the barrier from the ITS into the ATS.

Ted Taylor said by the time he reached the 40-hour test he no longer feared being scrubbed (a horrible thought) and felt capable of tackling all aspects of Wirraway flying

> The course at Uranquinty was quite exacting and I think all trainees felt the strain at various times. I had struggled to come up to standard in those first two months: however, instructors like Bob Paxton, Sandy McCulloch, Neil Funston and Murray Nash instilled a great deal of confidence and helped me to make greater efforts to overcome my weaknesses, such as flying in formation and slipping out of slow rolls.[12]

LAC F.E. Taylor, the first pupil pilot to solo at 5SFTS.

In October 1942 Clem Schmitzer's instructors on 27 course were F/L Jackson, F/Os Adsett, Fitton and Nolan, W/O Radkin, F/S Healy, and Sgts Birch, Donovan and Northover.[13] In June 1943 Bill Howard's instructors were F/Ls Bowman, Cullen, Milne and Tucker, F/Os Edwards, Whitehead and Joe Palmer, W/O Vonarx, F/Ss Henville and Sedwick.[14]

Service flying training in the Wirraway at ITS related to operation of the engine, undercarriage and flaps and the controls to enable all flying manoeuvres from circuits and bumps[15] to practising forced landings.

From the first flying lesson, a state of mind familiar to all trainees was expressed by Stephen Aboud[16]

> On course you seem to be either overconfident or underconfident and feeling that you are going to be scrubbed.

However one day he was doing circuits and bumps on his own and after two or three

> I thought this is pretty boring so I was giving it full bore and holding it down and releasing the u/c and there was a bit of a sag and it was exciting while unbeknownst to me the CO was watching. Anyway it was time to come in and land and with the two movements to put the u/c down, the second to lock, it did not work. I thought on landing the u/c will collapse so I did the usual alerting of the duty pilot at the control tower by coming in low and waggling the wings. The blood wagon and the fire engine came out. I tried to land the thing by awkwardly holding the lever down at the same time as manipulating the joystick and throttle. That was pretty difficult and the roughish landing was accompanied by a cloud of dust but the u/c held.
> Did I get a roasting – you overconfident young so and so!

In December 1942 LAC Nathan was fined five pounds for raising u/c at an unsafe height on take off.[17]

TEE EMM

Service Terms Illustrated
by
Well-known Newspaper Cartoonists
No. 2. ILLINGWORTH of the Daily Mail.

CIRCUITS AND BUMPS

The pupil pilot was required to sign as having read and understood Air Board and Station Orders relating to flying and operational limitations of Wirraway type of aircraft and Wasp engines. Starting the Wasp engine could be tricky especially on a cold morning when it was prone to catch fire. Earl Vonarx, out of the kindness of his heart, used to start the motor until his trainees gained experience.[18] On pressing the starter, smoke and flames would issue from the exhausts and if they did not subside the drill laid down was to keep the throttle advanced and the engine turning over until they died away. It was not always successful and it was reassuring to have an airman nearby on the tarmac with a fire extinguisher. However Gil Lundberg,[19] who had 2,000 instructional hours on Wirraways, remarked it was a nice judgement as to whether foam was needed because, if it was used, the engine required a day's cleaning down afterwards. Brian Crowley on a cross country exercise would not have forgotten restarting his engine at Parkes when the flames grew and swept back past his cockpit. The tarmac staff did not seem familiar with this quirk of the Wirraway. With flames enveloping the cockpit and the heat becoming unbearable, Brian continued with his drill until fire fighters, at last realising his predicament, helped him out under cover of foam.

The Wasp engine, made in Australia under licence, early on gave problems with spark plugs, cylinders and bearings which led to incidents arising from excessive oiling, engine failure and even seizure. During 1942 there were 18 forced landings attributable to engine problems.[20]

When failure was preceded by the engine running roughly, losing revs or blowing oil, there was time to follow procedure for emergency landing and the Wirraway might descend relatively unscathed onto one of the flattish areas characteristic of the Riverina.

13- 4-42   A20-242 forced landed 5 miles S Junee. Engine commenced to blow oil. LAC Bull 409023, LAC R Conroy 412113. Port oleo leg wrenched off, airscrew damaged, port wing tip and mainplane damaged.

22- 5-42   A20-28 forced landed at Bon Accord Siding due to engine cutting out. Sgt C Tucker 403887, LAC K Lafferty 414143. Damage airscrew, port and stbd mainplanes.

28- 5-42   A20-24 forced landed 20 miles from Deniliquin due to excessive blowing of oil. Sgt G Tucker, LAC J Carey 413166. No damage.

19- 7-42   A20-603 Forced landed 4 miles E of Lockhart. Engine ran roughly and pupil could not maintain height. On landing ran through fence. LAC C Hill 405855. Damage to left landing gear, port mainplane.

Ex Corporal Harold Hansen 5279, a fitter 2E, wrote it was part of his job to go out and recover the Wirraways which had belly landed in paddocks. The wings were removed and loaded onto a semi-trailer and, with the fuselage placed alongside, returned to the hangars for repair including bent propellers, damaged undercarriages and buckled cowlings.[21]

On three occasions during the first three months, engine cut occurred at take-off and the aircraft were badly damaged. With full power on and the pilot endeavouring to get the aircraft to a safe height, it is a bad moment when the engine cuts below a few hundred feet. It happened to F/O Paxton and Sgt McKissick in A20-216 on 16 April and F/Os Susans and Hartnell in A20-256 on 18 May.[22]

5- 7-42   A20-620 failed to rise during take-off and crashed through fence.
             LAC H Stone 412854. In addition to damage to airscrew, landing gear, wings and
             flaps, the fuselage was distorted.

Failure to rise was also a result of not brushing off the ice on the wings with glycol on winter mornings.

Engine reliability improved from then and the next entries in PORs[23] relating to loss of power are associated with instruction in simulated forced landings. In this exercise the instructor unexpectedly cut the engine back to idling necessitating the pupil selecting a paddock to glide into from several thousand feet. The pretended emergency occasionally turned into a genuine forced landing. It resulted from not occasionally giving a brief burst to the engine to keep it warmed during the descent, so that the cooled engine failed to respond when the practice was terminated near the ground.

11- 9-42   A20-31 Undershooting on practice forced landing.
              Instructor took over but although engine warmed
              at 1500ft engine did not respond and landed ahead
              with wheels up. F/O Butterworth, LAC F Lippiatt
              414579.

A steady stream of u/s aircraft flowed in for repair to the workshops and hangars from beginners' accidents like heavy landings; ballooning on landing; and holding off too high and stalling on landing, with damage to u/c, tail wheel, mainplanes, airscrew and twisting of fuselage; swinging on take-off or overshooting on landing and running through fences with damage to airscrew and mainplanes; too heavy application of brakes on landing with a/c tipping onto nose.

P.O. Prune's definition of a good landing is one you can walk away from.

P/O Prune's definition of a
good landing is one you can
walk away from.
(TEE EMM)

Wirraway A20-143 after a bad landing during 40 Course, 5SFTS, 1943.
(Donor R. Bowman).
AWM negative number P1167/45/42.

10- 7-42   A20-30 overshot on landing and ran through two fences. Damage airscrew, port mainplane.
12- 7-42   A20-427 overturned on landing during night flying due to pupil applying brakes too severely. Safety pilot and pupil both suffered shock and the latter amputation of little finger right hand, fracture of other fingers and severe gravel rash. Extensive damage to fin and rudder, propeller, instrument panel, windscreen, aerial fairings, port mainplane.
15- 7-42   A20-214 pilot held off too high and port wing dipped into ground.
29- 5-42   A20-531 heavy landing. Damage to u/c, propeller, mainplanes and tail wheel.

The pupil pilot of A20-476, which ballooned on landing with damage to airscrew (all blades) and starboard wing with twisting of fuselage, was scrubbed. Accidents, especially when coupled with borderline flying proficiency, made it likely that these pupils would be scrubbed. If the incident was avoidable, it was highly likely the pupil would be failed.

Before proceeding into ATS, ITS students were introduced by their instructors to formation flying and navigation exercises. Going solo on cross country, the trainee would have the course, allowing for wind drift, plotted on the navigational pad and computer strapped to one knee, and a map on the other. Checking both against landmarks like railway lines and road intersections, he would turn onto the next leg, while doubtless the locals at such vantage points, having witnessed Wirraway after Wirraway doing it before, must have anticipated and willed the rookie onto his new course. On the first leg of a cross-country Bill Merrett arrived at 5,000 feet over Narrandera and the motor stopped. He managed to get the u/c down and some flap and came in against red lights:

> Ruffled trainee Tiger Moth pilots appeared from everywhere. I was in the clear, a piston was hanging out of one of the cylinders. My instructor, Ralph Oberg, came over and picked me up in a Wirraway – a great morale booster – in lieu of a two-day trip in a train.[24]

Not in the clear, on a high level cross country, were the trainees who could not resist some unauthorised low level cross country and whose numbers were taken in the act[25]

9- 8-42   LAC Aircrew pilot awarded 120 hours detention by Commanding Officer in that he flew Wirraway Aircraft A20-57 over the town of Narrandera at an altitude within 500 feet of the ground in direct contravention of **A.F.O. 10/B/15 Para.2.**
9- 3-43   LAC Aircrew pilot awarded 28 day's detention by CO, 5SFTS in that he at Darlington Point flew aircraft A20-583 at a height of approximately 100 feet. **A.F.A. Section 39A (1) (b).**
            Contrary to **S.F.O. 3/A/57(b)** which directs that unauthorised low flying is strictly forbidden. **A.F.A. Section 11.**
            Contrary to **A.F.O. 10/B/15 (2)** which directs that flying within 500 feet of the ground, unless otherwise provided, is forbidden. **A.F.A. Section 40.**

There were four forced landings during early 1942 due to pupils becoming lost on solo cross country flights, with aircraft being retrieved from paddocks all over the Riverina.

7- 4-42   A20-217 forced landed 5 miles north of Canowindra due to pilot apparently being lost. LAC Cook 412399.
16-4-42   A20-556 forced landed at Harden due to pilot becoming lost. LAC J Scott 404939. Damage to airscrew and undersurface of a/c.
23- -42   A20-582 forced landed 4 miles NE Urana. Pupil 50 miles off course and lost. LAC H Watts 413296.
22-6-42   A20-441 precautionary landing 1 mile NE Adelong due to pilot being lost. Collided with fence. LAC R Griffin 413759. Damage to airscrew, mainplane.

There was speculation between the ground and flying instructors as to the reason for so many trainees becoming lost. The Navigation Officer, F/O Jim Dive, with F/L Cox as pilot carried out a number of experiments in the air with a Wirraway using an astro compass or sun compass.[26] Very accurate flying was required and use of the air almanac and trig. tables to work out the spherical triangle to set the reading. It was found that the compass readings varied slightly when the aircraft was level instead of tail down and also that raising the wheels had an effect. Thereafter compasses were swung on the ground with the tail lifted into the flying position by a group of sweating and profane trainees (F/L Steel later designed a sort of turn-table with a cradle to hold the aircraft which was constructed in the workshop with brass (non-magnetic) fittings). These innovations improved the standard of cross-country navigation and lowered the number of lost aircraft.

The training magazine, TEE EMM, made reference to one reason for navigational lapse with this classic example

THE MOST HIGHLY DEROGATORY ORDER OF THE IRREMOVABLE FINGER Patron;
(Pilot Officer Prune) is this month awarded to P/O — for completely Superfluous Devotion to Duty.

Dieu et Mon Doigt

THIS MONTH'S PRUNERY

THE MOST HIGHLY DEROGATORY ORDER OF THE IRREMOVABLE FINGER (Patron: Officer Prune) is this month awarded to P/O —— for completely Superfluous Devotion to Duty.

This officer on returning at night from a bombing raid in very poor visibility discovered he had accidentally set red on black and so had for some hours been flying on a reciprocal instead of the course for home. Realising his mistake he then set course for base (270°) expecting to get no further than Holland if lucky. When the fuel at last gave out—as he anticipated—he made a good forced landing and at once set fire to his aircraft to prevent it falling into enemy hands. He and his crew then made a quick escape across the countryside—only to find themselves almost immediately opposite the "Rose & Crown," Little Muddycombe, England.

TEE EMM'S COOKERY NOTE

A PUPIL asked to describe a SYKO machine did so quite efficiently, but finished up: "Codes are printed on rice paper to provide food for the navigator in case of capture!"

This officer on returning at night from a bombing raid in very poor visibility discovered he had for some hours been flying on a reciprocal instead of the course for home. Realising his mistake he then set course for base (270) expecting to get no further than Holland if lucky. When the fuel at last gave out – as he anticipated – he made a good forced landing and at once set fire to his aircraft to prevent it falling into enemy hands. He and his crew then made a quick escape across the countryside – only to find themselves almost immediately opposite the "Rose & Crown", Little Muddycombe, England.

Pilot wastage

In general about one third of the pupils coming from elementary flying training schools to service flying training schools were scrubbed and were posted elsewhere to train as wireless operator-air gunners or observers or to ground staff musterings. In the early courses the wastage rate was less and in the later courses approached 50 per cent.

Dick McKenzie, with 65 hours on Tiger Moths in his pilot's log book from Narrandera, started flying training at Uranquinty on 11 July 1943 and on 26 July, after 14 hours on Wirraways, the entry in his book read, "flying training discontinued."

The end of the world as far as I was concerned. Along with other scrub pilots I was assigned to guard duties on the station. We had time to collect our thoughts and consider our options to stay in aircrew. They were navigator, wireless operator or air gunner. The general thought among us was that if one proceeded with a long course like navigation the war would be over before we got there. So we chose air gunnery and left on 9 September for 1BAGS Evans Head. It was a whirlwind course totalling only ten hours flying time firing a machine gun from a Fairey Battle at the drogue behind another aircraft. I was presented with a half wing AG on 15 October and posted to embarkation. The embarkation age at this time was reduced to 18 years and nine months and just included me.[27]

Chapter 8   Avoidable Accidents

The first accident occurred on 28 November 1941 when A20-412, flown by a pupil, ground looped at the end of the landing run causing 250 pounds damage from the collapse of the starboard oleo leg. It was not due to lack of flying skill or experience but caused by failure to lock the tail wheel prior to landing, which was part of a set drill. It was a frequent cause of ground looping and, in June 1942, following several of these accidents in quick succession, the perpetrator was brought before the CO. 'For failing to properly lock the tail wheel of Wirraway A20-591 thus causing 350 pounds damage to the port mainplane, flap and oleo leg', he was awarded seven days CB and penal deduction of one pound from active pay. When it happened yet again, the pupil pilot of A20-385, who had failed to lock the tail wheel for landing causing the a/c to swing with damage to u/c and mainplane, was scrubbed.

Subsequently no more of these accidents appear in PORs[1] while the slightly less expensive but more

Is your accident really necessary?
TEE EMM

ignominious failures to lower the undercarriage prior to landing occur abundantly. The retractable undercarriage of the Wirraway was the bane of trainees at SFTS in converting from the Tiger Moth of EFTS with its fixed undercarriage. In addition to the more demanding flying of the Wirraway, when landing there were other distractions posed by new controls to be mastered; for the mixture of the engine, the pitch of the propeller, and the flaps, as well as the undercarriage lever.

The first letter "U" of the mnemonic of the cockpit drill "UMP fuel and flaps" for landing should have ensured that the undercarriage was lowered. If not, when throttling back on the final approach a warning horn would sound if the u/c was not down. The sound, loud as it was, might not penetrate the intense concentration of the trainee, away in the world of trying to cope with the many things happening at this time. The agitated pupil could still come up with "What are you saying, Sir ? " with the warning horn blowing in his ears and the instructor in the back screaming to put the wheels down.

> 8- 6-42. A20-420 Landed at Uranquinty with u/c retracted due to failure to complete "Before Landing" procedure. Damage to airscrew, flaps and oil cooler to the extent of about 30 pounds. Pupil pilot awarded 14 days CB and penal deduction of 5 pounds from active pay by the CO.[1]

LINES FROM PRUNE'S SHOOTING GALLERY

I'm not guilty of bad flying. Landing with one's undercart up is just a mistake.

Not all wheels-up landings were avoidable. Some were due to failure of the operating mechanism to bring the wheels down and some were the result of emergencies like engine failure, especially at take-off, when there was no time to select a suitable site for a forced landing. However an avoidable belly landing called for hefty punishment. The perpetrator also felt uncomfortable and was known as someone who had been awarded the order of the prune. P/O Prune, the legendary flying misfit of the training manuals, was even liable to pull up the undercarriage lever while on the ground in mistake for something else, and he wasn't the only one.

P/O Prune would have identified himself with the trainee who forced landed, with damage to the airscrew blade, after turning the petrol cock in error onto an empty tank.

Avoidable accidents were not only costly in the time expended in repairing the damage by groundstaff, but in the time lost to the flying program because of the aircraft being out of service. Other avoidable accidents resulting in unserviceable (u/s) aircraft, like those in taxying, were severely punished.

'On 2 January 1942 pupil pilot in A20-433 taxied into A20-451 which was stationary',[2] and this type of accident occurred many times with damage to the airscrew of one and some part of the other like the tail planes and elevators.

Yet more of these wasteful prangs required the imposition of stiffer penalties and greater precautions. By October a pupil pilot was given six days detention being the pilot of Wirraway A20-150, while taxying on the aerodrome failed to take adequate precaution to safeguard His Majesty's a/c as outlined in AFOs and taxied the said a/c within 50 yards of another a/c without having a safety airman at the wing tip.

By 1944 the precautions being adopted were still greater (even desperate) and the offence warranted a pupil pilot being awarded 14 days field punishment in that he did taxi aircraft A20-80 on the Tarmac area within 100 yards of other aircraft without a man on each wing tip contrary to POB. Part "A" Serial No. 15.[3]

On 16 April 1944 on taxying into A20-80, A20-103 sustained damage to the airscrew, engine, port wing tip, port aileron, centre section and engine cowl. A20-103 had served with 4Sqn in New Guinea when, on 16 December 1942, flown by P/O Archer and Sgt Coulston in the Buna area its guns had shot down a Zero, the only Wirraway in which this feat was achieved. Following repair at Clyde Engineering it was placed in the Australian War Memorial.

![Wirraway A20-103 in grass field with man approaching]

Wirraway A20-103 of 4Sqn at Berry (Bomana) Airfield, Port Moresby, New Guinea, 16 January 1943.
(Australian War Memorial negative number P02885.001)

Chapter 9   Trainees – Advanced Training Squadron

Yet the man who is the essence of caution and always plays for safety first will certainly not carry out his duties as it is intended that the Air Arm should be used.
RAAF handout on going to Elementary Flying Training School.

Most of those progressing from ITS into ATS, now with over 100 hours flying experience, successfully completed this final hurdle and graduated with their wings.

In ATS, the pupil pilot was only accompanied for about a fifth of the time in the final 50 hours of service flying training, either by an instructor or a safety pilot (another trainee). There was more instrument and night flying, including a night cross country exercise. The day cross countries were designed to test navigational skills at high and low level. There were aerobatics and the application of weapons in air to ground gunnery and dive bombing.

At the end of 1942 Clem Schmitzer's instructors were F/O Gardiner, W/O Lillie, F/S Young, and Sgts Boyd, Butcher, Connor, Conway, Dann, Hudson, Lambert and Lauder. Towards the end of 1943 Bill Howard's instructors were F/Os Whitehead and Wighton, P/O Bailey, F/Ss Fuller and Walsh, and Sgts Benson, Cook, Lewis and Wallace. During the time Bill was on course at 5SFTS there were eight fatal flying accidents and a few days after he left his instructor, F/S Fuller, was killed together with his pupil, LAC Nilon.[1]

The older men and CO were very experienced and had witnessed some dreadful flying accidents elsewhere. The flying instructors, under these leaders, had to strike a delicate balance between encouraging some dash in the flying of their pupils, while restraining young men in their late teens and early twenties from flying dangerously.

Alec Fitzsimons, on 38 Course, recounted how they looked forward to the solo low level cross country exercises.[2] One of the trainees returning with a dent in the wing tip explained that he had hit a bird. After leaves had been dug out of the cavity he was asked "was that bird in a nest ?"

Under the heading "Birds Cause Plane Mishap" a Sydney newspaper carried the par "Finding the rudder of his machine damaged after he had run into a flock of birds at 250ft in the south-west of New South Wales this week, an RAAF pilot, doing solo, low-level flying training, baled out. He landed uninjured." Richie Willcocks on 46 Course doing a low level X/country on 25 July 1944 remembered[3]

a terrific bang and a bit of a jerk. I started to climb and looked back to see about 100ft plus of high tension wire caught in a loop about one third of the way down the rudder which had been detached from its upper pinion. I continued to climb to about 3000ft because I felt if I tried to land the wire would get caught and pull the rudder off. I stood on the seat and went to get over the side but could not get out and sort of gave up. My next memory was floating down so my reflexes and training must have stood me in good stead.

THE ROO CLUB

C/o LIGHT AIRCRAFT PTY. LTD.
7TH FLOOR
GRACE BROS. STORE
BROADWAY, SYDNEY

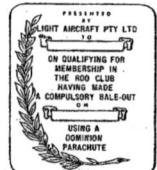

GNM:VS

8th August, 1944.

440112,
L.A.C. R. WILLCOCKS,
No. 5 S.F.T.S.
ROYAL AUSTRALIAN AIR FORCE,
AUSTRALIA.

Dear Sir,

On behalf of the G.Q. Parachute Company of England, we have pleasure in advising you that as a result of your compulsory descent from aircraft on the 25th July, 1944, you are now eligible for membership to the G.Q. Parachute Club, exclusive to those whose lives have been saved by the use of a G.Q. Parachute.

We are advising the G.Q. Parachute Company of your eligibility and on receipt of our application they will forward your Badge of Membership to us for presentation to you.

If at any time you are in Sydney and find time to pay us a visit, it would give us great pleasure to show you the intricate detail in the manufacture of a Parachute.

We would appreciate it if you would acknowledge receipt of this letter and let us have a forwarding address that we may forward the

PLEASE ADDRESS ALL CORRESPONDENCE TO P.O. BOX 98, BROADWAY

The Roo Club.
(R. Willcocks.)

These incidents occurred during authorised exercises. However as the trainees mostly flew solo in ATS there was a great temptation once out of sight to enjoy the thrill of unauthorised flying. At that time most young men had not driven a car, let alone a powerful flying machine, and accidents were bound to happen.

The engine and propeller recovered by Tim Hutchings, the son of an instructor,
form the centre piece of the RAAF Memorial unveiled in Wirraway Park, Uranquinty
on 19 September 1999 by His Excellency The Honourable Sir William Deane AC KBE,
Governor General of the Commonwealth of Australia.
(Jenny Lewington.)

Some of these accidents proved fatal. Neville Lamont, now 91 and formerly a cook in the officers' mess at 'Quinty, wrote[4]

I have very fond memories of the place tinged with sorrow from witnessing a fatal crash. It was a heartrending scene. The CO was in tears and we were all ordered back to whatever we were doing so that we would not see the bodies as they were extricated from the wreck. Many fine young men passed that way in the course of their training.

Unhappily many need not have happened.[5] Low flying with the thrill of speed near the ground continued to beckon the adventurous youth and sometimes killed them. Fortunate to have survived was the pupil pilot of Wirraway A20-450:

14- 9-42   During unauthorised low flying struck the water at Lake Cullivel.
             Fractures of maxillae and haematoma of face. A/c extensively damaged and engine
             affected by submersion.

The trainee in A20-566 engaged in unauthorised formation flying low over the water in company with A20-450 was given 28 days detention by the CO under:

AFA Section 11 - in neglecting to obey SSOs in that he at Lake Cullivel carried out unauthorised low flying contrary to **Unit Flying Orders 3/A/44(b).**

A.F.A. Section 39A(1)(b) – flew the said aircraft over Lake Cullivel at a height of approximately 50 feet above the water.

A.F.A. Section 39A(2)(b) – flew the said aircraft below a height of 500 feet contrary to **A.F.O. 10/ D/15/(2).**
A.F.A. Section 40 – flew the said aircraft beyond the boundaries of the Training Area laid down in **Unit Flying Orders 3/A/43.**

In the terminology of the RAAF, "the book had been thrown at him."

Nor were the youthful instructors immune to the temptation of indulging in unauthorised low flying, with the result on this occasion of a portion of the Riverina being blacked out:
17- 8-42.   A20-597 struck high tension power lines during unauthorised low
              flying 3 miles N of The Rock on main road.   F/L V.H. Polley,
              F/O R. Paxton. Damage to engine cowl, leading edge port side.[6]

LINES FROM PRUNE'S SHOOTING GALLERY

I never pull the stick back when flying low, in case my tail wheel hits the ground.

In ATS pupils had advanced to the stage when the next step was to operational training units and where low level flying, formation flying, air to ground and air to air gunnery, and dive bombing would be the prelude to active service on squadrons. These exercises were all practised with an instructor before the pupil was authorised to carry them out solo. When solo there were those who preferred the more exciting things when they should have been "practising their scales"[7]

For disregarding the instruction of their Flight Commander and the instructions contained in the Flight Authorisation Book, trainees, who had been sent off individually on a Navigation Exercise but arranged to meet and fly in formation, were awarded 72 hours detention under **A.F.A. Section 40.**

A trainee pilot was awarded 28 days detention to be served at Holsworthy
- neglecting to obey a local order in that he, not being a qualified pilot,
  was air fighting without his Commanding Officer's approval
  contrary to **P.O.B.**
- neglecting to obey a local order in that he at an altitude of between
  600 and 700 feet carried out aerobatics contrary to **S.S.O. 3/A/5.**

The second fatal accident occurred on the air to ground gunnery range, and there were more as trainee pilots endeavouring to smother the targets with fire came too close to the ground. Consequently authority was very sensitive to flying safety on the range. Ken Sly's enthusiasm to attack the targets from as close to the ground as might be required in action, earned him, together with another enthusiast LAC Inkster, 14 days in the guardhouse.[8]

30- 7-43.   LAC Inkster 432191 remanded to Commanding Officer in that he neglecting to the
              prejudice of good order and discipline flew aircraft A20-478 below a height of 200ft
              contrary to Range Standing Orders.

Both on 35 Course, they graduated in September 1943. During their time at Uranquinty the station suffered three fatal accidents. Posted to England they were not required to perform air to ground gunnery again as they became bomber pilots and adept at night flying.

Flying Officer JM Inkster, aged 22, was killed over Germany on 2 May 1945 flying Lancasters on 467Sqn RAAF.[9]

At Uranquinty pupils received just a few hours night flying. The instructors had the chore of test flying during the afternoon the aircraft to be used for the evening's night flying. Venn Cranmer[10] (40 Course) recalled it was the pupils' chore to put out the flare pots along the runway to be lit at dusk, because there was no sophisticated lighting system at Uranquinty.

On the night of 9 October 1943, Howard Dowker carried out a one hour exercise with F/O D.T. Burrows 408103. He was then replaced by LAC H.N. Slapp 432979 and told to assist the Duty Pilot in extinguishing the flares after the last detail of the night returned. F/O Burrows' aicraft A20-28 did not return.

> I waited until it was light, collected the flares and loaded them onto a tender. Wirraway 28 was found six miles from the airfield crashed and burnt out.

Night flying was at first stressful depending, as it does, on developing the skill to use visual aids and instruments to a larger extent than in daylight, coupled with underlying uneasiness that there might be engine failure. In the event once the trainee had settled down to solo flight, the engine sounded sweeter at night and the flying controls handled better, because of the lack of turbulence from hot air currents caused by the sun. Tom Glasson (23 Course) taking off on his first night solo struck a draught horse that had strayed on to the runway. The impact bent the propeller and dragged away half the undercarriage requiring a one-wheel landing after the runway was cleared of the obstruction. A laughing horse (it was no laughing matter for the horse) was sketched on Tom's flying suit by fellow trainee "Ace" Bates, a cartoonist in civilian life. Sgt Bates was himself to be killed just three months later at 2OTU Mildura.[11]

Dive bombing gave the exhilarating experience of a near vertical dive from 6,000ft. Rolling the Wirraway over to start was like the descent in a roller coaster except that the drop went on down and down until at 4,000ft it was time to release the 11½lb practice bomb and pull out of the dive. A white puff[12] in the target area could be seen over the shoulder as the aircraft pulled up to climb and do it again. After a while neighbouring farmers became used to these warlike practices so that a farmer ploughing a field might cast an eye at the moment of release just to be sure and go on with his task.

Exhilarations and vicissitudes, but mostly just plain application to hard work, culminated in the award of wings. The station stood by as all trainees paraded with rifles in their best blues in winter or drabs in summer. The CO inspected the newly fledged pilots at the head of the parade, gave a congratulatory address and pinned on the wings. "He made sure that there were personnel from every section of the unit at the parade and always started his speech by thanking all members for the overall effort in getting the trainees through their course."[13]

It was a great occasion, sometimes marked by the attendance of the great to present the pilot emblem.

The Governor-General, Lord Gowrie VC inspected the station and presented wings to the 58 graduates of 21 Course on 15 September 1942.[14]

The Governor-General, HRH The Duke of Gloucester
on arrival at Uranquinty.
(ACW EM Smith {Judie Trotter})

The outgoing trainees, on their part now awaiting posting, got around individually over the course of the next few days to personally thank their instructors, both flying and ground, for their patience and dedication in turning out another batch of "service pilots".

For Bob Davies the Wings Parade in December 1944 was probably the most memorable day of his life not only because he had always wanted to fly, but because of the presence of his mother and father, who had flown with the RFC in France after serving at Gallipoli.[15]

Parents were invited from Sydney for the Wings Ceremony and Jim Banyard's came up for 20 Course in their 1937 Oldsmobile which was fitted with a gas producer. They all drove back to Sydney overnight, having to find their way by the dismal light of slit lamps

Inspection of 22 Course by G/C Ewart during Wings Parade, 13 October 1942.
(W.K. Merrett).

because of the brownout and on arrival looked like coalminers from all the charcoal dust.[16]

A proportion only of those graduating received a commission. Four out of the forty graduating on 17 Course were made officers but on the late 48 Course there were only two out of 32. Some courses in between did better although it never reached as high as the third promised in the recruiting blurbs. That officers had better conditions, including higher pay and better clothing, was secondary to the artificial distinction imposed across aircrew members. Information available to higher ranks and discussed in commissioned messes and quarters might not fully reach the non-commissioned. Integration could not be complete within aircrews, closely knit while in the air, yet for most of the time separated by rank on the ground, and was of special import later on operations where gaps in communication impinged on tactics.[17]

For the great survivors at the end of all this turmoil, there was yet another round of breaking up of friendships, made during the four months of the course, by disparate postings to operational training units (OTU), instructing, staff jobs, and overseas. After being one of only four commissioned from 17 Course, Derek Beaurepaire, because of his 'above average' flying rating was posted to instructing.[18] Just before leaving 'Quinty, a clown on a bicycle rode in front of his Wirraway gathering speed for take-off. Although he did not turn over, the combination of hastily applied brakes and only a lapstrap retaining harness resulted in the permanent impression of the gunsight on his nose.

When Keith Pollard graduated on 34 Course, one question required to be answered in a questionnaire was, "do you prefer to go to the European war or the Japanese war"?
> Much as I hoped to fly Spitfires (like most other trainees) I thought that I had better nominate for the Japs. Ron Priestly, an Englishman, elected to go to England (he had lost a brother in the RAF earlier in the war). He went to Boomerangs in the islands and I went to England – so much for the option of posting![19]

Those going to active service were soon to be spread across scores of different squadrons in operations from New Guinea to Norway.

C hapter 10   Across the World

A few tens of Australian pilots fought in the desperate days of the Battle of Britain but tens of thousands of Australian airmen were to take up the air offensive in the Battle from Britain.

The young men trained under the EATS helped swell the air crew numbers of the squadrons in Bomber, Coastal, Fighter and Training Commands of the Royal Air Force and of overseas Royal Australian Air Force squadrons.

For the youthful RAAF personnel posted to Britain, there were oceans to cross in former luxury, but now utilitarian, liners which zigzagged and kept away from the direct sea lanes to avoid U-boats. Contingent after contingent of aircrews trained under EATS accompanied masses of troops, materiel and provisions.

About one quarter of 17 Course was posted to Bradfield Park where there was tight security surrounding the embarkation. The camp was locked up – no leave, no outward telephone calls, and no posting of letters. Ted Taylor recalled

On 15 May 1942, following equipment parades the contingent of about 180 pilots, observers and air gunners were assembled in the gym and the Padre held a service during which we sang "Abide with Me" and "For Those in Peril on the Sea".   Then to bed with our individual thoughts about our futures.[1]

The next day the draft boarded RMS *Ceramic*, a pre-WW1 cargo liner, which still offered to their surprise (and delight) steward service to double cabins. Five days later they disembarked in Lyttleton Harbour and were encamped for a week at a sister SFTS of the Royal New Zealand Air Force at Wigram where trainees and staff were very welcoming. Meanwhile the *Ceramic* had loaded 12,000 tons of valuable lamb and butter. After five weeks of steaming, the vessel was through the Panama Canal and awaiting the formation of a convoy to cross the Caribbean

We were attached to a small fleet of banana boats and proceeded at eight knots to Guantanamo, Cuba. There was no leave, this port being a very big American Naval Base with strict security and we sat it out on the decks for three days until the next convoy north. Three sloops took us up to Key West, Florida where there was another three-day wait. Due to the activity of U-boats in that area, we had to lay over in harbours at night. In Chesapeake Bay we stuck on a sandbank when the skipper took the wrong channel out. After two tugs dragged us through the bank, there was some hurried leave in New York while the damage to the hull was assessed before crossing the Atlantic. Then on to Halifax, New Scotia, where three days shore leave was more than sufficient. The city was drab and lifeless, for the most part seemingly peopled by sailors from the hundreds of ships awaiting convoy east or south.[2]

The convoy that **Ceramic** joined to cross the Atlantic was considerably better than the one from Panama. It comprised 32 ships carrying foodstuffs, fuel, ammunition and other war materials, and, escorted by five destroyers and four corvettes, sailed at 15 knots. Being the only troop ship, **Ceramic** had safest place in the middle lane, one ship behind the commodore

> We sailed into U-Boat Alley, the centre of the Atlantic, where our escort handed over to another which had been escorting a westbound convoy. It was Royal Navy, to take us through the Western Approaches. There were submarine scares and attacks. Seven ships were sunk, mostly at night and in fog. Across the water a big flash, a muffled report and we sailed on not knowing the details of the incident. At dawn on 15 August, three months after leaving Sydney, the **Ceramic** dropped anchor at the entrance to Liverpool, unable to proceed up the Mersey because a Jerry raid the previous evening had mined the river. The river was swept by midday and we moved up to Prince's Landing to march to the Town Hall for a Civic welcome by the Mayor at an afternoon tea.[3]

Following copious leave from Bradfield Park while awaiting embarkation, all of Jim Banyard's 21 Course of 68 pilots were sent to England.[4] Those posted through 2ED went from there in a large contingent of aircrew by double decker bus to board a Dutch ship. After all the secrecy concerning departure the ferry boats were piping cock-a-doodle-doo with people cheering good luck down to the Heads where the merchant cruiser **Westralia** met and escorted them for a few days. Although there was no information from the captain or the crew as to where they were going, the several hundred observers could guess.

Calling at Durban to recoal, the ship was inspected and condemned as unfit to carry troops because the life rafts were rusted and holed. At Capetown they were transferred to a holding camp next to the Simonstown Naval Base to await another vessel which was a South American banana boat, the **Highland Brigade**. Departure was delayed because the Orient Lines **Orcades** which had sailed before them had been torpedoed just out of Capetown. It was pitiful to see the wreckage floating, including tens of thousands of oranges for Britain. At Sierra Leone a convoy was being assembled and it was not until a few days later that they set sail, zigzagging and escorted by destroyers. Jim became ill with a fever which was thought to be meningitis. The sound of depth charges going off due to a sub scare barely penetrated the veil of his fever. Docking at Avonmouth near Bristol his first sight of wartime England was the aftermath of magnetic mines laid in the Mersey - ships lying at all angles above and below water. He was transferred to a RAF hospital at Weston-Super-Mare where, within less than an hour, he was told he had malaria.

Other contingents went by different routes and a variety of vessels.

The **Dominion Monarch** was armed with a naval gun manned by naval personnel while the 90 pilots on board, including those from 22 Course, took turns as gun crews for the Oerlikon guns mounted fore and aft. The ship called in at NZ to load meat, butter and cheese for the UK and, unescorted, then sailed to the UK through the Panama Canal.[5]

Dominion Monarch.
(W.K. Merrett)

Many courses made a journey to England similar to those leaving Sydney in August 1943 by the **Mount Vernon**. After two weeks, in which at first the vessel went well south away from submarines, it berthed at San Francisco; the trip across the States was by train in sleeping cars. Each lunchtime the train stopped to allow the boys in blue with the Australia flashes to march behind a band showing the flag through a town. Crowds of well-wishers would surround the train afterwards. In one Middle West town it is hard to give credence, in these days of internet and global TV, to being questioned as to whether our speech resulted from American missionaries teaching English. One questioner did not seem to know what it was all about by asking, "Why don't you guys get rid of King George and be independent like us ?" In Camp Miles Standish near Providence the march routine continued every day behind a huge band which played "While the caissons keep rollin along" and other unfamiliar tunes until it was persuaded to learn to play "Waltzing Matilda" and grudgingly "British Grenadiers". Invitations to local hospitality were so many (and so genuine) they could not all be accepted. New York on leave appeared as glamorous as anticipated and the sophistication and the skyscrapers amazed the boys from the bush. Many an RAAF contingent embarking from the New York docks for the Atlantic passage will remember the sabotaged **Normandie** lying on its side while at neighbouring berths the choice of transport lay between one of the ubiquitous **Queens** and other great liners.

The four-funnelled **Aquitania** embarked some hundreds of one lot of Australian aircrew in accommodation just where it was imagined a torpedo might hit, amidships at water level. Reputed to have the biggest roll in the service, her thousands of passengers who were mostly GIs anticipated sea-sickness. The soldiers slept in three-tiered bunks, one of which a man must share with three others by arranging eight-hour sleeping shifts. At other times men sat on the floor in corridors or stair wells wherever space might be found. On this voyage it was calm but it took six days. Unescorted because of her speed, she nevertheless at first went well south of her direct route before going well north. Approaching Britain towards evening on the last day she was shadowed by a Focke-Wulf 200 Condor four-engined reconnaissance plane spotting for U-boats. Coming up the Clyde many airmen have recalled that first sight of white crofters houses set among the hills, of a greenness never before imagined. As the ship came alongside a welcoming fife band played "Tea for two".

Among other vessels bringing RAAF contingents to Greenock was the **Nieuw Amsterdam**. This vessel brought David Currie's contingent in 1944 all the way from Australia via Durban: the year before in February, it was on this vessel that Sgt H.T. Taylor made a small fortune[6]

> I first broke the bank crossing the Pacific playing "Crown and Anchor" and bought the dice and ran the board on the Atlantic crossing. Landed in England with over a thousand pounds. I still have the board and the dice. There was a daylight bombing raid at Bournemouth on arrival and that night Lord Haw Haw announced that the Luftwaffe was greeting stupid Australians by killing them. It wasn't true of course, our radio admitting one Aussie dead and five wounded together with a number of civilians. I reckon normal everyday English civilians are the most stoical and brave people, equal if not better than any. We waited and waited, did a commando course at Whitley Bay and a lot of marching, and in a moment of boredom hearing that those who wanted to fight the Japs could volunteer, I did so. At last a posting was received to 17AFU Calveley near Nantwich.

The **Matsonia**, an American troopship, returning to San Francisco took 34 Course.[7] A Liberty ship took 35 Course:[8] the contingent's sleeping quarters were hammocks near the propeller to the noise of which was added the smell of the meals they had to bring back there for consumption. As well as keeping a lookout for subs they chipped away at the rust prior to repainting. Crossing the US by train, it was then respectively the **Queen Elizabeth** to Greenock, and the **Andes** to Southampton. The **Lurline** took 36 Course to San Francisco where they were encamped on

Angel Island before continuing on to New York by train and after eleven days on the *Mariposa* they arrived to a little welcome party at Liverpool.[9] Nearly all 38 Course were posted to embarkation, making the crossing to San Francisco on a Liberty ship.[10] Most of 40 Course also were posted to embarkation and they too made the voyage by Liberty ship, the *Cape Flattery*.[11] Crossing the US by train it was then by the *Andes* to Southampton for 38 Course, unescorted, while 40 went by the *Athlone Castle* in a convoy which included escorting destroyers. Four more courses went to embarkation and then postings overseas ceased in mid 1944.

John Wood has different memories of crossing to England, which he was to do many times as a member of RAF Ferry Command.[12,13] Eighty three Australian observers were posted to that command as navigators, and due to lack of experience of the horrific conditions often encountered across the North Atlantic, coupled with the relatively limited endurance of their aircraft, 29 of these airmen were lost.[14] In the total duration of Ferry Command about 9,341 aircraft were delivered and 175 did not make it.

Up to the beginning of the war there were no land-based aeroplanes flying the North atlantic. All travel between Europe and America was by flying boats. Thus, in the early days of the war American aircraft purchased by the British had to be disassembled after leaving the factory, lashed to the decks of freighters to cross the U-Boat infested Atlantic, and be reassembled. Due to the tremendous losses and costs incurred in this process, Lord Beaverbrook, who was in charge of Aircraft Production, decided that they should be flown across. Most did not have the capacity to fly this distance so extra fuel tanks had to be fitted. On 10 November 1940 Lockheed Hudsons fitted with additional fuel tanks set out from Gander, Newfoundland, and all seven aircraft made a safe crossing on this initial route to Prestwick in Scotland.

As many aircraft as possible were then able to avoid the hazards of sea transport. Because of the distance of the direct crossing, a northern route was opened from Montreal to Goose Bay in Labrador, then across to Bluie West in Greenland, then to Reykjavik in Iceland and on to Prestwick. Mostly the smaller aircraft like Bostons and Hudsons flew the Northern Route while the long range direct crossing was mainly used by the bigger planes like Liberators and later the Lancasters[15] when Canadian factories started to produce them.

The big challenge faced by Ferry Command was navigation, and with forecasting in its infancy, planes could be blown hundreds of miles off course. Radio signals were of no use beyond 100 miles from Great Britain or North America. So it was desirable to fly at night to enable a triangular fix from the stars.

John Wood measured against a Lancaster's landing wheel at Dorval near Montreal in November 1944.

John Wood recalls the long high flights at night over the North Atlantic using oxygen, with temperatures at freezing point, and particularly one frightening experience in a Lancaster:

Ice secretion is supposed to take place only between temperatures of 0 degrees Celsius and –20. This night we were flying from Gander across to Prestwick and had climbed to about 25,000 feet, but when we reached the front we were still climbing and the cloud was way above us still. We had the alternatives of turning back or going through cloud. The temperature was about –28C, which was well below the alleged ice secretion danger area, so we elected to fly through. In cloud for only a few minutes when ice was seen to be building on the wings at a colossal rate and on the engine air intakes. As the pilot swung around one of the engines spluttered and died and a second engine was spluttering before we emerged from cloud and headed for base.

Because of icing in winter on the northern routes a third route was opened from Elizabeth City in Carolina to Bermuda and then a long 25 hour trip to Largs on the Clyde. A fourth route was commenced when the Germans and Italians had control of North Africa and the RAF brought aircraft in from the south. It went down through Puerto Rico, Trinidad, to a spot called Belem near the mouth of the Amazon, and on to the east coast of Brazil. From there it was across to Ascension Island, a very small and extinct volcano in mid Atlantic. In those days there was no navigational aid to assist and to reach a little spot like Ascension required astro-navigation. A landing strip had been cut through the top of the volcano to allow refuelling before proceeding to Accra on the Gold Coast and then north to Libya and Egypt.

Late in 1943 the Portuguese allowed British planes to land in the Azores and this final route was used to avoid the nasty conditions in the North Atlantic and to take aircraft through Egypt to India. John Wood recalls:

We would fly from Dorval to Gander and on to the Azores, to a place called Lagens on the Island of Terceira, and then to Rabat in French Morocco, and from there to a little Bedouin town in Algeria called Biskra. On the flight to Cairo there was the sight of ships sunk in Tobruk Harbour. From Cairo to Habbaniyah in Iran we would then fly on down the Euphrates River and along the south coast of Iran and Baluchistan to Karachi.

Return to Montreal from the United Kingdom might be by troopship or the Return Ferry Service which used Liberators. There were no seats and the 20 or so passengers had to lie in flying gear on boards laid over the bomb bays. The flights were always at high altitude to minimise wind

TEE EMM

If you'd worn your oxygen mask you wouldn't be here.

resistance, with temperatures as low as −25 Celsius. With flight durations up to 20 hours and movement restricted by the need to wear oxygen masks throughout, the return flight from Prestwick was not a pleasant experience. On the other hand, on the Southern Route, the return from Accra in the Gold Coast was by American Transport Corps and these flights in a Stratocruiser at 10,000 feet did not require oxygen and were more comfortable.

The achievement of Ferry Command in delivering nearly 10,000 aircraft to the fighting zone had a profound effect on the length of WWII. However the lasting contribution of Ferry Command was the establishment of the network of transoceanic air routes, and the meteorological, communications and control procedures and ground facilities that were developed to support them. Created for wartime purposes, in peacetime this system formed the basis of the international grid of aviation services which is so readily taken for granted today.[16]

C hapter 11   Flying in England

The first sight of a nation involved in total war was affecting to the airmen as their vessels berthed along the bomb-scarred docksides of the Clyde, Mersey and Southampton. Until then the scenes of destruction in towns and cities had belonged remotely to newsreels. A new sound was the wail of the air raid siren. The whole country was blacked out each night. In seeking shelter from raids in the pitch black, care was needed to avoid stumbling over obstacles like large water pipes laid permanently along the pavements to fight fires. Overhead the searchlights coned and the anti-aircraft barrage replaced the siren. Emergency vehicles crawled about with their headlights confined by slits to a narrow beam. The streets emptied and it could be eery if one was late in finding cover. If the refuge was a tube station it was heart-rending to see the families who spent every night there already in their bunks along the walls.[1]

The Australian airmen were held in the aircrew pool at 3PRC Bournemouth and later at 11PDRC Brighton where the large waterfront hotels, the Grand and the Metropole, had been stripped of carpets and furnishings. The newly arrived in wartime Britain were likely to have a rude shock on pouring "milk" onto their cereal and liberally sprinkling it with "sugar". The first spoonful revealed the former to be watered and the latter salt. Large cruets of salt made up for the lack of sugar on the tables. Sausages, while tasty, were largely bread. The new comers, not very worldly wise, slowly learnt that Welsh rarebit was not rabbit from Wales and how to pronounce Bicester as Bister. However they very quickly got command of RAF slang,[2] a good deal of which was already in use in the RAAF, although there was always more to be readily assimilated by "sprog" pilots[3] eager to get into the "show".[4]

Over the next several weeks while awaiting the decision of the RAF equivalent of the "Man at Air Board" as to where they would go next, there were lectures on aircraft and ship recognition, route marches, pistol and trap shooting and on Sundays Church Parade. After the command "Roman Catholics and Jews fall out", the parade moved off, but not all reached the destination. If flying posts were slow in eventuating it could be off to an RAF Regiment where the hard training started early and finished late and included rifle, tommy and machine gun shooting, P.T. and route marches.

When Ted Taylor's contingent reached Bournemouth by train from Liverpool in August 1942 there had been no arrivals from the colonies during the previous two months, and their departure was quickly organised to training units, because replacement aircrews were badly needed by the RAF. However there was time to slip up to the sights of London and discover the hospitality of the many services clubs, not least the "Boomerang Club" at Australia House and "Cojers Club",

the unofficial HQ of the RAAF in London. On 30 August, Ted's posting was to AFU at RAF Tern Hill in Shropshire to refresh flying skills after such a long lay-off while travelling and to accommodate to English conditions[5]

> Supposedly the course was four weeks but it was shortened to one week because two more drafts had arrived at PRC and were pressing on our heels. So it was then on to RAF Calveley in Cheshire to convert onto Hurricanes through Miles Masters. Included in this course was night flying in daytime; achieved by lighting the runway with sodium flares and wearing very black goggles. The effect was incredible – the only visible factors were the cockpit instruments and the flares.

Night flying in England was facilitated by a system of lights called pundits and occults, which on recognition through the code for the night allowed identification of the location of the beacon (if the weather permitted). The occults, situated at a central aerodrome of a group of aerodromes, flashed white, while the pundits flashed red from the surrounding aerodromes. Disturbingly they could all go out if raiders were intruding in the area.

On 22 September 1942, Ted Taylor was one of a group posted to Spitfires on 53OTU Landow, South Wales.

> The CFI counted us and said "Thirty two ! Eight of you will kill yourselves by flying into the Welsh Mountains, more will fly into the Balloon barrage over Cardiff and more into the barrage over Swansea." We did not need a pep talk, the sheer joy of flying this sleek powerful machine, the ultimate goal of all trainees, was enough to make our conduct exemplary. Inexplicably we did lose Sgt McRoberts when flying four in my formation over a cloudy Irish Sea. [The death of Sgt B McRoberts on 3 November 1942 was the first overseas of a Uranquinty graduate. He was on 18 Course (see Roll of Uranquinty Graduates)]. Six weeks of OTU was followed by three weeks of battle tactics and it was off to a front-line squadron but not for me. I was separated from my mates to remain an instructor at OTU. In retrospect it was advantageous because I became part of a group of experienced pilots "resting at OTU" after service on Malta and who passed on their expertise.[6] Also several semi-operational squadrons were formed within OTUs and we became 553 Reserve Squadron. We did not get to participate in any raids but were able to combine convoy and shipping patrols and harbour protection in our training agenda.

For orientation and familiarisation with English flying conditions there were many paths through AFUs and OTUs to operations that could be taken by the recently graduated Australian airmen used to uncluttered and clear skies. One group of 'Quinty pilots went to RAF Station Clyffe Pypard in Wiltshire where the mists in winter regularly rolled over the aerodrome. Returning from a cross country several of them found the aerodrome and surrounding countryside obscured by fog and only one, by a chance break in the blanket, was able to get down on the home 'drome while the others landed elsewhere. The sole lucky pilot was unfairly rewarded with an above average assessment as a pilot/navigator and allowed abroad again under a lowering sky to search for the AIF insignia carved into the chalk cliff during World War I on Salisbury Plain. Over the plain a Messerschmit 109 observing army manoeuvres flashed underneath the Tiger whose pilot rapidly pulled it up into cloud and remained there doing a lot of IF on the way home.

On a familiarisation flight an Australian became hopelessly lost and as a last resort he sought directions by landing his Tiger with its wheels running along the furrows in a ploughed field near some habitation. Finding only the village idiot he trudged around before getting help. Arriving back at base many hours later he was credited with the longest flight ever in a Tiger Moth.

Jim Banyard (20 Course) was introduced to map reading around the relatively crowded countryside of England on a posting to a ferry pool at Dymchurch. There he became a passenger on a variety of aircraft delivered from across the Atlantic, which were then flown by older pilots, including a woman, to destinations in the United Kingdom. He progressed after a stint of flying Miles Masters to 7OTU at Hawarden near Chester where he converted to Mustangs[7]

> It was a matter of perfecting the cockpit drill and learning the essentials like take off speed, stalling speed, approach speed, amount of flap, trim and fuel cock whereabouts and when it was considered that enough theory had been absorbed it was into the aircraft and "have a go".

This moment of exciting conversion to another aircraft type was shared by many pilots, because many aircraft were single seater and others did not have dual controls. An hour or two of dual in another aircraft where the controls were not dissimilar was sometimes possible although some Beaufighter pilots felt there was no advantage in experiencing the controls of the heavier Beaufort.

Even arriving in Britain at the beginning of 1943 from as early a Uranquinty course as 22, George Clissold discovered his path to operations was longer than he had expected.[8] While undergoing flight familiarisation at 22EFTS Cambridge, he saw Geoffrey de Havilland testing Mosquitos, taking off on one engine and doing a roll on the way up. Delighted to receive a posting to 58OTU Balado Bridge, a satellite 'drome of Grangemouth for Spitfires, his excitement abated as he found that it was to fly Lysanders while the Spits fired live ammunition at the drogue he towed. After 200 hours he was posted to 59OTU Brunton on Hurricanes thinking he would soon be on Typhoons but, as they were in short supply, he got a further 300 very valuable flying hours of fighter affiliation experience at 14OTU Market Harborough "attacking" Wellingtons with cine cameras. At 3TEU Aston Downs on Hurricanes, and finally on Typhoons, he received training at bombing and on low level flying

> I was told not to get any higher than the spire on Salisbury Cathedral, and I was not a favourite with Land Army girls driving horses.

During Bill Merrett's operational training at Bruntingthorpe, he was test flying a clapped out Tomahawk from the Middle East which caught fire.[9] On baling out he was hung up on the aerial wire. Only able to open his parachute late he descended heavily, narrowly missing the burning circle around the aircraft crash. Suffering a spinal injury his upper body was encased in plaster and for six months he wore an outsize tunic through which he could beat his chest at the bar and give out a resounding boom. Refreshing his skills, this time on Hurricanes, he converted onto Typhoons in time to take part in D-Day.

In July 1943, Bruce Taylor was at 57OTU Eshott in Northumberland[10]

> I did one and a half hours learning to do Spitfire approaches in a Miles Master with an instructor, a couple of hours learning the controls, and then take a Mk1 Spit and fly it. XO-G was an old plane and I was only up for a minute and the cockpit was all smoke. Called Mayday and the tower, who had me in sight, said land or gain height and jump. No decision. I was scared of jumping, so landed and was out and running before the fire truck arrived.

Jack Chivers' mates left him behind when, during his familiarisation flying, he developed a pleural effusion and entered the hospital at RAF Wroughton in September 1943.[11] Months later he was found unfit for flying and in July 1944 he was on the way home on the **Queen Elizabeth**. She was carrying German POW from Scotland to the United States. Back in Sydney, a Medical Board found him fit to stay on in the RAAF and, because he had been a bank officer before the war, he was posted to a statistical job in HQ Melbourne. In April 1945, he managed to return to flying and to 5SFTS on a refresher course.[12]

From the latter part of 1943, because of the sufficiency of pilots trained on single engine aircraft, Uranquinty pilots were increasingly being directed towards multi engine aircraft and thence to bombers. From familiarisation schools like Carlisle, Clyffe Pypard, Fairoaks, and Theale the next step was to multi training on Oxfords at places like 15AFU Castle Coombe, 21AFU Wheaton Aston and 20AFU Kidlington. One spring day in 1944 a group of Australian sergeant pilots, lying about between flights on the grass at 20's satellite with a cup of tea and a bun from the nearby NAAFI truck, became aware of a strange aircraft overhead. It did not have the usual engine hum and there was a faint smoke trail behind it and it appeared to be propellerless. It passed quickly flying low, and as an unexplainable object was subject to disbelief. The news was yet to trickle down about the development of the jet.

The inventors of jet-propulsion have nothing on P.O. Prune : he, too, can fly without a propeller—for short distances.

Prune is modern
(TEE EMM)

There was an extra posting between AFU and OTU for those going to Coastal Command, a general reconnaissance course. On leave at the end of 1943 at the Trossachs Hotel on Loch Katrine, Peter Ilbery,[13] in RAAF uniform, had the waiter cross the dining room with a message from a couple to share a drink. Talking to the man afterwards and appreciating the kind gesture from someone who was apparently an Australian civilian, he explained that he and his friend, Bill Mitchell (32 Course), were frustrated SE pilots now in the queue for multi training for Bomber Command. The man came down to breakfast in RAAF uniform. It was Wing Commander Jack Davenport,[14] on his honeymoon. An EATS graduate from 1 Course, he was in command of 455Sqn, Coastal Command which was in the process of converting to rocket-firing Beaufighters.[15]

Consequently two SE pilots who had first looked longingly at a visiting operational aircraft, a Beaufighter, on the 'Quinty training tarmac were to reach that squadron after seven months further training on multies. The last instruction before OTU was at No. 3 School of General Reconnaissance Squire's Gate. Its salubrious location was at St Anne's on Sea, south of Blackpool, where the sun shone on the warm sands in June 1944. The school gave instruction in navigation using position fixing by very recent radio direction methods and the ancient art of night navigation by the stars.[16] Reconnaissance exercises were flown in Avro Ansons over the Irish Sea by day to intercept the Isle of Man packet. On night exercises, flying from blacked-out England, it seemed incongruous that the Irish with all lights blazing were ignoring the struggle against Nazi Germany. Graduating to the tune of "The RAF March Past", 2nd class navigators certificates were presented to the pilots, to the annoyance of the NavWs[17] with whom they now formed two-man crews and who had not received them at completion of training in Australia. Crews going to the strike fighter squadrons of Beaufighters then went to 132OTU East Fortune outside Edinburgh where, after converting through Beauforts, rocket and cannon attacks were practised on mock-up ships off Leuchars. Nothing however would prepare them for the precipitous descents into fiords after hidden ships, the spectacular glaciated heights of Norway, the Flak and fighters, and formation flying over the North Sea at 50ft.

Another pilot who had looked longingly at a visiting operational aircraft on the 'Quinty training tarmac, a Spitfire, was Denny Kingsbury. After OTU in Canada on Hurricanes, on arrival in England in February 1944 he went directly on to Spitfires at 57OTU Eshott in Northumberland. After further training at 1TEU (Tactical Exercise Unit) Tealing near Dundee he joined 126Sqn the day after D-Day.[18]

Dick McKenzie[19] and Bob Sloan, eliminated from pilot training on 34 Course at Uranquinty and trained as air gunners, decided to try and crew together.

Picking your own crew was encouraged by the hierarchy and Bob and I put our crew together in due course – Dick Hopman 35227, pilot (from 30 Course Uranquinty); Keith Sharp, navigator; and Frank Ferguson, wireless operator. Bob took the position of mid-upper gunner and I had the rear gun position. We were posted to 18OTU Finningley on Wellingtons where we collected our bomb aimer, Keith Martin of the RAF. Bob and I went to Ingham for gunnery exercises and finally after finding our seventh crew member (Englishman, Jock Gow, who was to be our flight engineer) we were transferred to the Sandtoft Conversion Unit to get up 30 hours on the Halifax.

Keith Pollard (34 Course) followed a multi path through 21OTU Moreton-in-Marsh on Wellingtons, where he "crewed-up", to 1652HCU Marston Moor on the Halifax. At first it was the Halifax MkII with Merlin engines but before leaving OTU late in 1944 there had been a change to the Halifax MkIII with Bristol Hercules engines giving 450hp extra to each engine.[20]

Ken Sly (35 Course) also followed the multi path after Miles Masters III in Wales through 20 AFU and beam approach instruction at 1521BAT, Wymeswold to 27OTU Church Broughton near Lichfield, Staff. He acquired 70 hours on Wellingtons, including operations to divert German fighters (called Bullseye), one of which was over occupied Europe. His conversion to heavies was at Lindholme, Yorks, at the end of the year and after 30 hours on Halifaxes went out on a special Bullseye during Lancaster conversion in January 1945 to the Friesian Islands. At 35,000 feet O_2 failure was brought to his attention by the rear gunner and in the emergency descent he suffered burst ear drums which ended his wartime flying.[21]

Bill Howard (36 Course) did 88 hours on Oxfords at 21AFU including 12 hours night flying before going on to 29OTU Bruntingthorpe on Wellingtons.[22] This large twin engined aircraft classed as a heavy bomber required a crew of five and in order to start training all the aircrew for the course were assembled one afternoon in November 1944

The time had come to acquire a navigator, bomb aimer, wireless operator and rear gunner. I knew nobody and this was the case with most of the pilots. A tall RAF bomb aimer came over and asked if he could join my crew. I looked him up and down and he seemed a reasonable sort of bloke. I said OK. It was a stroke of luck as he turned out to be an excellent crewman. I don't know what I would have done without him at times. Between the two of us we selected the other three crew members. This method of crewing up seemed to work fairly well. There were a few changes or swaps afterwards but it was the exception. We all got on well together – they were English by the way.

The exercises at 29OTU included high level bombing night and day and fighter affiliation when the bomber was "attacked" by a Hurricane fighter. The rear gunner used a cine gun and errors in aiming were pointed out by a gunnery officer from the film. While still training, flights were made over the North Sea to give the enemy the impression that raiders were coming in from that quarter. It was then off to Lincolnshire to convert onto four engined bombers at 1661HCU Winthorpe where training commenced on Stirlings and shortly afterwards on Lancasters

It was at this stage we received two more crew members, a mid-upper gunner and an engineer. They were simply told to join certain crews and that was it. There were long cross country night flights and a night "raid" on London to experience the joys of being caught by searchlights and to try and lose them by violently corkscrewing.[23]

Bill Howard's crew received its last training during two days at Feltwell when the navigator was given instruction flying about the district doing GH photography. GH bombing technique was used when the target was obscured by cloud.[24]

Jack McDonald (37 Course) after graduation in November 1943 was sent to West Sale to fly Fairey Battles.

Much to the chagrin of the other blokes who had been there for a year or more and were dying to get out, after only two weeks the "man at Air Board" posted me to embarkation. The voyage to England, arriving in March 1944, was a long one because the *Nieuw Amsterdam* was careened at Durban and then we went right over to the United States and up to Greenland to avoid German submarines. After refresher flying I did most of my time with 650Sqn RAF and then 577 on army and navy co-operation, first on Masters and then Hurricanes.[25]

By the beginning of 1944 the build-up of aircrew was such that the PDRC at Brighton was full and those at the top of the queue overflowed into a holding unit at Hednesford outside Birmingham while awaiting the call to continue training for operations. The EATS had delivered air superiority; there was now a sufficiency of pilots.

In June 1944 the Air Ministry was able to cable Australia not to send any more pilots. However pilots who had graduated from 43 Course on 4 June were on the way as well as a small number from 44 Course who had graduated on 1 July. For them it was a disappointing and frustrating time.

Stephen Aboud (43 Course) volunteered for any flying job and was told he was the umpteenth spare pilot in England.

I applied to be a glider pilot, didn't hear anything about that. Another on the notice board was the Fleet Air Arm, no didn't hear anything. Another was a flight engineer course and you will be in Burma within six weeks! He was accepted but on reaching the station in Wales he met a friend who had completed the course and had been digging the garden and mowing the lawns for a couple of months.[26]

The sufficiency of pilots trained under the EATS had become a surfeit.

hapter 12

Windows – Singles
United Kingdom, Mediterranean and the East

In the lines from Prune's shooting gallery
I leave my top button undone because I haven't got one: It was shot off in a dog fight.[1]

There was a national oneness, an uplifting, recalled with considerable nostalgia. The unity of purpose extended from civilian to sailor, soldier and airman. The RAAF and other Empire airmen experienced the same feeling in joining with the RAF. Irrespective of whether Australians happened to be posted to an RAF squadron, a predominantly Australian squadron or an Australian squadron, all flew His Majesty's aircraft with the same object - to put Nazi Germany back in its box, attacking the enemy as hard and as often as possible by all means available. The camaraderie of operational aircrews was above national identity.

Three RAAF fighter squadrons were formed in Britain in 1941; these were 452 and 457 Spitfire squadrons, and 456 Beaufighter/Mosquito night fighter squadron.[2] In May 1942, 452 and 457 Sqns were withdrawn to Australia. In June, 453Sqn RAAF was formed at Drem in Scotland armed with Spitfire IXs.

The first batch of 40 pilots graduated from 17 Course, 5SFTS on 23 March 1942 and the second from 18 Course on 18 May, so that, allowing for overseas travel and operational training, these EATS pilots from Uranquinty could not be in action until the second half of 1942.

However single-engine pilots[3] from earlier courses at other Australian schools had arrived in such numbers that the RAAF fighter squadrons could not absorb them and they were scattered over 51 day fighter RAF squadrons.[4]

The picture emerges that there were not enough Dominion squadrons to take the ever quickening flow of pilots from Australian, Canadian, and New Zealand schools "by the method of organising Dominion units and formations or in some other way".[5] In some other way meant that Australians, "placed at the disposal of the government of the United Kingdom"[6] wore distinguishing Australian shoulder flashes but were now being dispersed across the hundreds of RAF squadrons. There were relatively few Australian formations as such, but it has been considered that it was not a disadvantage

> Better, perhaps, for Australian aircrew to be more loosely integrated into the finest air force in the world and to gain operational experience under distinguished Royal Air Force officers.[7]

After the long journey to a squadron with the fragmentation of so many friendships along the path, the esprit of being part of a "mixed" squadron of Commonwealth nationalities was welcome. Indeed many preferred service in these squadrons to an RAAF squadron. Others have spoken of the friendly rivalry enjoyed when an Australian squadron shared an aerodrome with an RAF or RCAF or RNZAF squadron, and this situation achieved a peak in the RAF Dallachy Strike Wing, where all four air forces operated together in 1944.

Among the first pilots from Uranquinty available in the United Kingdom, Flight Sergeant Ted Taylor found himself on **The Monarch of Bermuda**, with 6,000 American troops, posted to North Africa in February 1943 with a group of Spitfire pilots. The soldiers and some pilots were disembarked at Oran and the remainder were landed in pitch dark at 2am off Gibraltar onto a tug heaving up and down in heavy seas

> Just grab a rope in each hand, wait for the swell to bring the tug to its highest point beside the ship and swing down onto its deck.[8]

From Gibraltar while awaiting posting to a squadron, Ted flew replacement Spitfires to Algiers and from there directly to the squadrons in the desert. The Allied forces, under the command of General Montgomery, had pushed the Germans out of Libya, past the Mareth Line, from Algeria into Tunisia. Bottled into the peninsula at Cape Bon the Axis forces in North Africa surrendered on 18 April 1943. During this time three Uranquinty graduates were killed. They were P.F. Burroughs on 232Sqn RAF, R.O. Sandell on 154Sqn RAF, and W.B. Ward on 3Sqn RAAF (see Uranquinty Graduates Roll). On 27 May Ted's posting to 154Sqn RAF came through together with rumours as to where the next campaign would be mounted

> For six weeks, from Ta Kali airfield on Malta, our wing of five squadrons of Spitfires joined 20 other squadrons, together with 10 squadrons of American fighters from Gozo just to the north of Malta, in escorting from first light to dark Liberators and Fortresses in their intensive bombing of the airfield network across Sicily. Flying in the first daylight formation on the morning of 10 July 1943, I found difficulty in comprehending the immensity of the invasion of Sicily. From Syracuse on the east, south and around Cape Passero, then north-west as far as the eye could see, stretched an armada. The battleships on the outside, the 15-inch guns pounding the shoreline, followed closer in by heavy cruisers, cruisers, destroyers, corvettes and sloops, all protecting the dozens of troopships disgorging British, Canadian, New Zealand and American soldiers being ferried ashore in TLCs and DUK-W small transports. Eight JU88s tried to penetrate the screen of fighters but turned and ran when challenged. For four days we kept up the pressure from Malta and then moved to a strip at Lake Lentini and continued our operations further north on the island. The Germans squeezed into the north-west corner of the island were running out of fuel. Intelligence reported a large number of transport aircraft assembling in Italy and Wing put up four squadrons to intercept. 81Sqn and 242Sqn flew in from the east along the north coast of Sicily, 81 at deck level and 242 as top cover. At the same time 232 flew in from the west with 154 as top cover. The four squadrons met over Milazzo Bay in time to see 17 JU52s going in to land on the beach and 81 tore into them shooting them down in flames, as they were loaded with drums of fuel, in a matter of minutes. Meanwhile 242 engaged the escort of 14 Me109s and Macchi202s promptly shooting them all down. From our vantage as top cover, we could only watch the battle which lasted about five minutes. Our Wingco got two JU52s, Gerry Whiteford from Canberra got two and Eric Doherty RNZAF of 242 shot down three 109s. That ended German resistance in Sicily – the island had been totally cleaned up in 38 days. In that time we lost one pilot from my squadron and he was subsequently reported to be a POW. A bout of malaria put me off flying from 9 August to 12 September.

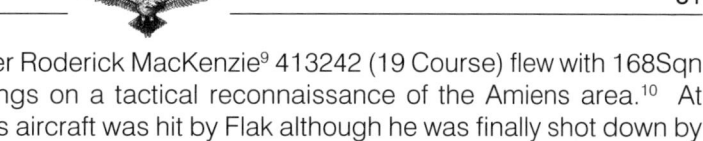

On 7 September 1943, Flying Officer Roderick MacKenzie[9] 413242 (19 Course) flew with 168Sqn RAF, ADGB, equipped with Mustangs on a tactical reconnaissance of the Amiens area.[10] At 1545, when north-east of Rouen his aircraft was hit by Flak although he was finally shot down by two FW190s. His aircraft had been on fire in the air in consequence of the Flak hits but on crash landing in a field the fire was out. Therefore he put one end of his parachute in the petrol tank and set the silk alight. He did not wait to see if the aircraft was burning well as he was being machine-gunned by the two FW190s.[11]

> I ran to some woods about 200yds away, still being machine-gunned. Crawling and scrambling through very dense undergrowth, I set course south using the small compass in my aids box. After about two hours, I concealed myself and waited for darkness, setting off at dusk again in a southerly direction. About 0230 on 8 September I came across a playing field pavilion and slept there until dawn when I resumed walking again. I knocked at two houses for food and assistance but the occupants seemed scared and refused.

That night he slept in an isolated barn and ate the chocolate from the aids box. At dusk on 9 September, he walked into Noyes and received a welcome at a farm labourer's house, sleeping there the night. With the aid of a dictionary in the house he explained his intention to them of heading for Spain which caused them to laugh. However in the morning the son gave him a beret and a packet of cigarettes and the old man a black pin-spot tweed jacket, and with his Australian dark blue air force trousers and battle-dress blouse under his shirt, he set off. At the Les Andelys crossing over the Seine he watched the procedure a few times and then went aboard the ferry with a crowd of farmers and bathers. No one seemed to notice his clothes. He walked to the outskirts of Louvres and again slept in a barn. Walking through the town the next day he saw many German soldiers (there was a large German camp in the vicinity) but he was not challenged. Until 16 September he took any road south, singling out farm houses en route for an occasional meal. It was obvious people would give him food but no other help. After spending 24hrs in a barn because his ankles gave out, he hobbled into St Eliph and going to the first house in the village was given a meal. They were dubious about him until he showed them his wings. He was able to wash and shave and the family washed his clothing. They bought him a ticket from Chartres to Saumer but he explained he was not keen to take the train as he had no papers. They provided him with a rather ramshackle bicycle and a cyclist's map and he set off armed with the dictionary from the first house on 17 September. He kept to the main roads, side-slipping the large towns and cycling through others at busy times until a series of punctures halted him just south of Noyant on the twentieth. It seemed a fairly wealthy district although no assistance was forthcoming from the chateaux. At a small house he received food and managed to exchange the bicycle for a better one. In France he decided a bicycle was better than a passport as he travelled unmolested through Miort and Bordeaux to Bayonne.

> On 25 September, I reached Cambo south of a frontier salient where there were Germans and gendarmes. It had been raining for a few days and the mountains were shrouded in mist. I left the bicycle behind a hedge and walked into the mountains, stopping at a farmhouse for a guide but was refused. A passing shepherd told me I was six kms from the frontier and to keep off the tracks as the police watched them.

On 26 September, a woman in a farmhouse indicated that he was just ¾km inside Spain. At Elizondo, the nearest town, he spent the night with some peasants before making for San Sebastian. A Spanish patrol stopped him and on being asked what was under his coat and his replying "pain", they seemed satisfied. At a jeweller's shop he sold his gold watch for 120frs where he was told to take the train to Pamplona. He chose the bus and was picked up by the Guardia Civil and interrogated at the police station. Taken to Pamplona and put in jail, he asked to see the British Consul. A week later the Uruguayan Consul, who did not speak English, came and he was placed in a hotel and then sent to Lecumberri. Returned to Pamplona on 27 October,

a Spanish Air Force officer escorted him and four others to a collecting centre at Alhama. They were then taken by lorry to Madrid and on through Seville to Gibraltar where they arrived on 31 October.

Jim Banyard (20 Course) was posted to 231 Sqn at York, then moved to Dunsfold, Guildford and Tenterden near Sissinghurst 20 miles inland from the Channel at Dungeness.[12] On the same airfield there was a Canadian squadron. The airfield was a bit hilly and had a runway with a wire mesh base. Living was in two-man tents, the mess was a bigger tent, the latrines and the ablutions were out in the open screened by a bit of hessian, the shower being some warmed up water in a canvas bag and string operated. A grim memory of that airfield was the dead airmen being brought out of Flying Fortresses, following a daylight raid far into Germany, which had managed to return from an operation beyond the range at that time of cover from Lightnings and Mustangs. The misfortune of this operation was compounded by adverse winds and a great number of B17s had dropped out in the Channel before some staggered ashore and others managed to reach even this little airfield. A move to Redhill meant altered circumstances into quarters which were commandeered luxurious houses and into the Tactical Air Force. The squadron flew low level everywhere making navigation difficult and only climbing up to enter the circuit for landing. More than once or twice Jim landed at an aerodrome to ask "where am I". Their TAF squadron did low level photography over the French coast building up information prior to D-Day. It was not known just what the casualty rate might be at the time of the invasion and by now air power was such that it was possible to take people out of the front line and create reserves. Jim became one of those and found himself posted far away to Montrose as an instructor.

Flying Officer K. Wilson 414449 (Course 21) posted to 3ED in September 1942 (Uranquinty Graduates Roll) was one of those from an early course who went to 453Sqn. On 21 September 1944, while flying a Spitfire IX over Holland, he was hit by Flak and crash landed at Waalwijk. He left his parachute, harness and mae west[13] in the aircraft and ran towards the village where a man called out and took him to some farmers. He was sheltered with two other airmen until liberated.[14]

Ted Taylor rejoined 154Sqn just as the invasion of Italy took place on 3 September 1943 at Salerno[15]

> Enemy aircraft were practically non-existent and our operations consisted mainly of beachhead and front line patrols, and escorting strike fighters (mainly 3Sqn RAAF). In late September heavy rains rendered our captured airfield at Gioia del Colle u/s. We had enjoyed this huge ex-Italian bomber base which allowed the Spits to take off at one boundary and cross the fence at the other end at 7,000ft. Deployed to Foggia we carried out weather recces along the Ligurian and Adriatic coasts and over Albania and Yugoslavia reporting if conditions were suitable for the American medium bombers, thus saving thousands of gallons of fuel in aborted bombing sorties. By the end of November, the weather was so bad Wing was moved east as far as Syria. There we were re-equipped with Spitfire IXs and, training intensively for low level operations, flying over the Sea of Gallilee where the Lord walked on water 2,000 years before, was a "buzz".
>
> In April 1944 came the long flight back to the reality of operations in the Western Med., three days and a few thousand miles put us back on Corsica. Our base at Falelli was shared by our wing of four Spitfire squadrons and another wing including 451Sqn RAAF. Our operational task was to patrol Northern Italy from Genoa down to just north of Rome, destroying enemy road transports. We attacked German airfields, bridges in Florence, Arezzo and Orvieto...., two or three times a day. The strain of ceaseless low flying, sometimes against heavy Flak,

began to take effect on pilots. However we were doing our best to prevent supplies reaching Monte Cassino where the Allied troops were held up and assist the British and American landing at Anzio. On 7 May 1944, fifty Luftwaffe bombers smothered our field with bombs ranging from 10lb daisy cutters to 1,000lb H.E. destroying 124 out of our 126 Spitfires. Squads removed unexploded bombs and all hands from the Groupie down walked and hand picked the shrapnel from the runways while trucks carried away the piled-up litter. There was no rest during the night as replacement Spitfires were flown in and by 0600 we had a full complement of 126 Spitfires, a tribute to the efficiency of the RAF and bouquets to the ferry pilots who made the long flights from North Africa.

Bombers were prevented by heavy anti-aircraft batteries from destroying the railway viaducts at Arezzo, located in steep, deep gorges. Four Spitfire squadrons (48 aircraft) swooping down from the top of the gorges blazed away at the German gunpits allowing the destruction of the main viaduct and the stoppage of supplies to Cassino. We lost six pilots.

Four days after the "Arezzo circus", we were briefed to escort "Thunderbombers"[16] in attacking a railway yard near Florence. Their attack was so successful there was no need to strafe, so as leader of the flight on spying on the way back some tanks sheltering in a copse near the Arno River, I decided to attack. On swooping in, my aircraft was hit by a shell which came up through the bottom of the cockpit, brushed my right leg, up through the hood and bursting, sent perspex and shrapnel into my face. Losing vision I reefed the stick back into my stomach and not knowing whether I was upside down or not frantically scraped at my eyes for some small degree of sight. It seemed that most of the eye trouble was coming from blood running into them from cuts on my forehead. My number 2 led me away and I had enough vision to formate on him, my engine was running sweetly and all controls seemed to be functioning but I had no instruments. No. 2 set course for Corsica, an hour plus away. Three months later, after several operations and removal of foreign material from my eyes I recovered 80% sight in one eye and 30% in the other.

Bruce Taylor (27 Course) in March 1944 had been posted to 186Sqn, a mixed squadron of Brits, New Zealanders, Canadians, Norwegians and Australians, stationed at Lympne (pronounced Limb) near Dover[17]

During a rest period I was sent to the Rolls Royce Engine Course at Derby, where if I didn't have it before I gained respect for the great Merlin. Back to ops on 130Sqn in 11 Group ADGB which was escorting anti-shipping Beaufighters; close escort on short range bombers, Bostons, Mitchells, Halifaxes and Lancasters; and general interdiction such as strafing trains, transport and Flak towers. We trained for the invasion and were allegedly the first day fighter low level support over the beachhead on D-Day. I know it was pitch dark flying across. We stayed, strafed a bit, got short of fuel and came back to our tented area near Bognor Regis to refuel and go back. Next little while was always exciting, one day we were close escort to 460 bombers when they flattened Caen before Montgomery's army went in. On 15 July the CO told me my posting to Asia had come through – I couldn't believe that my long forgotten application, in a moment of boredom, had fruited at the wrong time. W/O Taylor was off to India on the *Otranto* where I landed much richer from my trusty "Crown and Anchor" board.

A graduate from 22 Course Uranquinty, Bill Merrett, joined 164 Sqn RAF in time to take part in the historic invasion of France flying rocket-firing Typhoons from Thorney Island on D-Day, and had

An elevated view of the "Armada" already there or on the way to Normandy. The spectacular view of a lifetime.[18]

The squadron, with 183, 197, 198 and 609Sqns, was 123 Wing, part of the RAF's Second Tactical Air Force. The Typhoon Wings, with top cover of Spitfires and later Tempests to keep off the GAF, were used against tanks and transport, ammunition and fuel dumps, troop concentrations and headquarters. The Typhoon with a Sabre engine of over 2,000hp, a 4-bladed 14ft propeller, a speed of 400mph, with four cannons and eight rockets[19], was a fearful weapon platform.

A week after D-Day airfields were being bulldozed out of the Normandy farmland taken by the troops and 453Sqn RAAF, an Article 15 squadron, was one of the squadrons operating from these advanced landing grounds. On 27 July 1944 F/Sgt RA Dutneall from 27 Course Uranquinty was killed flying with this squadron over France (Uranquinty Graduates Roll).

With the beachhead firmly established, 164Sqn was operating from the wire mesh runways of the newly constructed B.7 Airfield[20] in support of the invasion armies at Caen. The 2nd TAF, as well as attacking targets of opportunity, used Visual Control Posts, usually an armoured car in the front-line, manned by a Forward Air Controller and an Army Liaison Officer in radio contact with the "cab-rank" of patrolling fighter bombers .

On 7 August under cover of darkness the German Panzers broke through at Mortain-Falaise. In the middle of the day when the fog lifted,[21] "The pilots spotted fifty or sixty tanks and 200 vehicles…..using classic fighter-bomber tactics they halted the column by attacking the lead and rear vehicles, and then set about those between."[22] By 1500hrs the 47th Panzer Corps was protesting bitterly about the lack of air cover, "The activities of the fighter- bombers are almost unbearable. The 1st SS reports that air attacks of such intensity have never before been experienced. Its attack has been stopped."[23] The figures for the German losses on the Mortain-Falaise operations were 10,000 killed in action, 50,000 POW including three generals, 187 tanks, 157 other armoured vehicles, 1,778 trucks, 669 cars and 252 artillery.[24]

The Typhoon operations had an unenviable reputation; among the Germans for creating mayhem and within the RAF as having a heavy casualty rate:

> There is no doubt that the Typhoon casualties had been very heavy, and by mid-February had included 20 squadron commanders and Wing leaders since D-Day, as well as large numbers of experienced flight commanders. Experience and flying skill were of some advantage when the deadly Flak was the main enemy, but chance and luck seemed to count for more.[25]

In Normandy the squadron lived in tents[26]

> We supplemented the mess with our own "boiling the billy style", buying, bartering and purloining. At night the Germans would drop a few 88s and the odd bomb into happy hour.

In Northern France, Belgium and Holland

> We got by in more salubrious style in old permanent Dutch and then German air force quarters. At Gilze-Rijen, sheltering from snow with wood at a premium, some furniture and fittings were burnt to keep warm. We were entertained nightly being in the path of V-1s launched against Antwerp by the Germans north of the Maas River as many of them misfired; living dangerously day and night.

For a while targets were limited by the covering of snow. On one flight a V-2 rocket emerged from the white misty ground to pass 100 feet from the aircraft and was in sight for about three seconds as it picked up speed for London.

POCKET CARTOON

" The 6.20 from Exeter and the West of England due on platform 5 will be 35 minutes late. . . . On the other hand, unless my ears deceive me, the 6.15 from the Pas de Calais will be dead on time."

Cartoon from Daily Express *or* Daily Mail *of 1944.*

One of the squadrons allocated to find and attack the launching sites of the V-1 and V-2 was Denny Kingsbury's[27] 126Sqn, equipped with Spitfire IXs, which he had joined a few days after D-Day. The squadron had flown initially on ground attack ahead of the invasion troops, mainly on road and rail targets, but later flew cover over the RAF's daylight bombing of Le Havre and Caen, and later Arnhem, and industry in the Ruhr as the Germans retreated.

Leaving in the dark to try and catch any Germans fleeing across the Zuyder Zee and coming back just south west of Utrecht, Bill Merrett's leader in the fighter pair decided to attack a train puffing out smoke. The moment they committed themselves to the dive the smoke from the train was lost in the Flak which erupted. He had never seen such Flak, which was coming not only from what now declared itself as an armoured train, but also from adjacent anti-aircraft guns – a fighter-bomber trap (Jabofalle)[28]. Bill lost sight of the leader as he continued down and out, but heard him say that he had been hit. He crash landed and was quite seriously injured. Picked up by the Germans, he was later roused out of hospital in their evacuation of this part of Holland and was put on the road to walk, where he died by the wayside.

The British and Canadian Armies in their advance left pockets of Germans behind. There was one large force near Dunkirk which had to be reminded it was not forgotten and attempt to breakout. During one attack a shell exploded behind Bill Merrett's armour-plating shield at the back of the cockpit, filling it with smoke and exploding the oxygen bottle. A quick descent was needed, and, with no hydraulics, a belly landing.[29]

British troops were being ambushed by 88mm guns secreted in windmills. As he was pulling out of an attack on one of these there was an internal explosion, and Bill heard his no. 2 call, and say, `You are streaming flames,´

> So hood, helmet, harness routine - get rid of hood, pull your helmet off and unplug yourself and release the harness - as your hood goes off so does your right side panel so as to vacate by the book - preferably step out on the right side - others push the stick forward and eject themselves - however being a bit circumspect having a four bladed prop on this occasion and having done it before – I stepped into the slipstream which was so fast it dragged me out snapping my left arm on the way. I drifted quite painlessly down into some French Canadians watching all this performance who picked me up and placed me in a "duck" with a couple of Germans who had been burnt when they had overrun the area. It was off to a casualty clearing depot and thence to an RAF hospital in Brussells and the broken arm meant extended leave in the UK and no more sorties.[30]

THE TATLER AND BYSTANDER, July 12, 1944

Yes, it was a bit of luck – not even singed!
(The Tatler, *1944*.)

George Clissold was separated from Bill Merrett on arrival in England, although they had been at 'Quinty together and come over on the same ship. On D-Day they were both on Typhoons but in different squadrons and different wings. Both RAF squadrons operated within 2nd TAF. Bill's was mostly Britons with a sprinkling of Belgians, Canadians, Australians and New Zealanders, while George's 245Sqn, again while mostly Britons, had some Argentinians, South Africans and Canadians, and with 174, 175, 185 and 247 squadrons comprised 121 Wing. The two wings supported the Allied Armies in the drive into France through the Falaise Gap destroying the *Adolf Hitler Panzer Division* with their low level rocket attacks.[31]

After accompanying the army through France and Belgium, 245 Sqn was based at Volkel in Holland, and billeted in a nunnery, where the nuns helped with the washing, but at a distance, and the locals were very friendly, especially the children.

> From there up to the time the Rhine was crossed, with hundreds of Horsa gliders towed behind DC3s, and thousands of paratroops, we attacked troops, tanks, trains and aerodromes. The Dutch underground notified British intelligence of a German train loaded with fuel moving east not far from Zwolle, near the Zuyder Zee, and 245Sqn was sent to attack it. Every second wagon was a flat top bristling with anti-aircraft guns which put up thick Flak, but the petrol tanks were left blazing. When listening to the BBC news four hours later, we heard a vivid account of the attack.

The following day, 25 March 1945, after attacking some half track vehicles and troop concentrations, George Clissold's aircraft was hit by ground fire and caught alight.

> I was forced to bale out and although shot at on the way down landed relatively unscathed apart from my burnt face and twisted knees. I was soon picked up by Germans, offered no treatment and it was no fun. Following interrogation, and while waiting at Ringenburg station to be loaded into vans marked "8 horses or 50 men", I saw eight Typhoons about to attack the train. I was under the platform very smartly. The attackers were from my 245Sqn and it was an experience to be on the other end of rockets and cannons. The noise from the rockets was deafening and the confusion of the German troops was terrible to see with many killed bodies.[32]

Eventually George Clissold was taken to a POW camp at Fallingbostle which he recollected as being Stalag 17. Some of the POW were Australian Army who had been taken in Greece and Crete, and they were a great team of men – great scroungers with plenty of experience. Soon after his arrival, with the Allies approaching very quickly, the prison was closed in haste, and everyone marched towards Hanover.

> Unlike the prison breakouts one reads about, a British officer and I decided to try it at one of the "comfort stops". Showing some newspaper we wandered off behind some trees and waited there until the group moved off. When it seemed relatively safe we moved off in the opposite direction. We hid in a very thick forest for several days, covering ourselves at night with pine needles. One morning on waking we found two men standing over us and thought our time was up, but they turned out to be Polish farm labourers. They were very friendly and after dark returned and took us to their house. We were put in the attic above where some German soldiers were living. Over the next few days we were given some milk and potatoes. By this time we could hear gun fire getting closer and our friends spoke excitedly about the "Americanos". However, when the Poles let it be known that there were two officers in their attic, it was British tanks that collected us on 26 April. It was then back to my squadron which had moved up in support of the army, but as I was not permitted to fly on ops, it was back to England, helped off the 'plane like the other POWs with a WAAF on each arm, and treated to some good food.[33]

The Spitfires of 126Sqn were required to escort bombers further into Germany, and, because of the restricted range of the Spitfire, 126Sqn converted onto Mustangs at Bentwater where six Mustang squadrons were stationed in December 1944. For the rest of the war the wing flew escort to Mosquitos and Beaufighters and the heavy bombers, Lancasters and Halifaxes. Denny Kingsbury's recollections of flying escorts to the heavies were of flying in all sorts of weather.

> At times we took off (in pairs) straight into cloud. On one show I remember we didn't break out of cloud until at 28,000 feet, and on another, the wing of thirty six Mustangs lost seven aircraft and five pilots due to weather alone.[34]

Warrant Officer Alan Clark 432122 (34 Course)[35] flew with 3Sqn RAAF. It was the first RAAF squadron in the Middle East, arriving in August 1940. In 1941, armed with Hurricanes, it covered the retreat of the armies including the 6th Division AIF across North Africa. It was re-equipped with Tomahawks for its army support role and in 1942 with Kittyhawks. After the defeat of the Axis forces, the squadron moved through Sicily into Italy, and were re-equipped with Mustangs modified to carry two 1000lb bombs.

W/O Clark on 3 April 1945 was flying Red 2 in a formation of six aircraft on an armed recce over Yugoslavia and Austria.[36] Near Maribor, a Fieseler Storch was sighted flying very low. They jettisoned their bombs and went after it. The enemy aircraft turned towards them but was immediately destroyed, crashing in flames.

> After this I was hit by 20mm in the wings, ailerons and engine, which started to pour white smoke. The ailerons were practically shot away but I was able to remain level by holding the stick hard over to the right. I climbed to 5,000ft, jettisoned the hood, trimmed the a/c forward and baled out. I got out easily enough, but on the descent noticed about a 5ft tear in my 'chute which caused me to hit the deck fairly hard. I landed in a field at approximately Sht. Y.2(R) E.3472, hid the parachute in a ditch, and headed for the nearest hills at a pretty fair pace. On the way I picked up some peasants who pointed to the hills and said "Partisani". Half way up one of the hills, I stopped at a farmhouse and was hidden in a concealed dugout nearby by the farmer. These people treated me very well for two days, until the partisans came for me on the night of 4 April. I was told that the Germans had been searching farms, and had found my 'chute and kite, which was nearby.[36]

Alan spent most of the night with Tito's Partisans, assisting them in sawing down telegraph poles as a communication-destroying operation. He was again hidden in a dugout for several days, until being taken to a Partisan station where he was told their courier lines had been disrupted by a big German offensive against them. Treatment and food was quite good, and he was able to get the wireless news. On hearing that two German divisions had pulled out of Yugoslavia, he and an American P38 pilot were able to start moving on the night of 14 April. They followed Partisan courier lines across the plain, heading NW to a mountain range called Pomerje. After several hours, they entered a house to enquire the way. Two German soldiers were sitting inside and there was a rush for the door. After running some distance, their guides decided to return and attack the house but the Germans, who were probably more worried than they, had left by the back door. They marched on for eleven hours and slept all the next day, moved again at night and reached the Partisans' 13th Brigade the following day. They seemed to be a pretty good fighting unit, well equipped with British and German weapons. They were informed that a mobile British Mission was close to the SW. On 21 April they met Major Owen and his staff, with whom they stayed for two days receiving the best of treatment. Then setting out south with a patrol, Alan walked the Savinja River to reach a Partisan division known as "Audret" where he met F/L Davies of 3Sqn who had been shot down earlier, two escaped English POWs from Stalag XVIIIA and a French Mission. On 6 May they watched two Halifaxes with P38 escorts dropping supplies to "Audret". On 9 May the Germans pulled out of Trbovlje so they entered the town where people were glad to see them, but quite a few were not so keen on the Partisans. There was then slow progress on a damaged train and a weak line to Ljubljana and a broken down truck towards Trieste where 6 N.Z.Field Regt received them. After interrogation a lift was arranged to Udine to join the Advance Party of 3Sqn on 16 May.

Jack Curtis, graduating from 39 Course in January 1944, made a circuitous route to 239 Wing Desert Air Force.[37] Posted to England, he was at 3EFTS Shellingford, followed by 5AFU Ternhill on Masters, and then embarked for the Middle East in January 1945 to 78OTU at Fayid, on the Suez Canal. He converted to Mustangs at 5RFU Gauda near Salerno in Southern Italy. A few weeks after joining 250Sqn the war ceased, and he was posted to the famous Desert Harrassers 450Sqn for service in the Pacific which did not eventuate.

In India Bruce Taylor found himself a field Test Pilot at 322MU Cawnpore. A highlight was testing the first MkXIV Spitfire in India on a detachment to 12CMU Santa Cruz[38]

> Next move was to 308MU Allahabad, one of the hottest, steamiest places in India. Dysentery, prickly heat, dhobis itch, heat stroke could not be avoided. Sitting in a shower reading a book sounds silly but eases prickly heat. Seemingly the only plane I had not been up in then was the Thunderbolt, and I even got to like them, but of course I never flew them on ops. Sitting for six hours in a single engine aircraft looking for enemy aircraft would not be like flying Spits where my longest trip, with a 90 gallon drop tank, had been two and a half hours. Had a couple of side detachments to Peshawar where we patrolled the Khyber Pass for a short time and it was the only operational flying I did in India. Uncomfortable, knowing there was no place for an emergency landing and one was issued with a Ghooli chit before take-off. It promised a lot of money to any tribesman who returned an airman alive and still with his testicles. He could keep the parachute as well.

Bill Cousens, after graduating on 19 Course Uranquinty in June 1942, was one of those who took a circular route to operations in the East. Arriving in the United Kingdom in November, he went through 5AFU Ternhill and 56OTU Tealing, to reach India in August 1943 on being posted to RAF Poona. In September he was flying Spitfires with 136Sqn in East Bengal. The first announcement that these Spitfires were in operation against the Japanese in Burma was a Press Note released in New Delhi on 6 January 1944.[39]

> It can now be announced that the RAF fighter squadron of the Tactical Air Force which so successfully intercepted a force of some 30 Japanese bombers and fighters off the Arakan coast on Dec. 31, destroying or damaging nearly the whole of the enemy formation, was a Spitfire squadron of 12 aircraft.

Bill's squadron became unofficially 'Churchill's own' following a special message from the Prime Minister – "My congratulations and compliments on your brilliant exploit." The squadron continued battles in the Burmese skies and covered the invasion in which General Wingate's forces were landed behind enemy lines.

Chapter 13   Windows – Multis[1]

For the EATS airmen in Britain the war became the Battle from Britain[2]

In the Battle of Britain, August to October 1940, the escalating scale of deaths in the air was a heavy demand on the fortitude of the pilots and their commanders. But it was for a shorter period than that required in the long sustained Battle from Britain, 1941-45, in which over 5,397 members of the RAAF were killed.[3] The majority lost their lives in Bomber Command. The night and day raids deep into Germany with severe and mounting casualties had to be endured by bomber crews. Akin to "going over the top" in the trench warfare of WWI, the challenge was also to be experienced a little later by the Americans in their daylight raids.

Insensitivity to the strains being placed on air crews during 1941-45 has been levelled at those in command in the grim exigencies of war, as criticism has always followed where the price has later looked too high. Airmen, while fearful, realised and accepted the inevitability of high casualty rates. At the Air Power conference a few years ago in Canberra, former members of Bomber Command, which had been led by Air Chief Marshal Sir Arthur Harris RAF, sharply rebuked the proposition that he had been culpable in asking too much of his aircrews. Harris, after the war, had received a standing ovation when he addressed an RAAF-over-Europe dinner in Melbourne.

By September 1941, sufficient Australians had arrived at Swinderby in Lincolnshire to render 455 Squadron, equipped with Hampdens. the first Australian bomber squadron operational under the EATS.[4] In common with Australian squadrons serving in the UK and Middle East, it had a considerable proportion of RAF support and ground staff.

The Australian contribution to Bomber Command increased with the formation of more RAAF squadrons, the second being 460Sqn[5] which was to fly Lancasters from Binbrook in Lincolnshire. Lincolnshire's position and terrain made it most suitable for bomber bases. Close to Lincoln itself were 463 and 467 RAAF Lancaster Squadrons. Two more RAAF squadrons, 462 and 466, were operating Halifaxes. The nightly drone of streams of departing bombers reminded the inhabitants that it was those airmen seen about the city on leave who were taking the war to the enemy.

After D-Day, the armies in France needed no reminding of the devastating role of heavy bombers. Chester Wilmot wrote "….on 7 July (1944), 467 Lancasters and Halifaxes dropped 2,560 tons of bombs on the northern outskirts of Caen. At dawn next morning, greatly heartened by this massive display of air power, I Corps attacked with three divisions: 3rd British on the left, 59th British in the centre and 3rd Canadian on the right."[6]

As with the fighter squadrons, the RAAF bomber squadrons were insufficient to absorb the number of available Australian aircrews. There was, as a consequence, widespread penetration of RAF squadrons.   Just how wide was their dispersal can be seen from the casualty lists (Uranquinty Graduates Roll). As more Empire airmen arrived, and with a sufficiency of reserves for Fighter Command, SE[7] pilots from Uranquinty found themselves late in 1943 directed onto further training as ME[7] pilots. Some were assigned to twin engined aircraft, but most went to the larger four engined bombers coming into service for the intensification of the bombing of Germany, the seven-man Halifax and the Lancaster (one of which belonging to 460 Squadron RAAF is preserved at the Australian War Memorial).[8]

Flight Sergeant R.V. Jubb 426609 (30 Course) progressed through 21OTU Moreton-in-Marsh and 1658HCU Riccall to 462Sqn equipped with Halifax III bombers. On 2 November 1944, his crew was briefed to depart their base at Driffield at 1700 for a raid on Dusseldorf. Shortly after leaving the target one of the engines and the fuselage were hit by Flak, and the plane caught fire. With the flames approaching the cockpit he ordered the crew out, and a little later, receiving no reply, he assumed they had all baled out and followed. He saw the aircraft crash and burn. It was about 20 miles south-west of Dusseldorf and the time was 1945.[9]

> I landed in a turnip patch. I expected to find some of the crew, but I never saw any of them. I buried my parachute, harness and mae west and then started due west guided by the moon and stars. For about the first hour I ran most of the way, going cross country all the time. Whenever I came to a road I crossed it very carefully …..a guard challenged me. It was foggy and I muttered something that sounded like German and he let me go. For a part of the day I followed some high tension wires. All of the cables but one were just hanging from the scaffold down to the ground…. I went on still cross-country ….and walked among some buildings on the outskirts (of a town)…. I saw a German military coat hanging on a line. I took it and put it on over my uniform. Then I went on and soon came to an area where there was a lot of artillery fire. It seemed to be coming from all directions. There was a village there and a small wood…. I decided to sleep there till morning. I didn't want to wander into some strongpoint of the Siegfried Line. The next morning early I started off again ….went down to the lake, filled my water bottle, and then started to pass by the barn of the house. Suddenly two Germans came around the corner of the barn. I started to twitch and looked as though I was crazy and said "Guten Tag". One of them stepped right up to me and said something and then walked on…. about five miles N.E. of Aachen. There seemed to be artillery coming from all over and there was a gun in the town…. I came to the outskirts and stood by a house for a while to get my bearings. Then a German walked out of the house without helmet or weapon. I put on the crazy act again and said "Guten Tag." He also paid no further attention to me. I walked carefully though the village. There seemed to be only one family left, and not many German soldiers. I came to the west side of the town and could see our artillery positions. During lulls in the firing I crawled through ditches till I got to the American lines and turned myself over to the artillery men. They took me to the Colonel, to whom I told the position of the gun in the village and that during my whole walk I had seen nothing of the famous Siegfried Line except a few empty infantry trenches in the fields and no concentrations of German troops. [The fate of his crew was unknown.]

Flying Officer D.G. Smith 428370 (32 Course) of 463 Sqn flying a Lancaster was shot down on a raid on Dusseldorf on the same night as F/S Jubb's Halifax (2 November 1944). He landed near a German D/F hut and started making westwards reached the outskirts of Neuss. He stayed in a haystack for a day and then, with the aid of his escape gear and compass continued west-south-west.[10] On 9 November he was caught by a German patrol while resting in a suburb of Aachen. After a spell in the German hospital, Duisdorf, he was imprisoned in Dulag Luft.[11] As the Allied Armies advanced they were moved to Stalag Luft III[12] and from there started marching on 28 December first towards Bremen and then towards Lubeck. He was liberated on 2 May 1945 by the 11th Armoured Division.

Stalag Luft III was the camp where 76 RAF officers escaped in March 1944. Later, on Hitler's orders, 50 were shot.[13]

Dick Hopman (30 Course), after 13 hours flying time converting from Halifax to Lancaster at 1LFS, was posted to 550Sqn, North Killingholme, on 16 July 1944. An RAF squadron, it had a sprinkling of Australians and others from Canada, New Zealand, the USA, and a black Jamaican air gunner. His crew included the two scrubbed pilots from Uranquinty as air gunners, Bob Sloan and Dick McKenzie. Their first operation on 5 August was a daylight trip to Paulliac, Brest Peninsula, bombing the U-boat pens. It was a longish trip (8.20hrs) via Lands End and at 500ft to avoid the radar and there was a diversion because of low cloud on coming home. Their tour of operations finished early in December after 31 ops. Twelve of these were over France and Belgium during the Normandy campaign (June to September) and 19 over Germany, mostly the Ruhr ("happy valley"). Dick McKenzie, the rear gunner, recalled some of the operations.[14]

> One of our trips was to heavily defended Kiel. The aircraft had been hit by Flak and on the approach to the runway at base it suddenly became nose heavy and went straight into the Humber hitting port wing first. The instructions on landing were to keep the gun turret fore and aft but, as the plane slewed around on impact with the water, the turret rotated leaving me an easy exit. I was able to climb onto the tail plane and then as no dinghy came out we swam for it. This Lancaster had previously completed 94 ops.

> On our second trip, a daylight to Caen on the Normandy battle front, we were accompanied by our CO, G/C MacIntyre. These trips were dicey in that we had to bomb at low level on the markers placed by pathfinders. This time the marker code read not to bomb. We were diverted, some 19 aircraft, on return to a US field named Oakley, much to the dismay of the Yanks when they found we had full bomb loads (they always jettisoned their left-overs in the Channel). Tired of the protests, the squadron leader on taking off for home base the next day, flew the force at low level over Oakley. The G/C was not pleased about it at all, especially as we had to again land with a full bomb load.

> On one of our sorties to the Falaise Gap, our instructions were to bomb from 500ft, which is pretty low for a heavy bomber. On our return I found a large hole in the tail plane (near my head) from which protruded a piece of the tail of a bomb which had bounced back at us.[14]

In February 1945, Bill Howard's crew were posted to 195Sqn Wratting Common, about 20 miles east of Cambridge. He arrived before the rest of the crew to allow him to do a couple of ops as "second dicky".[15]

> I remember the trip with an English crew well as I had nothing to do but observe what went on. It was a long night op to Chemnitz – 8½ hours. I took up a position beside the pilot in what would be described as the second pilot's seat but Lancs weren't equipped for second pilots. The engineer sat behind me in front of his instrument panel. It was still light when we took off. Over France ack ack shells started bursting near the Lancs ahead of us frightening

the life out of me as we weaved about. Darkness set in as we bored on into the night heading east. Every now and then the aircraft would stagger as we flew into the slipstreams of those in front.[16] Fighter flares appeared now and then hanging in the air in line about a few hundred yards apart illuminating a patch of air.[17] A bend of the Danube seen as a grey ribbon on a dark background gave a checkpoint against time – it was very important to be at certain points at specific times – to straggle behind was to ask for the chop.[18] Course was altered to the north west over Czechoslovakia and Germany with another alteration to the north as though to bypass the target and then a final sharp turn onto it to the east. Target indicators[19] were seen ahead and we could hear the master bomber instructing the main force to aim for the centre of the red flares where we released the bombs. Searchlights shining on wispy cloud below made the sky light as day – a FW190 slid past our wingtip going in the opposite direction – the sky was full of Lancs. I saw two strange lights in the sky which the pilot said were chops.[20] One aircraft wandered over Mannheim on the journey home and got coned by searchlights – the pilot threw the aircraft around as Flak sparkled about it like a Christmas tree – the rear gunner fired down the beams, the red tracers plainly visible – suddenly all lights were extinguished. I learnt on the news that 20 aircraft had been lost in the night's operation. Four days later I went with the same English crew to Wesel on the Rhine to bomb troop concentrations.

With his own crew Bill Howard's first raid was over Gelsenkirchen where the synthetic oil plant was bombed in daylight on 28 February.[21] Five days later they were over it again, the second of six raids on this target, well defended by Flak. In the flight commander's aircraft a crewman was killed. On 9 March, while on a sortie to Dortmund, a Lanc a few hundred yards ahead received a direct hit which demolished the fuselage, the wing portion tumbling down like a leaf below Howard's field of vision. On 11 March on the biggest daylight raid to that time, 1,000 plus aircraft, they bombed the railway marshalling yards at Essen escorted by three waves of hundreds of fighters. The following day was the heaviest raid of the war when 1108 aircraft of Bomber Command went to Dortmund. Other targets from Bill's log book were

    4 April   Marseburg near Leipzig oil plant at night
    13 April   Kiel dockyards at night
    18 April   Heligoland daylight
    19 April   Munich transformers and power station daylight
    22 April   Bremen FW factory in daylight
    24 April   Bad Oldseloe railway viaduct in daylight

Peter Collett flew with 101Sqn equipped with A.B.C. (airborne cigar). The equipment had the ability to jam German ground radio transmission to their airborne fighter aircraft directing them to the route and height of Bomber Command's aircraft.[22]

I VISH . . .

TEE EMM is proud to announce the appearance in its pages for the first time of a contribution from Germany. It is by Ober-Leutnant Otto Schitzenheimer of the German Air Force.

With large steins of lager beer (Ersatz) in view,
Two Jerries sat talking—the subject was *YOU.*
One said, " Fritz, you know I'm a night-fighter guy,
And nightly to strafe British bombers I try,
But I *vish* they'd fly level and straight as can be—
It makes things so very much simpler for me.
I *vish*, when I shoot at them, quarter or beam,
They vouldn't turn in, dodging my bullet stream.
I *vish* they'd all turn away *from* my attack—
There'd be more British bombers who vouldn't get back.
I *vish*, when their gunners are veary of eye,
They vouldn't still search every inch of the sky.
I *vish* they'd *all* bomb from incredible heights,
I shouldn't have nearly so many blank nights.
I *vish* they'd not *all* fly along the same route—
I've a veakness for stragglers, they're easy to shoot.
Ven the moon on the clouds makes the background all vite,
I *vish* they'd hug cloud-top, that suits me just right.
I *vish* they'd ignore what the ' old hands ' all say—
They'd be easier targets—I *like* it that vay."

205

Denny Kingsbury's enduring impression of flying above the bombers as escort with 126Sqn is of the heavy Flak over the targets, box barrage, through which the strungout gaggle of heavies flew to bomb[24]

Jerry heavy Flak was toward the end of the war "predicted" by radar, and it seemed remarkable that the bombers would survive their bombing run over the target. Many of course didn't, and the sight of a Lanc blowing up or spiralling down, often in flames, wasn't pretty.

When the "big boys" started to drop "window"[25], we, the fighter escorts became discernible targets and attracted a bit of attention. I remember remarking on the R/T that we were getting more flak than the "big boys" when one of the heavies came back with "good, it's your turn".

Early in 1944, 455Sqn converted from the Hampden bomber to adopt an even more hazardous, anti-shipping role in Beaufighter Xs. Delivery of cannon and rockets was head on down to 50 yards. Operating from Langham in Norfolk, their Rockbeaus[26] joined in the Anzac Wing with the Torbeaus[27] of 489Sqn RNZAF to attack German vessels in the Channel. As the invasion progressed and the Channel was cleared, targets were sought in the Skagerrak and the Norwegian fjords to interrupt the iron shipments from Scandinavia and the return of the German garrison in Norway to bolster their retreating armies on the western front. Towards the end of the year, the Wing moved to Scotland, combining with 144Sqn RAF and 404Sqn RCAF to form the Commonwealth RAF Dallachy Strike Wing and, with detachments to Sumburgh[28] in the Shetlands, the operating range was extended almost to Trondhiem.

The flight to Norway took two hours, and was made at 50ft to stay as long as possible under the German radar perched high on top of the cliffs at Stadtlandet. Preoccupation with flying so close to the huge wind-flecked waves of the North Sea was broken on one occasion by "Achtung Beaufighter", heard on the listening out channel by a freak of signals, a reminder of the watchful Nazis. As the squadrons emerged from the grey sea into the brilliance of the ice and snow-covered fjordland, they were acutely aware of being awaited. The following is abstracted from 455's Operations Book for that day, 8 March 1945:[29]

> Eight Beaus of this squadron, armed with 8 x 25lb armour piercing rockets, in company with eight Rockbeaus of 404Sqn, six Rockbeaus of 144Sqn, six anti-Flak Beaus of 489Sqn, one 455 outrider and one outrider from 489Sqn, escorted by 14 Mustangs of 65Sqn and two ASR Warwicks of 279Sqn were airborne Dallachy 1405-1410 on an Anti-Shipping patrol Sandoy to Svinoy. Outriders left the force making landfall 1615 four miles south of Sandoy and flew north over Askevold covering fjords to Midgulen. At 1625 outriders turned in south of Bremanger making for Midgulen and saw targets at bottom end of fjord, three ships and escort vessels including 'M'class Minesweeper.

As individual aircraft prepared to descend steeply on selected targets, the brooding picture became transformed with streaks of brilliant tracer and the white, grey and black puffs of light, medium and heavy anti-aircraft fire. The laconic log continued

> Attacked with rockets and cannon, failing to see results due to steepness of attacks and need to turn hard to port over land immediately after action but five vessels smoking and two on fire. Heavy Flak encountered from Askevold from four gun positions, accurate for height. During and after attack moderate Flak from escort vessels in barrage form and 20mm from camouflaged land positions both sides of Fjord and from town of Midgulen. Force landed Dallachy 1855. Of the 455Sqn aircraft, O/455 [flown by Bill Mitchell (32 Course) on his ninth operational sortie] failed to return; K, N, H and Z of 455 were all damaged.

After the action the Beaufighters, in a disorganised state, skidded and jinked through the Flak out to sea, as their crews' pressing state of murder and mayhem waned, and their rocket trails still hung in the air. The leader of the escorting fighters from 65Sqn saw red tracer arcing down to the sea[30] and two aircraft travelling fast towards the Norwegian coast, and on investigation found two partly inflated dinghies in the sea and some wreckage, but no sign of survivors.[31,32]

Rocket trails hang in the air after a strike in Midgulen Fjord, Norway

In March 1945, Keith Pollard and his crew left the UK on M.V. *Georgic* bound for Italy and 148Sqn Brindisi.[33] They flew six sorties dropping supplies (biscuit bombing) to Marshal Tito's partisans before converting from the old Halifax MkII bombers to Liberators, preparatory to switching wars to Japan. On 29 April, after a hastily arranged truce, Bill Howard took part in dropping food parcels over Rotterdam in operation "Manna". Every aircraft received at least one rifle slug from the Wehrmacht. Again on 2 May "Manna" was dropped over The Hague. On 12, 19 and 23 May they flew on Operation Exodus bringing back POWs from Juvencourt, 24 at a time. On the last

trip, having delivered the ex-prisoners to Ford Aerodrome, the airspeed indicator went u/s after take off for base. Base told him to land at Woodbridge which he found was a five-mile long airstrip for landing damaged aircraft.[34]

The wing of Mustangs which included 168Sqn, in which Denny Kingsbury served, escorted the Mosquitos which attacked the Gestapo headquarters in the centre of Copenhagen. It was "on the deck" and very successful but one Mosquito hit a tower on its approach and crashed with its bomb load on a childrens' school.

> On our last show of the war we escorted Beaufighters attacking shipping in the Baltic and during which we lost our CO, who I was following down to attack some subs. He was hit by an accompanying Flak ship. He would have been near enough to the last casualty of the war in Europe, as the armistice was signed by Monty on Luneburg Heath soon after we landed in Germany at a recently reoccupied Jerry aerodrome, also at Luneburg.[35]

Ern Dunkley, 19 Course, flew Mark VI fighter bomber Mosquitos with 464 Squadron RAAF from January 1944 to May 1945, after flying Mustangs with 4Sqn RAF. On 24 April 1944, Dunkley had to crash land Mosquito 4B-D after being hit by flak on a night Intruders sortie. On the night 5/6 July, during an attack on a rail junction near Tours, their Mosquito GB-L was badly damaged by flack and Dunkley and his navigator had to bale out, luckily over allied lines. Back on OPs, and in the rank of Squadron Leader, Dunkley flew on the successful attack on the Gestapo HQ at Aarhus, Denmark on 31 October, the all-out RAF effort on 22 February 1945 against German factories and communications, and numerous other sorties. He was awarded the DFC.

Sergeant Pilot Bill Mitchel, Brighton, 1943
(P. Ilbery.)

Chapter 14   Windows – South West Pacific Area

The Commonwealth …. supplies the pick of her young manhood, whose value to the nation cannot be measured in terms of finance.

Air Marshal Williams RAAF, 29 March 1941[1]

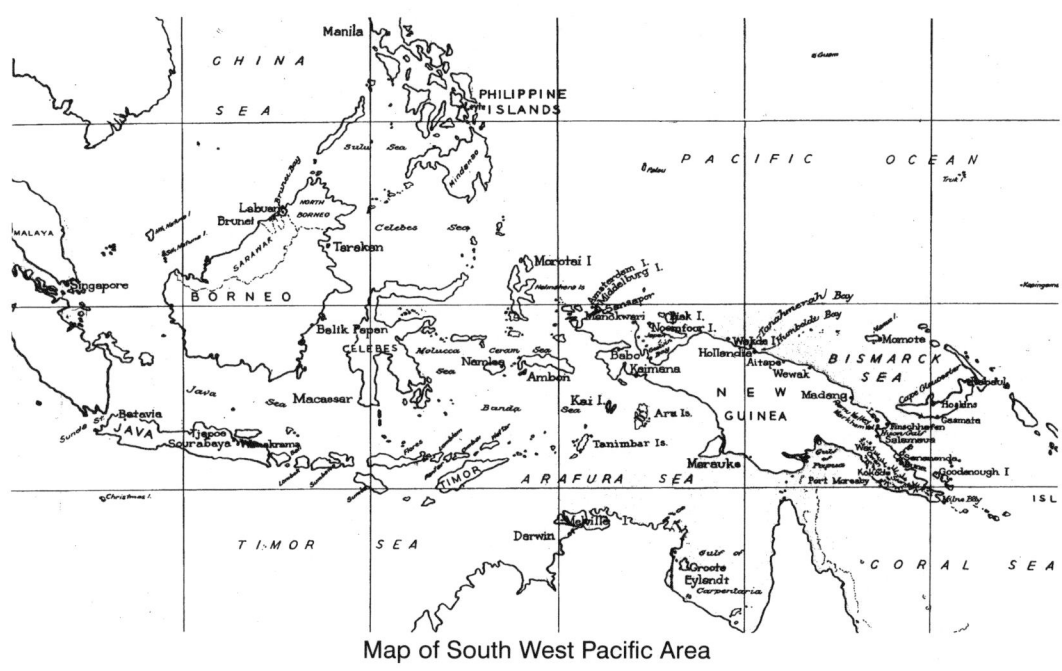

Map of South West Pacific Area

A large proportion of Uranquinty pilots, as late as 41 Course in April 1944, were sent overseas, as can be seen where initial postings are given in the Uranquinty Graduates Roll. Indeed in March, all of 40 Course had gone to embarkation. With the EATS aircrews accumulating in the United Kingdom in sufficient numbers for RAF requirements, and the RAAF gathering strength, more EATS aircrew were retained for service in the South West Pacific Area (SWPA). From 44 Course in July, smaller courses graduated from Uranquinty as the EATS schools in Australia were re-organised to satisfy RAAF needs only.

In the SWPA, the pilots trained on singles at Uranquinty flew mostly fighter aircraft, the Wirraways, Boomerangs, the Kittyhawks and Spitfires, although some did convert to multis.

Spitfire.
(C. Schmitzer)

One who did was Tony Christie (21 Course) whose initial posting after graduation had been to 3BAGS and then 1OTU Bairnsdale to fly Battles on drogue towing for Hudson and Beaufort trainees, and Oxfords for navigator training. After 12 months as a staff pilot

> I accepted that the chances of a fighter course were about nil and that the quickest way to operations was via a Beauforf Course. Completing 15 Beaufort Course at East Sale, I was posted to 6Sqn at Goodenough Island and teaming with Jock Davidson completed a tour of operations between February and November 1944. Our duties included bombing, often at night, targets in New Britain and Rabaul, and anti-submarine patrols and escorting shipping. We rarely had fighter escort ourselves as fighter opposition was of little consequence at that time and location.

Ian Reid (28 Course) also followed a circuitous route to multis. From an initial posting to a Vultee Vengeance OTU, he had a lengthy period instructing before converting through Beauforts to fly Beaufighters from Morotai with 30Sqn, part of 1TAF RAAF.

Beaufort

Clem Schmitzer (27 Course), after flying Kittyhawks at 2OTU, converted to the Spitfire Vc on 7 May 1943 during the formation of 79Sqn at Wooloomanata.[2] The aircraft were ferried through Richmond, Amberley, Townsville, Horn Island and Moresby to Milne Bay. Moving on to Kiriwina Strip through Vivigani, the squadron joined the Kittyhawks of 76Sqn.[3] In September Clem was on the first of his many scrambles. The squadron went on to fighter sweeps and strafing over New Britain and providing top cover for Beauforts. He completed his operational tour of 35 sorties and 56 flying hours in March 1944 from Manus Island with the Americans on one side of the runway and the Japanese on the other.

78Sqn's Kittyhawks formed up at Camden in late 1943, and moved to Kirawina in the Trobriand Islands and then to Nadzab in the Markham Valley inland from Lae. Its 24 Kittyhawks flew to New Guinea via Charleville, Townsville and Higgins at the tip of Cape York. But Derek Beaurepaire, having supervised the loading of equipment, went by ship[4]

> Spare parts, bombs, ammunition, 45 gallon drums of Avgas, transport including ambulance were loaded into the holds of the 4,000 ton ex German ship *Karsik*. It was hot, uncomfortable and smelly, for the Dutch officered Lascar crew carried their sacred sheep on various vacant spots of deck space. They killed one a day and made horrible looking curry. The captain's instructions, which he issued in a rare state of sobriety, were - never touch a sheep and don't stop them from killing them when and where they fancy. First night out of Sydney the convoy was attacked by submarines and the US Army gun crew frightened us more than the subs.
> The Squadron was probably the best equipped to leave Australia – 365 men all up, with equipment to totally provide for itself and be highly mobile. Most of the high mobility came from the strong working relationship between the ground crew and the pilots. At each move the pilots would load boxes of 50 calibre ammunition and 500 pound bombs on to trucks for shipment and it kept us fit.

> The squadron dive bombed and strafed and, particularly to the satisfaction of the AIF, held up by the Japanese on Shaggy Ridge, blew the enemy off the Pimple.

At Saidor the squadron pioneered belly tank bombing described by Derek Beaurepaire
> Use half a tank. Go into line astern when first man drops the tank, the next strafes it with incendiary bullets and so on. It worked like a charm !

At Aitape the pilots had two tents on a small patch of reasonably dry ground in which 28 fellows lived, slept and ate, being their own cooks on chuffas of copper tubing fed on Avgas 100 octane. The mosquito nets and camp stretchers had been left at Cape Gloucester and everyone had malaria. He continued

> In the heat we were hurling buckets of water over each other when it was announced that 100 plus were approaching. Take-off had to be immediate in a shirt and marine landing boots. Without underpants one feels a little vulnerable. It was a false alarm ! We were pleased to move to Hollandia which was relatively sophisticated. The squadron had a major victory from there destroying a record number of enemy aircraft in one sortie.

Leigh Hindley (29 Course) dates the action as 3 June 1944 when 78 Wing had scheduled 75Sqn for a barge sweep, 78 Sqn for high altitude patrol and 80Sqn for dive bombing and strafing over Biak Island. He wrote

> A Japanese force of 12 aircraft, eight Vals and four Oscars, were intercepted by 78Sqn over Biak Island. In the battle that followed the eight Vals and one Oscar were shot down for the loss of one Kittyhawk, making it probably the last time the enemy sent out a multiple force in the SWPA.

Manus 1944. In foreground, Spitfire of 79Sqn; in background, Kittyhawks of 76Sqn.
(C. Schmitzer).

After graduating from 28 Course in March 1943, David Yates did his operational training at Mildura before going onto the new P-40M Kittyhawks of 76 Sqn at Milne Bay.[4] The unit moved up to Goodenough Island as part of 23 Wing, which included 75 and 77 Sqns (Kittyhawks) and 79 Sqn (Spitfires). From their base at Kiriwina Island, the Kittyhawks, armed with six 0.5 guns, provided escort for Liberators, Bostons, Beauforts and Catalinas and, armed with 250 and 500lb bombs, carried out strafing and dive bombing. Completing this tour in April 1944, after a stint of instructing he was back in action within a year, posted to the SWPA with 457 Sqn at Morotai, in the Halmahera Group of the Dutch East Indies.

457Sqn had been the second Australian fighter squadron to be formed under the EATS in England. Returning to Australia with 452 and 54 (RAF) squadrons at the end of 1942, they made up Number One Fighter Wing. In 1944, 457Sqn was equipped with Spitfire VIIIs, and in company with 79 and 452 squadrons, were harassing the enemy on the ground, moving forward through Biak, Morotai, Zamboanga, Paluan and Labuan.

Ken Goldring,, after completing 31 Course in June 1943, went through 2OTU Mildura to Townsville where, in September, 80Sqn was forming with Kittyhawks.[5] The squadron completed training and deployed to Nadzab, New Guinea on 24 February 1944.[6] Ken described subsequent developments

In March 1944, The United States 5th Army Air Force had reduced their Kittyhawk squadrons to only two, the 7th and 8th Squadrons. At about that time it was determined that the Kittyhawk undercart could stand up to rough landing strips better than the other fighter types in service in the SWPA. As a result 80Sqn was taken out of 1st Tactical Air Force (TAF) RAAF and

Kittyhawks of 76Sqn 1944.
(C. Schmitzer)

attached to 78th Fighter Wing, 1st TAF, 5th USAF, and moved from Nadzab to Cape Gloucester in New Britain. The Wing covered the landings at Tadji in New Guinea, and in Dutch New Guinea at Hollandia, Wakde, Biak, Noemfoor, Middleburg and Morotai, and were the first aircraft to land subsequently on the new strips. Landing grounds, usually metal strips, were cleared from jungle or coconut plantations, about 300 to 500 yards in-shore from the beach-heads, and declared serviceable about D plus 2 or 3. The squadron operated in providing cover over the beach-heads, bombing and strafing around the perimeters, and 'softening-up' areas where further landings were planned. The squadron also provided cover for US bombers, B24s, B25s and A20s on raids over Balikpapan and the Southern Philippines to the limits of the Kittyhawks' range, then handing over to P38s and P47s.[7]

80Sqn at Noemfoor, 1944. Kittyhawks in middle ground and American encampment in background. L-R: Standing; R.G. Wallace, N.N. Knight (31 Course), J. Miller, G.C. Dengate (32 Course), M. Blake, L. Holtkamp, J.V. Read, J. O'Connor, L. Hindley, B.C. Carrol, L. Kilgariff,-, J. Lenneard: Sitting; D.M Craig, K.E. Goldring (31 Course), A.E. Watts (31 Course), D. Hillier,-, E.M. Fiane, W.C. Gates (Adj.), J.L. Waddy (CO), C.J. Winter-Irving, H. Roberts-Thomson (MO), N. Wright (Padre), D. Burston (Ops O), G.B. Downing (32 Course), L. Norton: In front; E.M. Robinson (31 Course), D.C. Hurst, - Mackay.
(K. Goldring).

John Humphreys gained his wings at Uranquinty with 45 other graduates on 37 Course in November 1943. Most of the course went overseas or straight to OTU, but John and four others were sent to a five-week course at the School of Army Air Co-operation in Canberra. A one-week high altitude course followed at Somers before entering the two-month course at 2OTU Mildura and a posting to 4 Squadron.[8]

4 Sqn AFC had been formed at Point Cook in October 1916, and after training at Castle Bromwich in England, flew first with Sopwith Camels from the end of 1917 at St Omer, France, and then Sopwith Snipes at Serny.[9] Between the wars it had been equipped with SE 5As and Avro Ansons but it was the sleek and gleaming silver Hawker Demons of 4 Sqn RAAF stationed at Richmond Base that had seized John's imagination and that of many a small boy.

In November 1942, flying Wirraways, No. 4 Army Co-operation Sqn went into action providing air to ground artillery observation for the AIF in the Buna area. As the Allied ground forces advanced they were informed about the position of enemy troops by the Wirraways' presence above the battlefield flying tactical reconnaissance. The squadron was also known as 4 TACR. In this role the aircraft were vulnerable to small arms and AA fire, but as opportunity and orders allowed they in turn strafed and bombed.

When John Humphreys joined the squadron at Nadzab in May 1944, the Wirraways had been replaced on army co-operation and tactical reconnaissance by the livelier Boomerangs, which entered operations conspicuously with the offensive on Salamaua in July 1943.[10] When 9 Div landed at Hopoi to invade Lae, 4Sqn spotted for the US warships. He did a nine months' tour of duty with 4Sqn, finishing in February 1945. Three months were spent with A Flight, operating from a dirt airstrip at Gusap in the Ramu Valley, supporting 5 Div AIF in driving the Japs from Madang to Hansa Bay and the Sepik River. In his last four months, A Flight flew from a coral airstrip at Aitape (Tadji, where relaxation was assured by a good surf), near the Dutch New Guinea border, working with 6 Div AIF in the campaign to force the Japs back to Wewak. The Boomerangs gave close support to the ground troops, in some cases within 200 yards, and

directed mortar fire. While dropping much needed supplies to forward troops, every opportunity was taken on the other hand to deprive the Japanese of their supplies by destruction of their landing barges. A particular memory of John's remains of dropping two 250 lb bombs from a Wirraway on Nambut Hill adjacent to the Japanese airstrip of But, one of the three around Wewak which included Dagua and Boram. B Flight served in New Britain and the whole squadron later went to Borneo. His final posting was to the School of Army Co-operation, Canberra before discharge in March, 1946.[11]

From 36 Course, Struan Robertson went to 4OTU Williamtown to do a dive bombing course on Vultee Vengeances.[12] It was one ride in the back seat then up and go on your own. The long bulky nose meant that it was side view only after checking for landing. Starting at 17,000ft the technique for dive bombing was to look for the target appearing behind the wing root and then

S.B. Robertson with his 5Sqn Boomerang with "P/O Prune" insignia at Tadji, 1945

wing over into a vertical dive. With the dive brakes out the aircraft descended at 300mph until at 4,000ft it was release bombs, dive brakes in and commence the pull out. Christmas 1943 saw another use for the bomb bays which could carry 37 dozen beer or 300 dozen oysters flown at high level from Moruya to keep them cold. The new year should have seen him operational with the RAAF Vultee Vengeance Wing (21Sqn, 23Sqn and 24Sqn) which had just started flying from Nadzab. However this wing, escorted by a wing of Kittyhawks (75Sqn, 78Sqn and 80Sqn) in dive bombing enemy airstrips, barges and Japanese troops and camps, had after seven weeks, been ordered by MacArthur's headquarters to return to Australia and the Kittyhawks to withdraw to the Cape Gloucester air field on New Britain. From the beginning of the New Guinea campaign there were never enough airstrips in the forward zone to accommodate the number of operational aircraft and the Vengeance was now an inefficient war machine compared to the modern aircraft coming from the United States (by March 1944 the US Fifth Air Force had 82 squadrons). The Vengeances were replaced by 22Sqn (Bostons), 30Sqn (Beaufighters) and 100Sqn (Beauforts).

Struan spent 1944 with 3 Communications Unit at Mascot before getting a posting to 5Sqn. The squadron was originally formed at Shawbury in England in September 1917, disbanded at the end of WW1, and reformed at Laverton in January 1941.[13] At Mareeba as a Reserve Operational Squadron it provided pre-battle training for those proceeding to 4Sqn, until in November 1944 it

became a combatant unit on relocation to Piva North airfield Torokina, on the island of Bougainville in the North Solomons. Tactical reconnaissance and army cooperation operations were flown in Wirraways and Boomerangs. The squadron spread its wings with a detached flight to Cape Hoskins in New Britain and then on to Tadji using the dirt strip at Wewak to pick up army observers for low level bombing and strafing in army support from Tadji to the Sepik mouth and inland for 50 miles. Incendiary bombs were used in clearing villages of snipers before troops assaulted the area. On the return to Bougainville the magnetic variation between New Ireland and the Solomons is so great that the course has to be flown by gyro compass only. During October "storepedoe" flights were made to the 27th Australian Battalion on Fauro Island.

Bob Davies went on to 8OTU Parkes, and clearly remembers the CO speaking straight from the shoulder to the new 40 Course that rules had to be abided by. He finished with the not original but nevertheless true adage: "Just keep in mind that there are old pilots and some bold pilots but very few old bold pilots." Concentrating on formation flying, air to air gunnery, air to ground bombing and strafing and very low level flying, the Wirraways were flown carefully but with more style and adventurous spirit, while every spare moment was spent over at the Spitfire wing. Bob said

> Sitting in the seat of the very ultimate of fighters, the cockpit drill was learnt in detail, awaiting the day to be sent off on the conversion flight. It is impossible to describe the feelings in March 1945 of a 19-year old, who did not have a motor car licence, to be at last at the controls of a Spitfire V whose straight and level speed, rate of climb and manoeuvrability took the breath away.

All his training was to be put to the test only three days and five flying hours later, when, at 10,000 feet and still climbing, his windscreen was covered in oil, and flames curled back from the motor, running very roughly. He called up the section leader who calmly assessed the situation as not requiring abandonment of the aircraft but to reduce revs and circle slowly down to the satellite at Forbes with the reminder that it was directly beneath him. Coming down to land he dropped the undercarriage while there was still power but with not enough height to cross over the fence he gave the throttle a quick burst. Blinded by the resultant discharge of oil, soot and flames he switched off the engine and, without brakes, went through the other end of the 'drome not seeing the fence in time to ground loop. On inspection it was found that the supercharger had blown up but the damaged wing was repaired and the aircraft flew again only to be crashed and written off a few months later.

> The incident was an example of the problems the RAAF was having with serviceability because worn out aircraft had to be kept flying. The accident rate was high at OTU and many young men were sacrificed because of this.

In April 1945, Bob Davies was posted to No. 80 Spitfire wing on Morotai, commanded by Wing Commander Ron Susans (one of the first instructors at 5SFTS), being flown up in a DC3 with five other pilots. Four went to 457 Sqn and Bob went to 79 Sqn. One day was spent converting to the Mark VIII, described by him as possibly the most beautiful and efficient mark of all the Spitfires, and two days later he was flying his first "barge sweep".

Being an NCO, Bob would normally have been in a Sergeant's Mess. However in this fighter squadron with only 25 pilots, there was the one Officer's and Aircrew Mess. It was both sensible and far better for the CO, S/L Ken James, to have all his pilots together, and it worked very well.

The CO's aircraft.
(C. Schmitzer)

Destruction of the barges cut off supplies to the Japanese from their submarines. The barges were cleverly hidden in the mangroves, necessitating flying low over shore lines, and when spotted climbing to 2000 feet, while not losing sight of the position, and diving into a strafing run. Although the war was drawing to a close, the Japanese were very active with anti-aircraft fire. The Spitfires' two cannons and four machine guns were set up by the armourers to fire incendiary as well as high explosive, so as to ignite the barges' fuel. The Spitfires could also carry two 250 lb bombs to dive bomb camps and bridges.

There was strong camaraderie between air and ground crew members. The demands on the ground staff were great. Apart from being able to tell which aircraft were serviceable for an early start, in that deplorable climate, they had to be run up during the night so that they would not overheat.

Prior to the landing at Balikpapan an enormous movement of equipment took place in ships from Morotai. Bob Davies recalled

> One convoy involved 40 plus vessels. In providing air cover for the convoys, addition of 90-gallon belly tanks increased their endurance to four hours, allowing them to meet and hand over cover of the convoy to 452 and 457 Sqns who had moved to Tarakan.

Servicing Kittyhawks.
(C. Schmitzer).

After the surrender of the Japanese forces, 79Sqn was one of those that dropped leaflets and supplies. On 17 August the squadron flew, without practising, a well performed BALBO of 17 aircraft in a VP formation to celebrate VJ Day, 15 August 1945.

Hundreds of POW were brought to Morotai in a dreadful state and dying. Bob and the other pilots spent nearly all their spare time at the AGH encouraging them while they were nursed to the stage where they could be carried home.

The squadron flew its aircraft home in two groups of 12 with a Beaufighter navigating for each. There was 18 hours of flying time over five days with overnight stops at Biak, Hollandia, Finschhafen, Townsville and Oakey.

At Oakey, Bob said, there seemed to be hundreds and hundreds of aircraft parked awaiting to be melted down.

79Sqn disbanded on 12 November 1945.

Peter Howard, 50 Course, was posted to 86Sqn at Bohle River, Townsville, and survived engine failure in a P-40 at 200 feet on take-off. On 3 November 1945, from Higgins field on Cape York, P-51s of 86Sqn made strafing passes along the river at Merauke, Dutch New Guinea, for the benefit of the local rebels, who had been sabotaging RAAF installations.

Spitfires on Horn Island.
(C. Schmitzer)

C hapter 15   Memorials *and* Return and Epilogue

The Battle of Britain led into the long haul of the Battle from Britain for the Empire Air Trainees from Australia and other Commonwealth countries. The majority of the RAAF airmen killed flew in the European theatre.[1] With the onslaught from Japan, the EATS in Australia was expanded to meet the needs of the new front in the Pacific, while continuing to meet commitments against Germany and Italy.

The young men of the RAAF had served as air crew members of the squadrons in Bomber, Coastal, Ferry, Fighter and Training Commands of the RAF and manned the RAAF squadrons in the UK; served with the RAF and RAAF squadrons in the Mediterranean and the East; and the RAAF and RAF in the Pacific; and other Allied squadrons.

Their path is marked by graves across the world from Norway to New Guinea. The War Cemeteries in which they are buried are listed in the Uranquinty Graduates Roll.

At the burial rites for two Australian Spitfire pilots on Morotai in October 1945, S/L K. James attended for the officer, F/L B. Newman, and F/S R. Davies for F/S E. MacLeod Stevenson. F/S Stevenson, after graduation on 37 Course 5SFTS in November 1943, had gone through 2OTU Mildura to join 452Sqn in March 1944 at Darwin. In December, 452Sqn moved to Morotai. On 13 January 1945 while flying No. 2 to W/O Byrne in a formation of four on a strafing sortie he went down near Ternate. Apparently unhurt on landing, he was to die following torture whilst a POW on 14 April 1945.[2]

Morotai, Netherland East Indies. 25 October 1945. The flag draped caskets of the remains of F/L Newman, 79Sqn, and F/S Stevenson, 452Sqn, are in between the chaplains, and F/S Davies and S/L James.
(R. Davies).

All Commonwealth servicemen and servicewomen who died during wartime are individually commemorated by name either at the gravesite or on a Memorial to the Missing.[3] The names of those without known graves are recorded on the Missing Memorials in the United Kingdom at Runnymede; in the Middle East at Malta; in the East and Pacific at Singapore, Ambon, Labuan, Lae, Moresby, and Rabaul; and in Australia at Adelaide River and Sydney.[4]

The Sydney Missing Memorial stands in the far right hand corner of the Sydney War Cemetery at Rookwood Necropolis. It commemorates 249 men and women of the Royal Australian Air Force, 259 of the Australian Army, and 242 of the Australian Merchant Navy lost in the eastern and southern regions of Australia and in adjacent waters south of 20 degrees S. Latitude, who have no known grave. The men of the Royal Australian Navy are commemorated on the Plymouth Naval Memorial in England, along with many of their comrades of the Royal Navy and of other Commonwealth Naval Forces.

The Northern Territory Memorial commemorates 154 members of the RAAF, 102 of the Army and 26 of the Merchant Navy (again the RAN are honoured at Plymouth) who lost their lives in operations in the Timor and Northern Australian regions and in waters adjacent to Australia north of Latitude 20 degrees South, and who have no known grave. It stands in the Adelaide River War Cemetery 116 kilometres south of Darwin.

The Singapore Missing Memorial in the Kranji War Cemetery overlooking the Straits of Johore.
(Imperial War Graves Commission)

The Singapore Memorial is in Kranji War Cemetery. A flat roof gives protection to the names, inscribed on twelve wide supporting columns, of over 24,000 soldiers and airmen of the British Commonwealth and Empire who have no known grave. Rising through the roof to a height of 24 metres is a great pylon surmounted by a star. The airmen named on the Memorial died during operations over the whole of southern and eastern Asia and the surrounding seas and oceans.

On the first terrace of the Ambon War Cemetery stands the Ambon Missing Memorial to Australian forces who have no known grave. Nearly 300 are to the Australian Army and over 170 to the RAAF. Of the 2,327 missing at the Labuan Missing Memorial, 51 are RAAF. Of the 1,225 without known graves inscribed on the Rabaul Missing Memorial, 104 are RAAF; of the 744 at the Moresby Missing Memorial, 126 are RAAF; of the 348 at the Lae, among the Australian Army and Australian Merchant Navy, 173 are RAAF. The Lae Missing Memorial is inscribed

AD MAJOREM DEI GLORIAM
1939-HERE ARE RECORDED, THE NAMES OF THE OFFICERS
AND MEN WHO DIED IN NEW GUINEA, ON LAND, AT SEA AND
IN THE AIR, BUT TO WHOM THE FORTUNE OF WAR DENIED THE
KNOWN AND HONOURED BURIAL GIVEN TO THEIR COMRADES
IN DEATH-1945.

The small island of Malta was awarded the George Cross for the steadfastness of its people during World War 2. More than 2,300 airmen, including 211 members of the RAAF, died in raid and sortie over and around Malta, and have no known grave. The Missing Memorial is easily identified by the golden eagle which surmounts the column outside the King's Gate, the main entrance to Valetta. The 15-metre column of travertine marble with a reticulated pattern stands on a circular base around which are the names on bronze panels. Commemorated are those who lost their lives whilst serving with the Commonwealth Air Forces flying from bases in Austria, Italy, Sicily, islands of the Adriatic and Mediterranean, Malta, Tunisia, Algeria, Morocco, West Africa, Yugoslavia and Gibraltar, and who have no known grave.

The Malta Memorial to Airmen who have no known grave. Unveiled by the Queen in 1954.
(Commonwealth War Graves Commission)

The Air Forces Memorial is at Runnymede in Surrey where Magna Carta, enshrining man's basic freedoms under law, was sealed by King John in 1215. Anyone who has experienced the emotional impact of seeing war cemeteries in Europe with their row upon row of crosses, some with a personal inscription from the family, will understand the need for this memorial and its stark loneliness. It commemorates the 20,401 airmen, who have no known graves, lost during operations within the British theatre of war in 1939-45 and is an enduring mark of respect for each airman's sacrifice. They were from all parts of the British Commonwealth and Empire and from countries which had been over-run but whose airmen continued the fight in the ranks of the RAF. The memorial takes the form of a shrine as a place of contemplation with a court enclosed by a cloister in the stone of whose walls are cut their names including those of 1,396 members of the RAAF. The great north window in the shrine has engraved words from the 139th Psalm (sometimes called the Airman's Psalm) "If I climb up into Heaven, Thou art there...." and above the angels flanking the text are represented vapour trails taken from actual photographs of the sky during the Battle of Britain. Over the portico of the shrine are the stone figures of Justice, Victory and Courage[1].... If ever there was a just cause this was it.

The Air Forces Memorial at Runnymede to the 20,401 airmen without known graves lost from the United Kingdom in WWII unveiled by the Queen in 1953. Design: Sir Edward Maufe.
(Commonwealth War Graves Commission)

The extent of the beautiful memorial at Runnymede is testimony to all those airmen flying from the United Kingdom who do not have a known grave. However the memorials in the countryside of Britain from where the flying took place have added poignancy and there is sustained local sentiment as expressed by the organiser of the 1997 Anzac service in Scotland; "be assured of the lasting goodwill of the people of Moray and Banff towards the gallant young men who left their own countries to come to help us defend ours."[5] EATS airmen with similar associations in many places around the British Isles will empathise with this sentiment and on their part retain a depth of feeling for those they helped in waging the Battle from Britain.

There were hundreds of wartime aerodromes dotted over Britain and the local communities were conscious of the airmen in their midst. Aircraft were constantly overflying them, if indeed runways did not actually abut the towns and villages. There are many churches close to airfields and former airfields which have plaques, banners and fitments such as kneelers embroidered with squadron crests. In the church near RAF Langham, Norfolk there is a plaque to the Anzac Wing (455 Sqn RAAF and 489 Sqn RNZAF) which reads:

> From the fields between this church and the sea, during the wartime summer of 1944, a small band of young men flew in defence of these islands. Most of these ardent volunteers had journeyed across half the globe to our aid in a time of desperate need. Sadly many of these young men were destined never to return home again, but to be lost somewhere across a waste of seas with their final resting place remaining unknown to this day. May their sacrifice for us never be forgotten."[6]

RAAF Lancaster Squadrons 463/467, in which 986 airmen gave their lives, were based a few kilometres outside Lincoln at Waddington.[7,8] Lincoln Cathedral, a soaring landmark imprinted on the minds of those returning from raids deep into Germany, now contains an Airmen's Chapel housing the Memorial Books of 1 and 5 Groups of Bomber Command. The book, a page of which is turned every day, contains the names of nearly 22,000 who did not return: 1,368 are Australians. A service is held there in their memory each Thursday at 10.30 am.

Smaller memorials abound in the countryside such as the one in East Yorkshire to the 482 airmen who lost their lives while flying the Halifaxes of 466/462 Squadrons RAAF.[9]

In the desire to leave the war behind it was not until 1992 that the spontaneously felt need by the local populace and the surviving airmen caused a memorial to be raised to the 35 crews of Bristol Beaufighters killed and missing from air operations in the winter and spring of 1944/45 from the RAF Dallachy Strike Wing, a British Commonwealth affair, in northern Scotland. It is made from local stone in the shape of an aircraft tail fin and also contains stones flown from Canada, Australia and New Zealand.[10]

Looking out between Scots pines to the North Sea – the RAF Dallachy Strike Wing Memorial.
memori - dallachy (R. Tustin).

Between Scots pines where the old guardroom once stood on the road between Fochabers and Spey Bay the memorial looks out to the decaying concrete control tower, still standing, and mouldering runways. On this memorial there are often fresh wreaths. In the local museum there are photographs and memorabilia from those times including the flags of these Commonwealth nations. In 1997 a suggestion to quietly raise the RAAF flag at the memorial on Anzac Day met with an astounding local response. A spontaneous wave of enthusiasm swept across many people and organisations to honour the day. Though only a part of the complex fabric uniting Britain and the Dominions, the reaction is indicative of its deep and abiding nature. Australian and New Zealand flags flew in the village and over the hotel. A guard of honour from neighbouring RAF Lossiemouth, the base for the RAF's current strike wing of Tornados,[11] was drawn up at the memorial at 0900 on a chilly morning. The Lord Lieutenant of the county was present to represent the Queen and there were representatives from the Gallipoli Association, the RAF, the Royal British Legion, the Western Front Association, the Air Crew Association and the RAAF as well as local bodies. The RAAF ensign was raised and there was a short but moving service for those lost on air operations and whose graves are the waters of the North Sea beyond the memorial.

In the address it was recalled that the genesis of Anzac was the Australian and New Zealand Army Corps formed of divisions from the two dominions in Egypt in 1915. In the Great War most of the 60,000 dead of the Australian Imperial Forces were soldiers. Many of the battlefields of the western front remain familiar and affecting to this day - Passchendaele, Pozieres, Mont St Quentin, Ypres and Cambrai. It was Gallipoli where the spirit of Anzac started and the mystique created was about soldiers. There is no hallowed RAAF equivalent.

In the Second World War many more Australian participants were airmen[12,13] and by the end of the war the RAAF had become the world's fifth largest airforce. Except for the Battle of Britain in which some Australians took part, the RAAF's engagements are largely unknown by name because of the very nature of their diversity and multiplicity. More Australian lives were lost in the air than on Gallipoli and nearly as many airmen in the Battle from Britain as soldiers in the legendary campaign. Rather than a number of well known encounters the air war was one of attrition across a broad canvas. Losses ranged from one or two aircraft failing to return from an operation to one of the largest losses on one day from a Royal Air Force station of nine aircraft.[14] As so often happened many of those who flew into battle were never seen again, their end for us only to imagine in their uncontrolled descent to earth or into the sea, killed, wounded or ablaze.

For many of the RAF and Commonwealth air forces the most significant day on looking back may not be Remembrance Day or a national day but the fifteenth of September, Battle of Britain Day. For Australians, while acknowledging the few of the Battle of Britain, remembrance extends to the many of the Battle from Britain, and the EATS aircrews from the Middle East to the South West Pacific and beyond. All those airmen who were lost are in the thoughts of those gathered at the Australian War Memorial in Canberra each September on the fifteenth when the High Commissioners of the Commonwealth and Ambassadors of the Allied Nations lay wreaths, the RAAF parades and the modern jets fly over.

Return and Epilogue

After the war some pilots found positions in airlines and a very few only were kept on by the RAAF, in the throes of running down. Many had no desire to fly again. Those who had joined the RAAF straight from school had to find a job and in learning a trade or vocation they were supported by another great plan, the Commonwealth Reconstruction Training Plan (CRTS).[1] Others had their previous occupations to which to return and in doing so they could also benefit from retraining with the CRTS.

CRTS figures prominently in the rehabilitation of many of the Uranquinty graduates.[2,3] Those entitled to training were
- those whose training had been interrupted by the war
- those too young to have started training when they went to war.
- those whose careers had been jeopardised by war-caused disabilities
- those needing refresher courses.

After termination of the EATS in February 1945, the service flying training schools were disbanded, with the exception of 5SFTS Uranquinty which became 1SFTS providing refresher courses for qualified pilots. It relocated in 1948 to Point Cook as No. 1 Flying Training School (FTS). Uranquinty became a migrant centre in 1949.

In 1951, the Prime Minister, Mr Menzies, informed the chiefs of staff that Australia had three years to prepare for a major war. Accordingly the Minister for the Navy and the Air, Mr McMahon, wrote to the Minister for Immigration on 17 September 1951

> The overseas commitments of the RAAF in Korea and Malaya and the state of the international situation, which has made it essential to bring RAAF strength up to establishments as quickly as possible, have all combined to necessitate an expansion in aircrew training activities.... Under this expansion, it has become necessary to re-open the RAAF establishment at Uranquinty, which is now occupied by your Department on a permissive occupancy basis. The proposed date of re-forming this RAAF unit is March 1952.[4]

In reply, Mr Holt:
> At present some nine hundred migrants are housed at Uranquinty (Immigration Holding Centre), but arrangements will be made for their transfer to another Centre and this movement could be completed in quite a short time.[5]

In the event the transfer was made to Bonegilla Centre between 17-19 October and the Secretary of the Department writing to the Director-General of Works in October mentioned, as well as Uranquinty, the return of Mallala and Kapooka.[6]

Wirraways were again flying at Uranquinty, as part of 1FTS became No. 1 Basic Flying Training School (BFTS).

Extension of the runway for jets was being considered in 1956 and the Lewington family were concerned at the possibility of an additional portion of land being acquired.[7] There had already been a problem with disposal of stormwater.[8] Further, the runway would have to cross the Uranquinty to Kywong railway.[9]

The Department of Civil Aviation objected to
> The establishment of a jet training school adjacent to a civil trunk air as route would create a potentially dangerous air traffic situation....
> and expensive air line diversions would be necessary.[10]

Nethertheless a decision was made for the re-equipment of the AFTS at Pearce with Vampire Mk 33 aircraft and movement to Uranquinty as soon as the runway was constructed and the BFTS moved to Point Cook.[11] In fact the AFTS was to remain at Pearce and on 19 December 1958 because of a diminishing need for aircrew there was once more a decision to move Uranquinty to Point Cook.[12]

In 1952 Bruce Taylor rejoined the RAAF as a flying officer in Equipment Works, having taken up and finished an electrical apprenticeship started before the war. Full circle, he was appointed Barracks Officer to Uranquinty and then as Works Officer at Forest Hill from 1956-59. He had the sad task of finally organising the closing down of his former SFTS. He retired as S/L Equipment in 1975.[13]

At disbandment during 1959 there was a move from NSW to take over the Base as a Child Welfare Institution.[14,15] Mr Bourne had the grazing licence in 1960 and Mr Walkley in 1961.[16] In 1962, the base was acquired on tender by Crestbrook P/L, a development company based in Sydney, which placed a deposit of 10,000 pounds on the 404-hectares property in order to develop it as an aero club. The firm failed to raise the necessary funds to complete the deal even after selling off most of the buildings and surplus land. The private airfield did not eventuate and the Air Force was forced to resume the land and put it up for auction. The Lewington family bought back the land at auction in April 1964 for fifty pounds five shillings an acre.[17]

In 1978, when Lou and Jenny Lewington moved back to live on the former base, they named their house, Churchill Square, as it is sited opposite the parade ground which bore that name. All the streets of the base were once named, mostly after aircraft.

Wirraway A20-719 was bought in March 1960 by CAC to assist in the development of a crop sprayer, the Ceres.[18] It was modified with a slightly larger wing to consequently achieve lower stalling speed. It was acquired later by Pearce Dunn, an early collector, at Mildura, before passing into the hands of the syndicate referred to at the end of Chapter 2.[19]

Jim Banyard's father had an agent in London who lived in a big block of flats in Dolphin Square. He invited Jim for 1944 New Year's eve party to which he had also asked a WAAF officer living there who worked in Air Ministry. Rather at a loose end Jim decided to attend and finding his way through the corridors in the large building he passed a woman in black evening dress and said to himself, "I would like to spend the evening with you". Eventually he got up to the right flat and the girl he was introduced to was not in WAAF uniform but the same girl dressed in black, and 54 years later they now live in Canberra. In December 1945 he returned aboard HMS *Victorious*, sailing from Plymouth home through the Mediterranean and the Suez Canal. Just outside Trincomalee about 20 brand new Spitfires were dumped over the side. At 0700 one morning they found themselves in Sydney Harbour, transferred in ferries from Atholl Bight to Bennelong Point at Man'o War Steps, bussed to Bradfield Park, discharged, and home by midday: All an anti-climax at the end.

Derek Beaurepaire returned from New Guinea to a posting on Test and Ferry at Laverton, and did some long range deliveries of Kittyhawks from Laverton to Morotai. After a series of bouts of malaria he finished service flying on a refresher OTU at Mildura. He later flew light aircraft when expanding the family's Beaurepaire Tyre Service from 25 to 175 branches in all States.

Ira Bensley seemed far from the war on 21 May 1943, flying in an Avro Anson from GRS Bairnsdale to Melbourne. It was a day of heavy low cloud and on descending, instead of being over the sea as reckoned, the hills and trees about Yarram loomed through the mist. Five of the six crew were killed in the crash and Ira suffered fractures of both legs and multiple injuries. Ira went on to fly with PTU Richmond (paratroop training) during 1944 and at the end of that year to 38Sqn (Dakotas) operating as far as the Halmaheras and supply dropping to Wewak (biscuit operations).

Jack Chivers had been a banking officer, and he went back to the Bank of NSW. He retired in 1981 having managed branches at Echuca, Glen Waverley and Richmond.

Bill Cousens returned to be with his father in their real estate business in Tamworth (later Bill relocated the business to Yamba). As well as being a swimmer of note, he had considerable talent as an actor and singer. He and his wife, Marjorie, were members of the Tamworth Musical Society. Their son, Peter, is a well known music theatre actor, notably being the phantom in the London production of "The Phantom of the Opera" two years ago.

Venn Cranmer took advantage of the Commonwealth Reconstruction Training Scheme[16,17] to do Industrial Chemistry at Sydney Technical College. He worked in Taubmans, Atlantic Union Oil Co (which later became Esso), ICI, and then the Research Department of CSR, identifying the virus in sugar cane. He has remained in touch since 'Quinty with John McCosker who piloted flying boats on the Lord Howe Island run, brought out the first Fokker jet from Europe, flew with East West Airlines, and has accumulated 26,000 hours.

Jack Curtis flew with TAA for 35 years, being First Officer on many aircraft including the DC3, Viscount, Bristol 170, Lockheed Electra, DC9 and B727. On retirement he was soon back in the air with Rebel Air, Dakota Downunder, Desert Air Safaris, and Air North, flying Australia's oldest DC3, VH-MMA with 68,000 hours on the airframe. It had 150 engine changes during its lifetime. In 1991 he began flying an immaculately restored Lockheed 10A (Electra) VH-UZO) which was Reg Ansett's first all metal retractable undercarriage airliner, delivered to Ansett Airlines in July 1937. It saw service during WWII in Northern Australia including the evacuation of Darwin during the Japanese bombing in 1942. Jack said he was fortunate enough to have flown it for 18 months and 150 hours, including flights to Darwin and Townsville to commemorate respectively the 50 year anniversary in Darwin and the 50th anniversary of the Battle of the Coral Sea. Having

been Chief Pilot DC3 for five operators, he is now the Chief Pilot and Check Captain for Dakota National Air. As well as the above types he has flown Navy Museum's Neptune, Lodestar, Trojan, Beech 18, Winjeel, Boeing Stearman and finally his own Wirraway A20-719 VH-WRX.[1]

Bob Davies returned to his old job in an accountancy office in Wagga and qualified as a chartered accountant through the CRTS. He then went into the family real estate business and on retirement lives in Canberra.

Keith Doyle OAM did a B.Ec. through CRTS at Sydney University, and after an accounting degree established his own insurance brokerage, Sold it to Lloyds and entered State Parliament as Member for Vaucluse 1965-74, becoming Parliamentary Secretary to the Premier in 1976. He has been fund raising Director for "Odyssey House" and NSW Society for Crippled Children and chairman of Vaucluse House Trust.

Ern Dunkley worked post-war for the Sydney County Council and Electricity Commission of NSW, before retiring to the Gosford area. He wrote the Forword to the history of 464 Squadron, "The Gestapo Hunters", published in 1999.

Bruce Emmerson, Peter Ilbery, Douglas Mackenzie, Struan Robertson and Richard Willcocks became medical practitioners, and Bill Wileman, a dentist, through the CRTS at Sydney University.

Ken Goldring, originally in the firm of Magnus Goldring, established his own venture in Japan. For the past many years he has been a Japanese resident, perhaps nominally only as it seems home is a Cathay Pacific aircraft with an average of two visits each month to offices in Korea, Taiwan, Hong Kong and less regular visits elsewhere in the East.

John Humphreys had the misfortune to contract poliomyelitis in 1952. In the less usual form it left him paralysed in his upper limbs. Despite this handicap he worked as purchasing manager with the supportive firm of Unilever, until retirement, sustained by Jean, his wife of 54 years.

Bill Howard sailed for home on the *Stirling Castle* in October from Liverpool. There was an RAF Air Marshal to wave farewell from the dockside to the large RAAF contingent. He had enlisted from Gilgandra, where he was a farmhand on his father's property. After his return he tried growing wheat on shares with his brother, but there was a bad drought in 1946, and 1947 was very wet at harvest. However, he was fortunate in a ballot for a soldier's block on Wantabadgery West Estate near Wagga. It had no buildings or improvements although there were plenty of rabbits. The grazing enterprise was successful, helped along by the wool boom of the 1950s.

Denny Kingsbury did a Building Diploma at Sydney Technical College through CRTS, but later ran the hotel at Tumut and enjoyed fishing. Always wanting to meet someone he had escorted, following the Battle of Britain ceremony at the Australian War Memorial in 1997 he talked with a Beaufighter pilot whose anti-shipping wing had been escorted by his Mustangs on their mutual last operation of the war.

Jack McDonald went back to being a clerk at the Sydney County Council, but becoming dissatisfied, applied for a CRTS grant on 30 June 1948, the last day on which application could be made. He qualified for the NSW Teaching Service and retired as a principal in Canberra in 1983.

Dick McKenzie returned to his old job as an audit clerk with a firm of chartered accountants, and then took a commercial position with a firm importing textiles, before finally settling full time into the share market.

Keith Pollard came home on the **Stirling Castle** in August from Suez. He would have liked to enter commercial aviation, but, in his words, "pilots were two bob a dozen." Since 1895 his family had been butchers and he joined his father's business in Queanbeyan.

Vern Polley, on leaving the RAAF in late September 1942, joined ANA and during the next four years flew and instructed on DC2, DC3, DC4 and DC5. He was then with TAA as first instructor and flew their new DC4s mostly to Perth. On Anzac Day 1948 he flew British Commonwealth Pacific Airlines' first flight to America in a DC4. BCPA obtained new DC6s in 1949 and he flew the Pacific for 5 years, until Australia bought out New Zealand and the United Kingdom, and Qantas operated the route. He joined Pakistan International Airlines as Senior Instructor for the new airline. Based in Karachi, he flew Superconstellations all over Middle East, Europe…. In 1964 he joined Trans Mediterranean Airline, Beirut, flying DC6s and was mixed up in the Israeli 6-day war. In 1968 he flew DC6Bs for Transavia Holland and was involved in the Biafran War of 1968-70. As Chief Pilot he was responsible for training and operations. He evacuated mercenaries, from the Congo and did 71 flights (all night) into the ULI Strip.[20] He was attacked on the ground at ULI by MIGs flown by mercenaries and later shot down on 2 June 1969 in a DC6. He then flew jets, Caravelles, B707 and B737, until forced to retire in 1978. He flew in the World Vintage Air Rally in 1990 from England to Australia in a Cessna 120. At 81 he is still flying and has 32,000 flying hours and nine log books. Last August he wrote off his CT4 (ex RAAF trainer) after engine failure over Evans Head.

Heather Schmitzer spoke about her husband Clem who died two years ago. As Heather Spires she married him in 1950 following their meeting at the Royal Naval Air Station at Culham where she was a WRNS. He had been practising deck landings at Yeovil and was ferrying Sea Fury aircraft while awaiting posting to **HMAS** *Sydney* (**HMS** *Terrible*). She said that Clem had completed his service with RAAF at the Test Flight at Bankstown and, looking together at his log book, we saw where he had flown the following types - Avenger, Corsair, Hellcat, Martlet, Reliant, Firefly, and Seafire. He had joined the RAN in 1948, after a spell back with the family building company at Taree. His naval career started in the Fleet Air Arm with seamanship training at **HMAS** *Cerberus*, and then it was off to England. In 1949 he was at **HMS** *Chatham* before joining **HMAS** *Sydney*. In 1950 he flew Firefly aircraft from the Australian carrier while she was carrying out exercises in the North Sea with the 21st Carrier Group. In 1951 he was back in the SWPA with the navy at Manus. By degrees his service became administrative and in 1967 he was appointed to Navy Office, Canberra as Director of Personnel Services. He retired in 1973 as Commander.

Manus Island 1951 –
"This is an old Spitfire that used to belong to my squadron – I'd flown it many times".
(Clem Schmitzser.)

Ken Sly met his wife, Olga, at RAF Lindholme when reporting the loss of his gear to the Orderly Room, where she was Senior NCO WAAF. After their marriage in the UK, they were sent from London, where he had a position with Bank of NSW in Threadneedle Street, to Suva. Serendipitously following a meeting with CO of the RNZAF Catalina Base there, he joined that air force. Changing to the RAF, he became a flying instructor with 1FTS Moreton in Marsh to again fly the Wirraway in the form of the Harvard, and later Meteor and Vampire aircraft. He commanded a RAF unit in Hong Kong after a year learning Mandarin at London University, later transferring to the Foreign Office where a period followed travelling between the UK and China concerning MOD sales to the PLA. In 1980 he was seconded to British Arospace as resident representative in China, based in Beijing, and during the sale of the BAE 146 aircraft to China he was their consultant. They now live at 33 Gotha Street, Cleveland 4163.

Ron Susans after the war commanded the RAAF Base at Parafield, and in 1946 commanded 77Sqn in Japan with BCOF. In 1948 he was Senior Staff Officer in BCAIR Headquarters at Iwakuni, returning to Australia to command 25Sqn at Pearce. In 1950, while serving as Staff Officer Fighter Operations, he was posted to again command 77Sqn which was then with a USAF Wing in Korea. Flying Mustangs, W/C Susans was awarded an immediate DSO for his outstanding leadership of 77Sqn, during which he engaged in 110 rocket and strafing attacks. Returning to Australia he represented the RAAF on the Joint Planning Teams for the Pacific treaties. As G/C Susans he was Deputy to the Head of the Australian Joint Services Mission in Washington. In 1957 he became Senior Air Staff Officer at Headquarters RAAF Edinburgh, where he was associated with the provision of air support and trials for the guided missile program at Woomera. In 1961 he was in Paris in connection with the purchase of the Mirage fighter, and was later RAAF Air Attache in Paris during their testing. Before retirement as Air Vice Marshal Susans CBE he commanded Williamtown and Butterworth.[21]

Ted Taylor before leaving England, married Pat Longley, a young lady met in London in 1942, and with whom he had corresponded all the time he was in the Middle East. They lived in Temora and Dungog where he was a Crown Land Agent, then in Cooma where he was a Field Administration Officer on the Snowy Mountains Scheme, and finally in Canberra as a builder. On retirement, they live on a rural holding near Bungendore.

W.M. Williams from 48 course became Chief Manager Branch Operations for the T & G.

Ken Witt from 57 Course became a stockbroker and has been programming computers since 1948. Being on the last course at 5SFTS few flying hours were achieved but a friend on the course, "Aussie" Miller, became a cropduster and got up 25,000 hours.

Bruce Gogery, 36 Course, continued to fly in the post-war RAAF, and on 1 December 1951, destroyed a Mig-15 in an intense combat when 40 Migs attacked 12 Meteors of 77Sqn RAAF. Three Meteors were lost. Gogerly, as a F/L, flew on the last RAAF strike in Korea on 20 July 1953. He received the DFC.

Tony Christie joined the RAAF Active Reserve and flew Dakotas from 36Sqn Richmond between 1950 and 1953 until the scheme was wound up. For 21 years he was an examiner for the old DCA based in Victoria and Western Australia. "In order to be placed on the civil register aircraft have to meet certain performance standards and my job was to establish take off and climb performance, t/o and landing distance charts, payload dump rate in an emergency. The Ceres was a good concept, carried about one ton of fertiliser with the likes of the DH Beaver."

Gorden Harvey, 28 Course, flew Mustangs with 75Sqn RAAF in Korea, was shot down by ground fire on 19 January 1951, captured, and released on 29 September 1953. He was awarded the DFC, the US DFC and US Air Medal.

Fred Hanson on 26 Course became a Commissioner of Police.

Leigh Hindley undertook a five-year electrical course under the CRTS but in 1951 accepted one of the permanent positions in the RAAF being offered to wartime aircrew. From an exchange posting to an RAF Mosquito squadron in Malaya, a return to Wirraways at Uranquinty as an instructor, and transport duties with Dakota squadrons, his career altered with conversion to helicopters. Initially based with 9 Helicopter Squadron in Canberra, he was appointed CO of 5Sqn, equipped with Iroquois, at Butterworth, performing combined operations with British and New Zealand forces, and then with American forces in Vietnam. His DFC citation read in part, "He participated in a large number of the more hazardous missions flown by the squadron, and on many occasions his helicopter came under direct small arms fire from the Vietcong." He retired from the RAAF in 1968, obtained a commercial licence and flew helicopter for numerous companies and authorities in New Guinea and Australia, achieving 9,000 flying hours on the Jet Ranger helicopter alone. In his 18,000 hours he rated the de Havilland Hornet the best aircraft.

R oll

Uranquinty Graduates Roll
Graduates of No. 5
Service Flying Training School, Uranquinty[1]

The list of those awarded their Wings at 5 SFTS, Uranquinty is as complete as it has been possible to extract from the combined photographed records in Rolls 370 and 371 of Personal Occurrence Reports (PORs) and in Station Daily Records (DROs). These records are held at the RAAF Historical Unit, Canberra (filmed by HPA for Department of Defence (Air Force Office) and where documents had poor legibility the best possible reproduction had been obtained).[2] The photographed records are consequently at times of poor quality and difficult to discern. Further the data appeared sometimes incomplete and occasionally incorrect. Some inconsistencies are to be found when comparison is made with the names in the separate books of Grave Registrations for officers and airmen who died on service 1939-1947, held by the RAAF Historical Unit, which total 10,953.[3]

Comparison of the list of graduates with the separate books of officers and airmen who died on service has allowed some brief details to be given concerning age, rank, formation at the date of death, and in the case of those who have graves, where buried. The location of the cemeteries has also been obtained from records in the RAAF Historical Section, compiled by Jock Ross, and the list and key is at the foot of the Roll. For those without known graves the location of their missing memorial is shown. Where initial postings have been found they have also been included. The key to these movements is within the List of Abbreviations.

In performing the not inconsiderable task of extracting these records I have been conscious that my own fallibility in making interpretations from the material available may have resulted in errors. The state of preservation was such that inevitably there must be some inaccuracies.

The listing of graduates is by course and includes where available, after each name, the following in order – initials, number, and first posting, and where killed or missing - (age), rank, formation, where lost and the date, and finally the key to the place of burial or the missing memorial on which the name is recorded, as listed on pages 150 - 160
for example, on 17 Course:

     Ainslie HG;   Air Force No 405814; to 3ED; Died age 21, Rank of Flying Officer;
                111 Sqn Italy, Died 2 Oct 1944; Buried in Florence War Cemetery,
                Shown as It1.

17 Course, 5SFTS. L-R: Back Row; R.N. Spowart, D.C. Logan, H.E. Williamson, K.W. Ashmead, R.O. Sandell, C.N. Smith, D. Keane, S.L. Jay, S.J. Donellan, B.H.0 Hall, A.W. Ward, E. Marsh, K.B. Morgan, D.R. McCarthy, F.A. Hewlett, R.J. Shumack, D.B. Beaurepaire: Centre Row; F/L V.H. Polley, R.R. Bladwell, R. Ambler, R.H. Hodges, K.E. Spedding, J.C. Irvine, M.A. Kilpatrick, H.G. Ainslee, J.F. Howell-Price, A.W. Walker, R.H. Small, J.W. Thorncraft, J.J. Parker, K.J. Dawes, P.E. Whitehead, F/L E. Cooke: Front Row; A.J. Noldart, C.G. Walford, S.L. Porter, F.E. Taylor, S/L T. O'Connell, S/L C.F. King, S/L F.G. Huxley, J.I. White, D.L. Nelson, G.B. Rich, T.R. Davies. (F.E. Taylor).

17 Course (P): Commenced 16/11/41and awarded flying badge on 23/3/42:

Ainslie HG, 405814; 3ED; (21), F/O, 111 Sqn, Italy, 2-10-44. It1.

Ambler R, 412227; 2ED; (24), F/S, 2 Flying Instrument School, Angus, UK, 4- 8-43. UK8.

Ashmead KW, 41 093; 3WAGS.

Bladwell RR, 411988; 2CF.

Davies TR, 409094.

Dawes KJ, 411486; CFS.

DeBeaurepaire DB, 411754; CFS.

Donnellan SJ, 411879; 2ED.

Hall AH, 408830.

Hewlett FA, 412511; 2CF.

Hodges RH, 411912; 2CF.

Howell-Price JF, 411914; 2CF.

Irvine JC, 415911; CFS.

Jay SL, 411915; CFS; (20), Sgt, 10EFTS, Temora, NSW,8-12-42. A11.

Keane D, 411917; 2CF.

Kilpatrick MA, 409056; CFS.

Logan DC, 412068; 2ED.

Logan RD, 405929; 3ED.

Marsh E, 412820; CFS.

McCarthy ER, 411923.

Morgan KB, 412019; 2AD.

Nelson DL, 412653.

Noldart AJ, 411937; 2CF.

Parker JJ, 412829; 2ED.

Porter SL, 412681; 2CF; (23), F/O, 23 Sqn, off Qld coast, 4- 5-44. A9.

Rich GB, 412695; 2CF.

Sandell RO, 411608; 2ED; (22), F/S 154 Sqn, Tunisia, 20- 4-43. T1.

Small RH, 412727; (22), F/L, 229 Sqn, France, 23-6-44. F1.

Smith CN, 412275; 2CF.

Shumack BJ, 412036; 2AD.

Spedding KE, 412205; 3WAGS; (20), Sgt, 12 Sqn, Northern Territory, 1- 4-43. A12.

Spowart RN, 412736; 2AD.

Taylor FE, 412210; 2ED.

Thorncraft JW, 412214; (23), F/O, 5 Sqn, Toowoomba, Qld,25-10-42. A13.

Walford CG, 412773; (25), F/S, 2 WAGS, Parkes, NSW,4- 1-44. A8.

Walker AW, 412285; 2CF; (21), F/O, 250 Sqn, Italy, 24- 2-44. It2.

Ward WB, 411622; 2CF; (22), Sgt, 3 Sqn, Middle East, 6- 4-43. ME1.

White CI, 412781; 3WAGS.

Whitehead PE, 408942; (32), F/O, 75 Sqn, New Guinea, 21-10-43. NG2.

Williamson HE, 412290.

18 Course (P): Commenced 14/12/41 and awarded flying badge on 18/5/42:

Atwell GJ, 411673; 2ED; (27), P/O, 614 Sqn, off Italy, 20-4-44, Malta Missing Memorial.

Bell MH, 405995; (21), P/O, 19 Sqn, Holland, 9-9-44, Runnymede Missing Memorial.

Bull DWW, 409023; (21), F/S 56 OTU, Scotland, 27-4-43, Runnymede Missing Memorial.

Burroughs PF, 412383; 2ED; (22), F/S, 232 Sqn, Middle East, 13-4-43. T1.

Calvert WV, 412387.

Carrick RM, 412804; 2ED.

Connor EG, 412609; 1ED.

Curtis JF, 412231; 2ED; (27), P/O, 1661 Conversion Unit, United Kingdom, 3-9-43. UK9.

Conroy RJ, 412113.

Darbishire DD, 411874.

Devine PE, 405788; 3ED; (22), P/O, 1492 Target Towing Flt, United Kingdom, 24-6-43. UK6.

Douglas HA, 405843; 3ED; (21), W/O, 53 OTU, Scotland, 18-3-44. UK10.

Farrell JW, 412419.

Filshie LR, 414012; 3ED.

Fletcher DG, 412579; 2ED.

Foran MT, 412240; 2ED.

Fuller B, 412427; 2ED.

Gray CH, 412312.

Hibbett FJ, 405481; 3ED.

Hinton JE, 412446; 2ED.

Jekyll GD, 405914; 3ED; (30), P/O, 102 Sqn, United Kingdom, 9-6-44. UK2.

Jennings EC, 412539; 2ED.

Kingston CC, 414046; 3ED.

Lowe RN, 412257; 2ED.

Luke CS, 412461; 2ED; (21), W/O, 43 Sqn, Middle East, 5-2-44. It3.

Markwell IA, 414054; 3ED; (24), F/O, 452 Sqn, N.E.I., 24-12-44. Ambon Missing Memorial.

Matthews FG, 412465; 2ED; (25), P/O, 214 Sqn, France, 13-8-43. F2.

McAuliffe L, 412624; (24), F/Lt, 222 Sqn, Holland, 17-3-45. H1.

McIntyre AWB, 412635.

McIver KA, 412636; 2ED; (25), P/O, 467 Sqn, United Kingdom, 3-10-43. UK11.

McRoberts BOK, 412563; 2ED; (21), Sgt, 53 OTU, United Kingdom, 3-11-42. Runnymede Missing Memorial.

Morris SN, 412619; 2ED.

Munson RW, 414065; 3ED.

Murphy FD, 408608; 2ED.

Neilson RC, 412652; 2ED.

Pendrick KR, 413247; 2ED.

Racklyeft PM, 412691.

Ranson KJ, 412267.

Rivett PE, 414084: (23), F/L, 71 OTU, Middle East, 18-5-44. ME2.

Scanlon AR, 403535; 2ED; (29), F/L, 620 Sqn, Holland, 20-9-44. H2.

Sheekey TB, 412720; 2ED; (24), P/O, 114 Sqn, Italy, 16-12-43. It5

Simpson TH, 408609; 2ED; (27), F/O, 88 Sqn, France, 5-8-44. F3.

Stuart DC, 412279.

South RF, 412345; 3ED.

Taylor AJH, 414100; 3ED.

Travers A, 412762; 2ED.

Tucker C, 414278; 3ED.

Twigg HR, 412470.

Vance RL, 407769 .

Whiteman AL, 412782; 2ED.

Williamson DC, 412786; 2ED; (21), Sgt, 52 OTU, United Kingdom, 15-10-42. UK12.

Wright GE, 412794; 2ED.

Woodey JE, 411625; 2ED; (24), W/O, 131 Sqn, France, 7-6-44, Runnymede Missing Memorial.

53/93

19 Course (P): Commenced 8/2/42 and awarded flying badge on 23/6/42:

Atherton HM, 414123; (21), F/S 55 OTU, United Kingdom, 23-3-43. UK13.
Bell RC, 412884; (20), 57 OTU, United Kingdom, 27-2-43. UK14.
Bermingham GR, 409072
Burney SW, 412896
Carter JW, 412912; (22), P/O, 137 Sqn, United Kingdom, 1-4-44, Runnymede Missing Memorial.
Clark PM, 412903; (22), F/S, 55 OTU, United Kingdom, 23-6-43. UK15.
Cook LT, 412399; (20), F/S, 55 OTU, United Kingdom, 23-3-43. UK13.
Cotterill AJ, 412909
Cousens WL, 412911
Curling R, 409088
Cuthbertson RH, 413355
Dripps DC, 409392; (27), P/O, 550 Sqn, Germany, 24-12-43, Runnymede Missing Memorial.
Dunkley EH, 413358
Evans R, 413481
Fleming RC, 413113; (26), F/L, 101 Sqn, Germany, 9-7-43, Runnymede Missing Memorial .
Gow DM, 413306; (24), F/O, 242 Sqn, Italy, 25-4-44. It4.
Gilbert RD, 413188; (22), W/O, 181 Sqn, France, 19-8-44, Runnymede Missing Memorial.
Grady JC, 413202; 2ED.
Gullan MJ, 409045; 1ED.
Guthrie DD, 413376; 2ED.
Haley JP, 412432; 2ED.
Halloran SC, 414230; 3ED.
Hewitt KH, 413380; 2ED.
Kevin FJ, 413140; 2ED.
Langford F, 412976; 2ED.
Layfield RS, 414244; 3ED.
Low JC, 413129; 2ED; (28), F/O, 168 Sqn, France, 8-6-44. F4.
Lowder LS, 413086; 2ED.
Lowe JC, 409420; 2ED.
MacKenzie RM, 413242; 2ED.
Mackintosh HCL, 414052; 3ED; (28), P/O 630 Sqn, Germany, 21-2-44. G4.
Marshall AL, 33391; 2ED.
Mason DW, 413220; 2ED; (25), P/O, 198 Sqn, France, 18-6-44, Runnymede Missing Memorial.
Maxwell JH, 413388; 2ED.
McMahon M, 414070; 3ED; (30), P/O, 103 Sqn, Germany, 24-12-43. G3.
Murray SW, 412622; 2ED; (23), F/S, 56 OTU, Scotland, 11-10-43. UK8.

Myers NL, 413088; 2ED; (22), F/L, 242 Sqn, off French Coast, 13-8-44, Malta Missing Memorial.
Neal C, 413230; 2ED.
Oliver JK, 414075; 3ED.
Palesy RV, 413027; 2ED.
Paton JM, 411600; 2ED.
Patton HA, 414262; 3ED.
Payne TH, 413418; 2ED; (27), F/S, 295 Sqn, United Kingdom, 24-7-42. UK16.
Pearsall AL, 408266; 1ED; (28), F/O, 16 Sqn, English Channel, 8-3-44, Runnymede Missing Memorial.
Pilling RK, 413096; 2ED.
Precians RK, 413097; 2ED.
Robinson NJ, 413271; 2ED.
Ryall JL, 413262; 2ED.
Scott JW, 405939; 3ED.
Semadeni CJ, 413436; 2ED.
Simpson AS, 412723; 2ED.
Stanley J, 413099; 2ED.
Stockdale WH, 409455; 2ED.
Stubbs JD, 413275; 2ED; (29), F/L, 168 Sqn, Holland, 2-1-45. H3.
Te Kloot J, 414276; 3ED.
Templeman ND, 413279; 2ED.
Thynne EA, 414103; 3ED.
Wallace-Wells HG, 32266; 2ED.
Watts H, 413296; 2ED.
Webster HL, 413461; 2ED.
Weeden J, 413054; 2ED; (20), F/S, 58 OTU, United Kingdom, 2-7-43. UK17.
Westgarth DD, 413463; 2ED; (22), P/O, 261 Sqn, Burma, 25-4-45. Bu1.
Wright EC, 413813; 2ED.
Wright H, 413067; 2ED.
Ulrick BL, 413048; 2ED; (22), W/O, 146 Sqn, India, 5-6-44. I2.
Young HK, 414148; 3ED.

66/159

20 Course (P): Awarded the Flying Badge on 22/7/42:

Atkins R, 405897; 3ED.

Baetz HL, 414379; 3ED; (20), F/S, 184 Sqn, Atlantic, 12-3-43, Runnymede Missing Memorial.

Ball E, 405991; 3ED; (24), P/O, 4 Sqn IAF, 14-8-44, Singapore Missing Memorial.

Banyard JR, 413333; 2ED.

Barlow JC, 405992; 2ED; (35), F/L, 106 Sqn, Germany, 6-10-44. G5.

Barnes BK, 405898; 2ED.

Bartlett SW, 405994; 3ED; (19), F/S, 58 OTU, United Kingdom, 5-5-43, Runnymede Missing Memorial.

Bennett WR, 414189; 2ED.

Bowen JA, 414334; 4ED.

Buchanan JT, 405998; 3ED; (31), P/O, 467 Sqn, Holland, 28-7-43. H5.

Cann MJ, 411678; 2ED.

Carey CT, 413166; 2ED.

Charles EL, 412108; 2ED.

Clark AN, 414126; 3ED.

Coward CT, 414003; 2ED; (22), F/O, 42 Sqn, 22-12-43, Singapore Missing Memorial.

Davis SH, 412934; 2ED.

Dunn CD, 408824; 4ED.

Durance AJ, 409207; 4ED.

Emslie AW, 414130; 3ED.

Farrell AC, 414216; 3ED.

Foley BL, 414398; 3ED.

Galletly AW, 405847; 3ED.

Healy HG, 414235; 3ED.

Hensel MR, 416573; 4ED.

Hill CH, 405855; 3ED.

Holland EJ, 416500; 4ED.

Hooper WM, 416577; 4ED; (20), F/O, 5 AFU, Stoke-On-Trent, UK, 26-2-43. UK18.

Jackson JW, 416579; 4ED.

Kewish WK, 414409; 3ED; (21), W/O, 215 Sqn, India, 3-3-44, Singapore Missing Memorial.

Lafferty KA, 414143; 3ED.

Laman SM, 405196; 3ED; (24), P/O, 198 Sqn, France, 13-1-44. F5.

Lawrence KK, 5358; 4ED.

Lee WR, 405693; 3ED.

Mackay JD, 405864; 2ED; (23), F/O, 129, France, 6-9-43. F6.

Matthews FJ, 408859; 2ED; (26), F/S, 27 OTU, Chester, UK, 4-8-43. UK19.

McIlroy AW, 409430; 4ED.

McLean AA, 405694; 3ED.

McMinn RL, 412646; 2ED.

McQualter MS, 413014; 2ED; (21), F/O, 55 OTU, Cumberland, UK, 27-5-43. UK20.

Nalder NR, 412650; 2ED.

Negus BL, 414072: 3ED; (26), P/O, 207 Sqn, Germany, 18-10-43, Runnymede Missing Memorial.

Nicholson NA, 413019; 2ED.

Nixon NH, 4717; 1ED.

O'Connor NT, 413413; 2ED.

Ogilvie VC, 413392;2ED.

O'Reilly TB, 409535; 2ED; (23), F/O, 61 OTU, Oswestry, UK, 2-6-43. UK21.

Osborne ET, 409272; 4ED; (24), F/S, 198 Sqn, Holland, 2-9-43. H4.

Owen EC, 409438; 4ED.

Patterson EJ, 413028; 2ED.

Percival WF, 5478; 4ED.

Pile DZ, 408511; 1ED; (27), F/O, 63 Sqn, Costorphine, UK, 26-10-43. UK22.

Pym CR, 409066; 2ED.

Rasmussen ER, 412692; 2ED; (24), W/O, Grp Support Unit, Surrey, UK, 9-6-44. UK3.

Refshauge JH, 409477; 1ED.

Robinson KA, 416614; 4ED; (28), P/O, 199 Sqn, Marseilles, France, 16-2-44. F7.

Sheekey ID, 413439: 2ED; (24), F/O, 168 Sqn, Sussex, UK, 28-2-44. UK24.

Simpson AB, 408881; 4ED.

Steel TJ, 405701; 3ED; (21), F/O, RAAF Survey Flight, off Qld Coast, 23-7-45, Sydney Missing Memorial.

Sorohan KE, 405772; 3ED.

Stone HD, 412854; 2ED.

Taverner WC, 416464; 4ED; (21), F/S, 59 OTU, Harrogate, UK, 26-7-43. UK2.

Townend JD, 413148; 2ED.

Turner CG, 408939; 4ED.

Vanrehen WP, 409258; 1ED.

Vercoe AJ, 405532; 4ED.

Vicary ET, 414370; 3ED.

Webster AC, 408940; 2ED.

Wraith A, 408994; 1ED.

21 Course 21(2P): Awarded the Flying Badge on 16/9/42:

Bailey KJ, 31540; 1BAGS.
Bartrop BW, 413725; 1BAGS.
Bates JC, 409495; 3BAGS.
Boyce RF, 413520; 3BAGS; (21), F/O, 78 Sqn, 29-10-44. Lae Missing Memorial.
Brocklehurst J, 413729; 1BAGS.
Burke WN, 413161; 1BAGS.
Callan HM, 413821; 3BAGS.
Christensen PL, 409082; 3BAGS.
Christie AS, 413824; 3BAGS
Cook FH, 409868; 3BAGS.
Costello TJ, 414203; 3BAGS.
Crow TJ, 409818; 3BAGS.
Deal DA, 409820; 3BAGS.
Demedici JR, 11142; 1ED.
Dewar M, 409523; 3BAGS.
Durbidge J, 412929; 1BAGS.
Ellis NR, 413183; 1BAGS.
Fischer FE, 414031; 1WAGS.
Gourley G, 413572; 3BAGS.
Griffen RE, 413578
Guy JJ, 413581; 3BAGS
Higgins VP, 409116; 3BAGS
Hipgrave GF, 420195; 3BAGS
Houston JW, 409475; 3BAGS; (28), F/O, 5 OTU, Tocumwal, NSW, 19-6-44. A14.
Hudson JK, 413770; 3BAGS.
Lanham OA, 414411; 3BAGS.
Law CW, 414048; 3BAGS.
Longmore RE, 409559; 3BAGS.
Madigan WJ, 416507; 3BAGS.
Matley GE, 412992; 3BAGS.
Mulholland JO, 413006; 3BAGS.
Mullavey JM, 409571; 3BAGS.

Neall CJ, 413651; 3BAGS.
Phillips AR, 414078; 3BAGS.
Proudfoot AR, 412266; 3BAGS
Pryor MA, 412685; 3BAGS.
Rae RV, 413139; 3BAGS.
Read WA, 414366; 3BAGS.
Robertson AS, 409596; 1WAGS.
Schmidt LF, 414265; 3ED.
Scott KC, 412848; 2ED; (21), F/S, Advanced Flying Development Unit, Cambridge, UK, 18-12-43. UK1.
Sinclair CM, 8849; 1WAGS.
Stevens RP, 414110; 3BAGS; (20), Sgt, 3 BAGS, Sale, Vic, 5-6-43. A7.
Stokes GJ, 412727; 2ED.
Tamlyn JD, 409613; 7SFTS; (22), W/O, 5 SFTS, Uranquinty, NSW, 26-3-45. A1.
Taylor AV, 413042; 2ED.
Taylor CA, 413620; 2ED
Taylor IC, 413590; 1WAGS.
Thomson RB, 413689; 2ED; (27), Sgt, 50 Group, Reading, UK, 14-3-43. UK25.
Thompson WK, 409351; 1WAGS; (21), F/O, 5 Sqn, Rocky Creek, Qld, 17-3-44. A20.
Tippett JH, 414174; 1WAGS.
Trumper SN, 413692; 2ED; (22), F/O, 4 Sqn, New Guinea, 30-10-43. NG1.
Wallace RH, 414178; 7SFTS.
Wilson KA, 414449; 3ED.
Wilson NG, 409866; 1ED.
Wilson DJ, 414286; 2ED; (23), F/L, 130 Sqn, Germany, 8-12-44. G2.
Wiskar DA, 414180; 7SFTS.
Woods RD, 413496; 2ED.

22Course: Awarded the Flying Badge on 13/10/42:

Bath RW, 420116; (22), F/O, 75 Sqn, Dutch New Guinea, 9-8-44. NEI3.

Beggs KM, 409878.

Bolton RH, 420121.

Bridgford KJ, 205876.

Bull DJ, 420133.

Chappell AL, 413737; (23), W/O, 615 Sqn, India, 10-8-44. I1.

Christie BH, 420336.

Clarke RB, 420149.

Clissold G, 420150.

Cornish KS, 420204.

Edwards GA, 41311.

Gale JF, 409682.

Goodwin AG, 413985; (24), F/O, 2 Aircraft Depot, Morotai, 21-9-45. Ambon Missing Memorial.

Haggarty J, 414556.

Job R, 409702.

Kelly WP, 420208.

Kennedy RC, 409840; (22), F/L, 274 Sqn, Germany, 24-3-45. G2.

Knodler KJ, 420211; (22), W/O, 30 Sqn, India, 14-8-44. I2.

Merrett WK, 420231.

Ricketts RJ, 420057; (19), Sgt, 58 OTU, Grangemouth, UK, 10-6-43. UK17.

Roberts AE, 409775; (26), F/O, 164 Sqn, France, 6-6-44. A21.

Staff RC, 409608.

Stokes CK, 409765; (22), F/S, 58 OTU, Grangemouth, UK, 29-6-43. UK17.

Tapp CS, 420298.

Thomson RJ, 409862; (25), F/S, 622 Sqn, France, 18-11-43. F9.

Torpy JL, 420306.

Ware JB, 420311.

27/312

23 Course, 5SFTS, 13 October 1942. E.F. Glasson with dog. (Alma Stump).

23 Course: Awarded the Flying Badge on 13/10/42:

Bates AF, 413510; CFS; (19), Sgt, 2 OTU, Mildura, Vic 21-1-43. A5.
Blom GH, 420525; CFS; (25), P/O, 450 Sqn, Italy, 11-9-44. It5.
Blumer GM, 413517; 2ED.
Bousfield HT, 420530; CFS.
Bradley J, 415463; GRS.
Buck EE, 409984; CFS.
Burfield NM, 416027.
Carter RC, 412901.
Catford GS, 416826; CFS; (27), W/O, 222 Sqn, Germany, 17-3-45. G2.
Clark PW, 420459; GRS.
Commons MF, 409468; CFS.
Dohrman JF, 409822.
Eckert RA, 416838; 4ED.
Flanagan MW, 415471; CFS.

Gadd WC, 416946; 4ED.
Glasson EF, 416951.
Krogdahl ML, 413716; 5ED.
Munro HC, 10941; (25), F/O, 4 Sqn, off New Guinea, 26-11-43. Lae.
Pratten ME, 416994; CFS; (26), P/O, 463 Sqn, NW Europe, 22-5-44. Runnymede Missing Memorial.
Roberts HW, 409225.
Stewart R, 408505; GRS.
Straughair EA, 409860; GRS.
Sullivan N, 420297; 2ED.
Watt A, 10973; 1ED.
Wilson E, 409624; CFS; (26), W/O, 450 Sqn, Yugoslavia, 23-2-44, Malta Missing Memorial.

24 Course: Awarded the Flying Badge on 4/11/42:

Allen RC, 409980; 2OTU.
Bartels AT, 409652.
Connell SJ, 420448.
Cornally FJ, 420450; 2OTU.
Freeman WJ, 15763.
Gilmore WE, 8685; (27), W/O, 78 Sqn, off Kai Is, 14-10-44. Ambon Missing Memorial.
Glasson MR, 420657.
Harper WG, 409696.
Hart CJ, 420665; 2OTU.
Holmes HS, 420752.
Jones EL, 420569; 2OTU; (26), F/S, 83 Sqn, Lutwyche, Qld, 10-11-43. A3.
Kerrigan AI, 420681; (24), F/S, 11 PDRC, Bournemouth, UK, 23-5-43. UK26.
Kershaw HB, 420570; 2OTU; (31), F/O, 8 Communication Unit, New Guinea, 24-12-43. NG2.
Lippiatt FW, 414579.
Mann DR, 420423; 2ED.
McGlinchy L, 420483.
McLeod CN, 410007; 2OTU.
McNeil DL, 414815.

Miller CE, 420424; 2OTU; (23), F/O, 452 Sqn, Morotai, 22-5-45. NEI1.
Morroy JH, 420477.
Patterson GR, 408870; 2OTU.
Pine NH, 420400.
Robinson LG, 429274.
Sephton D, 420603; 2OTU.
Shipley HJ, 420284; 2OTU.
Turnbull JW, 414515.
Turnbull WJ, 420719; (23), F/S, 85 Sqn, Karrakatta, WA, 27-12-43. A2.
Venn KA, 420721.
Walsh RJ, 420087; (29), F/O, 466 Sqn, Germany, 25-7-44. G4.
Weatherstone AG, 420414; 2OTU.
Webb NE, 420726; (27), F/O, 463 Sqn, France, 4-7-44. Runnymede Missing Memorial.
Williams BP, 410024; (20), Sgt, 85 Sqn, Karrakatta, WA, 28-5-43. A2.
Wright LS, 410026.

33/370

25 Course: Awarded the Flying Badge on 1/12/42:

Biggs JC, 12413.
Burrows FR, 416824; 4ED; (29), P/O, 622 Sqn, France, 11-4-44. F10.
Chatillon FJ, 420860; 2OTU.
Faria R, 421045; 2ED; (23), W/O, 3 Sqn, Italy, 25-9-44. It6.
Gould GE, 414682; 2OTU.
Hall TT, 409993; 2ED.
Halpin CT, 420746; 2ED; (26), W/O, 3 Sqn, Italy, 21-8-44. It5.
Heap KA, 414936; 3ED.
Laybutt NK, 21165; 2ED.
Mainwaring W, 421044; 2ED.
Marr R, 421121; 2ED.
Marshall JS, 410359.
McNulty FP, 420588; 2ED.
Nixon WB, 420986; 2ED.
Normoyle FR, 420905; (28), F/L, 268 Sqn, 8-2-45, Holland. G7.
Poate JH, 421042.

Rossow VJ, 414835; 3ED.
Sheldon GC, 420282; 2ED.
Shipway G, 421132; 2ED; (22), F/S, 71 OTU, Middle East, 4-11-43. F2.
Simpkins W, 420502; 2OTU; (19), Sgt, 2 OTU, Mildura, Vic, 6-1-43. A5.
Steele RA, 421055; 2ED.
Stephens RV, 420631; 2ED.
Stove RG, 421098; 2OTU.
Stubbs GH, 420296; 2ED.
Taaffe GE, 421099; (23), P/O, 2 OTU, Mildura, Vic, 21-1-43. A5.
Turner GC, 420082.
Ware JP, 420311; 1ED.
Watson MJ, 420610; 2OTU; (20), W/O, 453 Sqn, France, 14-8-44. (the day before his 21st birthday). F13.
Webb RC, 420316; 2ED: (21), F/S, HQ Desert Air Force RAF, Italy 14-6-44. It2.

29/399

26 Course: Awarded the Flying Badge on 17/1/43:

On 21/9/42 74 LACs Aircrew 11 were posted in from 1, 5, 8, 10 and EFTSs.
Wastage – Scrub rate = 21/74 = 28%

Anderson RR, 420371; 2ED.
Andrews JL, 421003; 4OTU.
Barratt CA, 421148; 3WAGS.
Bechtel LC, 414882; 2OTU.
Callaghan FJ, 20203; 4OTU; (28), Sgt, 4 OTU, Sandgate, NSW, 3-3-43. A4.
Cole GL, 417262; 2OTU; (27), P/O, 25 OTU, Finningley, UK, 3-8-41. UK27.
Cook HHT, 416933; CFS.
Cowley JD, 421188; CFS; (23), F/O, 31 Sqn RAAF, North Borneo, 11-6-45. Labuan Missing Memorial.
Cowling WJ, 425428; 3ED.
Decourcy-Ireland BK, 417163; 2OTU.
Ellis FH, 417167; 2OTU; (23), Sgt, 2 OTU, Mildura, Vic, 13-4-43. A5.
Everett K, 420927; GRS.
Faulks NS, 420930; 2OTU.
Ford CH, 425294; CFS.
Gard H, 417066; 2OTU.
Garrett NR, 417173; 4OTU.
George WP, 414927; 2WAGS; (22), W/O, 76 Sqn RAAF, North Borneo, 19-7-45. Bo1.
Grant WG, 420936; 1WAGS.
Hanson FJ, 407958; 2ED.
Hatcher IC, 417183; 2OTU; (20), F/O, 86 Sqn RAAF, off Merauke, 8-9-43. Port Moresby Missing Memorial.
Hodgkinson AJ, 425160; 3ED.
Hogg WD, 420401; 2ED.
Johns AP, 417209; OTU.
Johns DC, 421019; 2ED.
Keenan TP, 425022; 1WAGS.

Keyes RJ, 420571; 3BAGS; (21), W/O, 76 Sqn RAAF, New Guinea, 28-1-45. Lae Missing Memorial.
Knapton PC, 413777; 3WAGS.
Knocker LB, 425026; 3BAGS.
Lang SB, 417268; 2OTU.
Layton DA, 417269; 2OTU.
Limbrick GA, 420894; 4OTU.
Martin R, 420974; 1BAGS.
Mauch AC, 425453; GRS.
McKay CG, 421492; CFS.
McKenzie C, 421493.
McKenzie DG, 421700.
Nicholls ES, 420706; 4OTU.
Orr WL, 420993; CFS.
Parks LC, 417231; CFS.
Peters TH, 421384; CFS.
Rich AB, 421466; 2BAGS.
Roulston AS, 421127; 2ED; (31), F/O, 587 Sqn RAF, United Kingdom, 11-5-44. UK9.
Salter AJ, 414841; 2OTU; (22), F/S, 4 Sqn RAAF, New Guinea, 26-11-43. Lae Missing Memorial.
Saywell GW, 414962; CFS; (22), F/L, 2 AD, Kyushu, Japan, 18-3-46. Labuan Missing Memorial.
Sellick BC, 417239; 1BAGS.
Shephard RF, 417241; 2OTU.
Shepherd RJ, 420403; 2BAGS.
Shoesmith JW, 421404; 2OTU.
Smith K, 421476; 4OTU.
Sparrow WF, 421092; 1BAGS.
Sullivan HJ, 420362; 4OTU.
Watts JL, 414855; 3BAGS.
Wrightson DT, 425400; 2WAGS; (21), W/O, 1 AD, Exeter, NSW, 20-3-45. A15.

53/452

27 Course, 5SFTS, 9 February 1943. (H. Schmitzer).

Group from 27 Course, 9 February 1943. L-R: Back Row; M. Walker, R.E. Ayre, E.R. Newberry, A. Frost, C.C. McKinnon, A.B. Todd, S. Bradford, H.H. McMullin, R.V. Nathan, D. Proctor: Middle Row; B.H. Waldin, R. Badly, R.R. Hartman, G.R. Balcombe, R.F. Badman, J. Donald, A.L. Langford, C.H. McCosker, H.T. Taylor: Sitting; C. Warren, E.F. Wright, W. Marsh, J.W. Mossop, A. Pacie, P. Day, D. Blackwell, O. Cormack: In front; J. Leyden, -, J. Poynden, C.J. Schmitzer, J. Preston, W. Parkes-Monty, J. Auld, J. McCarthy, L. Whitby. (H. Schmitzer).

27 Course. Awarded the Flying Badge on 9/2/43:

Allen TH, 421875; 2ED.
Allsopp RW, 418044; 2OTU.
Altoft RH, 425478; 3ED; (22), F/O, 450 Sqn RAAF, Italy, 29-5-44. It7.
Ayre RE, 422095; 2OTU; (23), F/O, 83 Sqn RAAF, Melville Bay, NT, 22-5-44. A12.
Badman RF, 420824; 2WAGS; (20), F/S, 25 Sqn RAAF, Karrakatta, 25-4-44. A2.
Balcombe GR, 420825; 2ED; (22), F/O, 100 Sqn RAF, Germany, 15-2-44. Runnymede Missing Memorial.
Ball CG, 425582; 1ED.
Becker RE, 425565; 3BAGS.
Blackford WF, 425589; 1ED; (24), F/O, 21 Sqn SAAF, Yugoslavia, 8-3-45. Y1.
Bradford S, 422114; 2WAGS.
Bridgeman RW, 422117; 2ED.
Carnell RW, 414899; 1ED.
Chamberlain JW, 24216; 3BAGS.
Chomley GA, 418232; 2OTU.
Collins JW, 421571; 1ED.
Copeman HA, 425607; 1ED.
Cormack O, 422263; 3BAGS.
Delbridge NS, 421893; 7SFTS.
Dickson C, 422038; 1ED; (23), P/O, 467 Sqn RAAF, France, 4-5-44. F12.
Douglas TH, 425620; 1ED.
Dowding AW, 425139; 1ED.
Dunk JH, 421845; 1ED.
Dutneall RA, 418083; 1ED; (21), F/S, 453 Sqn RAAF, France, 27-7-44. F3.
Evans J, 421896; 1ED.
Faddi RA, 422154; 2OTU.
Fay BJ, 422266; 1ED.
Frost A, 422164; 3BAGS.
Gracie A, 420935; 1ED.

Hampstead LJ, 421805; 2BAGS; (21), Sgt, 2 BAGS, Port Pirie, SA, 20-5-43. A16.
Hartman RR, 422178; 4OTU.
Harvey MM, 421976; 2OTU.
Hedger JH, 418114; 1ED; (23), W/O, 3 Sqn, Italy, 6-9-44. It5.
Hilyard LF, 420194; 3BAGS.
Hunter RJ, 425664; 3WAGS.
Inglis BS, 418230; 1ED.
Keene JC, 412554; 3BAGS.
Kellet NB, 418255; 4OTU.
Langford AL, 418131; 1ED.
Lee J, 421810; 2WAGS.
Liddicoat FJ, 425799; 4OTU.
Markey EJ, 13051; 3WAGS.
Martin KA, 418140; BAGS.
McCosker CH, 422032; 2OTU.
McDonald FG, 418154; 4OTU; (21), F/S, 23 Sqn RAAF, New Guinea, 31-1-44. Lae Missing Memorial.
McKinnon CC, 422082; 1ED.
McMullin HH, 425732; 3ED.
Morgan MD, 425718; 2OTU.
Mossop JW, 418148; 7SFTS.
Nathan RV, 418458; 2OTU.
Newberry ER, 421753; 1ED.
Parkes WG, 420497; 2ED; (20), F/O, 198 Sqn RAF, Brookwood, Surrey, 9-3-44. UK23.
Schmitzer CJ, 421830; 2OTU.
Taylor HT, 421770; 1ED.
Todd AB, 418208; 4OTU.
Waldin BH, 422014; 2Ed.
Walsh HJ, 421479; 2WAGS; (20), F/S, 84 Sqn RAAF, Gulf of Carpentaria, 10-3-44. Sydney Missing Memorial.
Wannan CW, 421948.
Wright EF, 422015.   58 /510

28 Course: Awarded the Flying Badge on 9/3/43:

On 23/11/42 71 LACs Aircrew 11 were posted in from 5, 8, 10 and 11 EFTSs
Wastage – Scrub rate = 22/71 = 31%.

Ainsworth AJ, 422364; 1BAGS.
Alexander JS, 410935; 3BAGS; (23), F/S, 3 BAGS, Sale, Vic, 17-11-43. A7.
Baker GL, 422097; 2OTU.
Barraclough GW, 412865.
Bash FD, 422380.
Blackwell D, 421842; 1BAGS.
Butcher WE, 417154.
Conway D, 426246; 3WAGS.
Cripps CM, 410955; 2OTU.
Crossing GW, 422442; 2OTU.
Denham MJ, 410960; 4OTU.
Edwards D, 417467; CFS.
Ellis FL, 426069; 4OTU.
Emmerick AF, 422469.
Evans PR, 422541; 1BAGS.
Ferguson DA, 422474; CFS.
Fitter WR, 422159; CFS.
Fletcher J, 410967; 1WAGS.
Gill JH, 425144; 1BAGS.
Griffith M, 422503; 2OTU.
Harvey GR, 422516; 3WAGS.
Henry WV, 422272; 3BAGS.
Holliday RW, 422561; CFS.
Hutchinson HW, 422543
Jago K, 422191; 2OTU.
Lees N, 422276.
Lucas FA, 425102; 3WAGS.
Martin SP, 421815; CFS.

Maunsell CR, 435711; 1BAGS.
McGilvrey GC, 422638; 4OTU.
McIntyre JW, 422657.
McKay MJ, 422240; 7SFTS.
Mills FE, 422228; 4OTU.
Mutch R, 422236.
Olson RW, 422672; 1BAGS.
Parton FL, 32589; (27), P/O, 5 Sqn RAAF, Mareeba, Qld, 12-6-43. A20.
Rea MW, 422358.
Reid ID, 422719; 4OTU.
Reynolds WB, 422705; 7SFTS: (22), P/O, 80 Sqn RAAF, Celebes, 8-3-45. NEI1.
Roantree N, 422300; (20), F/S, 76 Sqn RAAF, New Britain, 23-9-43. Rabaul Missing Memorial.
Rothe CJ, 422713; 2WAGS; (21), F/S, 4 OTU, Williamtown, NSW, 30-10-43. A4.
Sherman G, 422701.
Simpson PW, 422308; 1BAGS.
Spargo KE, 418016; (20), P/O, 82 Sqn RAAF, Sydney, NSW, 14-7-43. A17.
Vaughan MT, 30201; 3BAGS; (26), W/O, 2 OTU, Mildura, Vic, 14-2-45. A5.
Wells AJ, 422789; CFS.
Weymouyh AG, 418029; (26), F/O, 82 Sqn RAAF, NEI, 18-10-44. NEI3.
Wright AC, 422789; 7SFTS.
Yates DE, 422331; 2OTU.

29 Course, 5SFTS, 9 April 1943. (R.J. Chivers).

29 Course Group, 5SFTS, 9April 1943. L-R: G.E. Gibson, D.J. Sheahan, I.G. Hunter, R.J. Chivers, L.D. Heath, A.D. Rose, B.A. Armstrong, D.R. Hare. (J. Chivers)

29 Course: Awarded the Flying Badge on 9/4/43:

Adams DB, 418043; 2OTU.
Armstrong BA, 423581; 2OTU; (22), P/O, 85 Sqn RAAF, off coast of WA, 3-10-43. Sydney Missing Memorial.
Baskerville AM, 426281; 3ED.
Bridgett CJ, 426299.
Campbell IR, 418521; 1ED.
Chivers RJ, 422420; 2ED.
Covill CJ, 426429; 3ED; (22), F/S, 5 AFU, Chester, UK, 30-1-44. UK19.
Eddy LG, 422465; 2OTU.
Ferguson EK, 423090; 2ED; (21), F/S, 14 OTU, Oxford, UK, 27-3-44. UK6.
Fleming AJ, 426222; 4ED.
Gibson GE, 423704; 2OTU.
Gray VW, 421802; 2ED.
Hare DR, 423202; 2OTU.
Heath GL, 423114; 2ED; (20), P/O, 166 Sqn RAF, Germany, 25-7-44. G4.
Heath LD, 423305; (21), P/O, 166 Sqn RAF, Baltic Sea, 30-8-44. Runnymede Missing Memorial.
Hindley LA, 421905; 2OTU.
Hunter IG, 423379; SAC.
Jessup AL, 30055; 2BAGS.
Lambert RJ, 419271; 2OTU.
Lewis A, 422590; 2ED; (22), F/O, 635 Sqn RAF, Germany, 31-3-45. G6.
Liggins AW, 423143; 2OTU.
Maskey BW, 426231; 2OTU.
Mason WR, 418446; 1ED.

McCosker GB, 421999; 2ED.
Murphy SI, 423307; 2OTU.
Ninness GN, 423173; 2BAGS; (19), Sgt, 2 BAGS, Port Pirie, SA, 27-8-43. A16.
O'Brien AH, 423253; SAC.
Preston JRR, 421756; 2OTU; (23), F/O, 51 Sqn RAF, Germany, 11-9-44. G2.
Rattle WF, 423256; 2OTU; (29), F/O, 622 Sqn RAF, Holland, 13-6-44. H3.
Richards JJ, 418466; 2OTU; (20), F/S, 21 Sqn RAAF, New Guinea, 5-3-44. Lae Missing Memorial.
Rose AD, 422711; 2OTU.
Sheahan DJ, 426395; 2OTU.
Simmonds JA, 423409; 2WAGS.
Smethurst SW, 418014; 2OTU; (20), Sgt, 78 Sqn RAAF, Camden, NSW, 30-9-43. A18.
Smith CL, 423328; 2OTU.
Stuart JF, 423314; 3BAGS.
Taylor LCA, 425812; 2OTU; (28), F/L, 514 Sqn RAF, Belgium, 28-5-44. B2.
Thomas PR, 426243; 3ED.
Tudberry J, 423357; 2ED.
Turvey RG, 421645; 2ED.
Ward SS, 423430; 2ED.
Williams JL, 418475; 1ED.
Windrim BC, 423965; 2ED.
Wolf BO, 423274; 2OTU; (20), Sgt, 85 Sqn RAAF, Guildford, WA, 22-9-43. A2.
Woods BA, 423375; 2ED.

45/604

30 Course: Awarded the Flying Badge on 30/4/43:
On 20/12/42 74 LACs Aircrew 11 were posted in from 5, 8, 10 and 11 EFTSs.
Wastage – Scrub rate = 23/74 = 31%.

Arnott ARA, 426819; 2OTU; (19), P/O, 2 OTU, Mildura, Vic, 16-7-43. A5.
Bailey FC, 423584; CFS.
Beddoe RH, 418717; 1ED; (21), F/O, 463 Sqn RAAF, Scotland, 31-8-44. UK1.
Bishop NA, 426520; CFS; (28), Sgt, 10 EFTS, Temora, NSW, 14-8-43. A19.
Beeck NK, 427286; SAC.
Cameron JD, 6074; SAC.
Campbell JM, 426532; 1ED; (22), F/S, 457 Sqn RAAF, Darwin, NT, 6-10-44. A12.
Chambers RJ, 426287; 1ED.
Clark AN, 426864; 3ED.
Corbett WE, 426542; 3ED.
Crebbin RC, 423656; 3OTU.
Dale JF, 37917; 2OTU.
Dane FL, 422140; CFS.
Devine EN, 426556; 3ED; (21), P/O, 622 Sqn RAF, Germany, 12-2-44. Runnymede Missing Memorial.
Dodds JR, 427072; 5ED.
Downes CR, 426560; CFS.
Eddison ED, 563; (24), F/L, 30 Sqn RAAF, New Guinea 72-5-53, Lae Missing Memorial.
Fenton RB, 423694; CFS.
Fletcher AD, 427080; 5ED.
Hall MA, 426573; CFS.
Hamilton DB, 423722; 2ED; (21), F/L, 460 Sqn RAAF, Germany, 20-1-44. G4.
Hansen G, 426586; 3ED.
Hardie JB, 424178; 2ED.
Harvey JN, 423998; 2ED.
Hopman R, 35227; 2ED.

Houghton RC, 422542; 2ED.
Jubb RV, 426609; 3ED.
King AC, 422575; CFS.
Lemon KJ, 424300; 1ED.
Martin SB, 418860; 1ED.
McKinley D, 426654; 1ED.
Middleton JH, 423153; 2ED; (21), F/O, 207 Sqn RAF, Germany, 6-10-44. G6.
Middleton WJ, 426366; 3ED.
Noon TW, 426668; 3ED.
O'Bern M, 410369; 1ED.
O'Connell EJ, 423858; 1ED; (20), F/S, 2 OTU, Wentworth, NSW, 25-10-44. A5.
Palmer AH, 426948; 2ED.
Perry WK, 418564; 2ED.
Philip H, 423880; CFS.
Rice RG, 417889; 1ED.
Righetti JI, 418980.
Schadel WJ, 423905.
Sleeman JD, 423912; 2ED.
Smyth DA, 424311; 1ED.
Stewart SW, 418018; 1ED.
Sullivan PS, 412855; 2ED; (21), F/S, 9AFU, North Wales, 8-6-44. UK19.
Thomas RE, 424242; CFS.
Thwaites HW, 426710; CFS.
Tuckey B, 423942,; 2ED.
Warren KM, 417254; 1ED.
Williams GP, 424328; 1ED.
Wilson TD, 426735; 1ED.

51/655

31 Course, 5SFTS, 1 June 1943. L-R: Back Row; 1st T.G Trask, 2nd N.N. Knight, 5th A.H. Dennett: Centre Row; E.N. Robinson, J.R. Rose, A.K. O'Gower, R.W. MacAlpine, 6th D.D. Charles, 10th T.W. Collis, 11th J.W. Ahern: Front Row; 1st D.J. Murray, 2nd W.D. Kentish, 3rd K.E. Goldring, 4th D.J. Wallace, 5th R. Sears, 6th A.D. Marshall, 10th A.E. Watts: Seated; 1st L Hanson, 3rd W.J. Moran, 5th F/O G. McInerney, 10th K.H. Moeser. (K.E. Goldring).

31 Course: Awarded the Flying Badge on 1/6/43:
On 15/2/43 69 LACs Aircrew 11 were posted in from 5, 8 and 10 EFTSs.
Wastage – Scrub rate = 30/69 = 43%.

Ahern JW, 426817.
Andrews WW, 423596.
Charles DD, 426993.
Collis TW, 424150.
Crampton GH, 424983.
Dennett AH, 423669.
Donald KJ, 424389.
Goldring KE, 424906.
Hanson L, 25485.
Heath EW, 429562.
Irwin FR, 424186.
Kentish WD, 423757.
Knight NN, 424420.
MacAlpine RW, 428726.
Marshall AD, 429469.
McKee JJ, 424304.
McLean JD, 428761.
Moeser KH, 424434.
Moran WJ, 423822.
Murray DJ, 424203.
Murray PF, 429616.
Nicholls GC, 424511.

O'Gower AK, 424448.
Oliver GJ, 422876.
Orr RB, 424544.
Perske RL, 425895; (20), Sgt, 4 OTU, Williamtown, NSW, 6-8-43. A4.
Redwood HG, 428804.
Robinson BB, 434026.
Robinson EN, 424464.
Roeder RF, 424465.
Rose JR, 424548.
Sears R, 424565.
Taylor LF, 424514.
Tedd JJ, 428812.
Trask TG, 419921.
Trewenalk, 424337.
Wallace DJ, 429418; (20), P/O, 80 Sqn RAAF, New Guinea, 24-8-44. Lae Missing Memorial.
Watts AE, 424486.
Whitwell DM, 428841; (19), F/S, 3 Communication Unit, Mascot, 28-2-44. A17.

32 Course: Awarded the Flying Badge on 28/6/43:

Abrams CA, 428747; 2ED.
Bromhead SJ, 33011.
Burns WJ, 428754.
Carter JB, 418719.
Clarson AJ, 426251; 3ED.
Clemens MK, 424971; 2ED.
Cousins AY, 424737; (20), F/S, 450 Sqn RAAF, Italy, 5-11-44. It6.
Dengate GC, 424388.
Deramore-Denver IH, 422844; 2ED.
Dever NP, 429527; 3ED.
Downing GB, 424899.
Ellison GR, 424292; 2ED.
Fagg EG, 429542.
Feddersen MJ, 419989; 1ED; (20), F/O, 467 Sqn RAAF, Germany, 11-11-44. G5.
Forge RS, 418263.
Gray-Buchanan PR, 429554; 3ED.
Green G, 422949; 2ED.
Grose K, 424901; (21), F/O, 51 Sqn RAF, Germany, 11-9-44. G7.
Harkiss RC, 429559; 3ED.
Heathcote JR, 419648.
Hocking JW, 429321; 3ED; (21), P/O, 1651 Conversion Unit, RAF, United Kingdom, 28-7-44. UK1.
Hutchins TM, 422956.
Jaensch RA, 417583; 3ED.
Jones JR, 428767; 2ED; (21), F/O, 100 Sqn RAF, Germany, 19-7-44. G2.

Long FM, 418287; 1ED.
Lorimer PD, 424773; 2ED.
Lynch J, 424270; 2ED.
McKay NH, 422972; 2ED.
McKenna KB, 428342.
McKinnon TH, 428760; 2ED.
McPhee AL, 423552.
Mitchell WD, 422968; 2ED; (21), P/O, 455 Sqn RAAF, North Sea, 8-3-45. Runnymede Missing Memorial.
Murphy TW, 428338; 2ED.
Nisbet AH, 422975; 2ED.
Parker IS, 429480.
Paull IG, 428351.
Regan LJA, 424798; (22), F/O, 80 Sqn RAAF, New Britain, 5-4-44. Rabaul Missing Memorial.
Russell TR, 428852.
Sanderson RW, 428797; 2ED.
Simpson GE, 428802; 2ED.
Smith DC, 424860; 2ED.
Smith DG, 428370; 1ED.
Souter MI, 428369.
Stewart CB, 422892; 2ED.
Tubman RV, 428830; 2ED.(20), F/S, 84 OTU, Oxford, UK, 11-4-44. UK6.
Wheatley CM, 425994; 3ED.
Williams RJ, 419684; 1ED.
Withers RG, 418728; 1ED.
Youll JT, 424540; 2ED.

49/743

33 Course Group, 5SFTS, 29 July 1943. L-R: Back Row; 4th J.D. Humphreys, 5th G.J. Stuart: Middle Row; 6th P.A. Peirce, 7th K.F. Robinson, 10th W.L Ives: Sitting; 4th N. Fernley-Stott, 5th P.L.T. Ilbery, 6th A.C.F. Klingner, 7th B. Rawlings, 11th B.R. Crowley. (P. Ilbery).

33 Course: Awarded the Flying Badge on 29/7/43:

Bailey VT, 425821; 3ED.
Bayliss HM, 425823; 3ED.
Cornwell DG, 422431.
Crowley BR, 428756; 2ED.
Dickie JL, 429496; 2OTU.
Dollison JT, 422845.
Ellis JS, 424618; CFS.
Evans TE, 429220; 2ED.
Fernley-Stott N, 429281; 2ED; (20), F/O 463 Sqn RAAF, Germany, 13-2-45. G1.
Frost KA, 422944; CFS.
Gill RD, 417299.
Henderson JR, 422953; 2ED.
Hillman JS, 429565; 3ED.
Horne AR, 429283; CFS.
Hurst DC, 425854; 2OTU.
Ilbery PLT, 422957; 2ED.
Irving DM, 424038.
Ives WL, 434232.
Joel SP, 424765; 2ED.
Klingner ACF, 425945; 3ED; (26), P/O, 260 Sqn RAF, Adriatic Sea, 29-4-45. Malta Missing Memorial.
Lanham NA, 424770; CFS.
Leamon FN, 425861; 3ED; (21), W/O, 332 Sqn RAF, Germany, 25-3-45. Runnymede Missing Memorial.

Maunder EJ, 422967; CFS.
Maxwell LK, 426130; 3ED; (21), F/S, 27 OTU, United Kingdom, 19-6-44. UK6.
McCulloch DW, 425878; 3ED; (21), W/O, 164 Sqn RAF, Germany, 10-4-45. G2.
McKimm RJ, 429262; 2OTU.
Moore RW, 424533; 2ED.
Nicol AH, 426979; 3ED; (20), F/O, 50 Sqn RAF, Germany, 14-1-45. G1.
Parry RW, 434265; 1BAGS; (20), F/S, 80 Sqn RAAF, New Guinea Area, 13-1-45. Ambon Missing Memorial.
Peterswald JS, 424921; 2ED.
Ranger LR, 432011; 2OTU.
Robinson KF, 428861; 2ED.
Rothwell JM, 422886; 2OTU.
Schlink HJ, 423557.
Shanahan PK, 425902; 3ED.
Stephenson DH, 429248; CFS.
Storr AF, 425983; 3ED.
Stuart GJ, 425909.
Swain RE, 422911; 2ED.
Thomson SM, 21582; 2ED.
Utting WT, 426785; CFS.

34 Course, 5SFTS, 25 August 1943. L-R: Back Row; 2nd E.J. Ingram, 4th B. Heffer, J.E. Laffan, R.L. Priestly, A. Smith, K.G. Pollard, R.T. Brunskill: Fourth Row; 1st K.W. Sullivan, last R.E. O'Donnell: Third Row; 3rd A. Clark, 5th J.R. Brauze: Second Row; 1st B.J. Thewlis, 6th H.H. Beveridge, 10th G.H. Jones, 11th W.R. Wileman, 13th G.O. Webb: Front Row; none. (K.G. Pollard).

---

34 Course: Awarded the Flying Badge on 25/8/43:

Beech C, 426450; 2OTU.
Beveridge HH, 422923; CFS.
Black RL, 429276; 1BAGS.
Bownas AA, 422925; 1BAGS.
Brauze JR, 422834; CFS.
Brown LB, 432127; CFS.
Brunskill RT, 432106; 2ED.
Casey TK, 432119; CFS; (21), W/O, 75 Sqn RAAF, New Guinea, 22-3-45. NEI1.
Clark A, 432122; 2WAGS.
Clark FJ, 424623; 1BAGS.
Crone JH, 419521; (21), F/O, 15 Sqn RAF, United Kingdom, 17-1-45. UK1.
Dalton GW, 430015; 1WAGS.
Eagle JA, 418652; 3BAGS.
Edmonds CJ, 419802; 2OTU; (21), F/S, 84 Sqn RAAF, NT Area, 23-3-44. Sydney Missing Memorial.
Fulton AMcR, 419122; 1WAGS.
Gibson RG, 419089; 2OTU.
Gorman JV, 423457; CFS.
Hall DL, 423162.
Haslope LC, 428073; 1WAGS.
Heffer B, 422952; 2ED.
Hum JD, 432187; CFS.
Ingram EJ, 424587; 2WAGS.
Jolly DA, 432198; 2ED.
Jones GH, 432316.
Laffan JE, 432212; 1BAGS.

Linklater LW, 428723; 2ED; (20), P/O, 1667 Conversion Unit, United Kingdom, 30-10-44, UK2.
McFadden JD, 422971; 1BAGS.
McLaughlin PJ, 425894; CFS.
Meares CJ, 429287; CFS.
Menzies LG, 425865; 3ED.
Middleton JL, 418291; 2OTU.
Murray DR, 421747.
Nielsen RC, 429263; 2ED.
Norton LJ, 432248.
O'Donnell RE, 422875; 2OTU.
Pitt AF, 432259; CFS; (22), W/O, 5 OTU, off Williamtown, 21-9-45. Sydney Missing Memorial.
Pollard KG, 422883; 2ED.
Pontifex RB, 422981; 3BAGS; (20), F/S, 75 Sqn RAAF, Celebes, 5-1-45. NEI1.
Poulton M, 428565.
Priestly RL, 424090.
Scott WH, 426982; 3ED.
Shelton HJ, 408470; 2OTU.
Smith A, 423519; 3BAGS.
Sullivan KW, 422988; 1BAGS.
Thewlis BJ, 430069; CFS.
Thompson RB, 432380; 1BAGS.
Webb EA, 428883; CFS.
Webb GO, 424688; CFS.
Wileman WR, 424603.

34/35 Course Group, 5 SFTS. L-R: Back Row; Wicks, R.B. Thompson, L.J. Norton, D.A. Jolly, E.J. Ingram, G.O. Webb, P.J. McLaughlin, R.L. Priestley, K.B. Sly, B. Riley and W.E. Wearne: Third Row; B.J. Thewlis, H.J. Shelton, H.N. Trowbridge, J.D. McFadden, Meredith, D.R. Murray, J.E. Laffan, R.E. O'Donnell and K.W. Sullivan: Second Row: D.J. Murray, W.D. Kentish, K.E. Goldring, D.J. Wallace, R. Sears, 10th A.E. Watts: Front Row; Veitch, R.B, Pontifex, A.S. Whitmarsh, W.R. Wileman, A. Smith, C.J. Meares, Mann, J.M. Inkster, A.F. Pitt, E.A. Webb and R.N. Stokes. (K.B. Sly).

35 Course, 5SFTS, 23 September 1943. L-R: Middle Row; 3rd K.B. Sly; Front Row; 5th P.A. Peirce, 11th N.A. Emery (K.B. Sly).

35 Course: Awarded the Flying Badge on 23/9/43:

Andrews HR, 429060.

Bennett KW, 432472.

Breusch KL, 426477.

Buckland J, 430104.

Bullock PW, 434617.

Caddy PO, 432340: (20), F/S, 19 OTU, UK Coast, 28-8-44. Runnymede Missing Memorial.

Crawford KP, 424739.

Dibden EJ, 432490.

Elliott JA, 432140.

Emery NA, 432141.

Fleming JG, 429180.

Goold DC, 428598.

Hickson RJ, 428044.

Holmes JH, 429054; (20), F/L, 460 Sqn RAAF, Germany, 2-3-45. B1.

Inkster JM, 432191; (22), F/O, 467 Sqn RAAF, Germany, 2-2-45. G4.

Kirk EG, 426808.

Layzell FW, 432214.

Newbiggen R, 414673.

Nicholls AG, 419839.

Peirce PA, 432016.

Reed JV, 419833; (20), F/O, 5 SFTS, Uranquinty, NSW, 15-6-45. A1.

Roberts JL, 432618.

Shelton AP, 428602; (21), F/O, 466 Sqn RAAF, United Kingdom, 4-3-45. UK2.

Sly KB, 422890.

Spencer GG, 432345.

Steele AG, 426985.

Stokes RN, 430066.

Symons PW, 432616.

Thornton EH, 430271.

Trowbridge HN, 21587.

Wearne WE, 428838.

Webb WN, 430077.

White CO, 432321.

Whitmarsh AS, 422995.

Woodward RH, 429185.

Wright AG, 432328 .

36 Course, 5SFTS, 20 October 1943. L-R: Back Row; 5th C. Rasmussen, 7th Bell: Third Row; D.G. Harden, E.P. Simpson, S.B. Robertson, N.J. Mackay, -, D. Knudson, S.K. Biggs, 12th Searle: Second Row; C.C. Taplin, 5th R.N. Roberts, 8th B.R.McK. Emmerson: Front Row; F.J. Squire, 7th S/L Sturgon. (S.B. Robertson).

36 Course: Awarded the Flying Badge on 20/10/43:

Armstrong NB, 432468.
Barsby EA, 434121; (20), F/S, 575 Sqn RAAF, United Kingdom, 6-2-45. UK3.
Biggs SK, 432740.
Borrett DR, 427371.
Boyd GD, 432444.
Boyd RJMcK, 429170.
Bycroft CM, 434446.
Cameron RE, 430248.
Cohen JA, 424974.
Cullen AJ, 434512.
Davis ANH, 428956.
Edmonds JD, 424653.
Emmerson BRMcK, 432775.
Fiveash RA, 432145.
Gogerly B, 434681.
Haddon SO, 9407.
Hamlyn JMcP, 426959.
Hannan JT, 432791.
Harden DG, 432792.
Horsman WC, 432804.
Howard WN, 428710.
Hurworth GE, 434135.
Jacob EH, 432578.

Kelleway IL, 432208.
Knudsen D, 432957.
Lane R, 432523.
Laurie JT, 434140.
Mackay NJ, 432527.
Marchant ES, 434510.
McGilvray JRN, 432539.
Nielson SW, 2678; (30), P/O, 550 Sqn RAF, Germany, 7-3-45. G1.
Oswald BA, 434650.
Parker KE, 432563.
Patrick NG, 434651.
Powell LG, 434653.
Raftery BA, 432264; (23), P/O, 5 SFTS, Wagga, NSW, 27-9-44. A1.
Rasmussen C, 33273.
Roberts RN, 432274.
Robertson SB, 432976.
Robinson RB, 432572.
Simpson EP, 432886.
Smith NL, 426984.
Squire FJ, 432587.
Taplin CC, 27709.

44/913

37 Course, 5SFTS, 18 November 1943. L-R: Back Row; 6th A.L. Shaw, 7th J. McDonald, 8th J.D. Humphreys: 3rd Row; 2nd P.N. Joubert, H.S. Macneil, 5th J.R. Carroll, B.A. Nall: 2nd Row; E.N. Ball, 7th A.C. Britton: In front; 9th H.F. Luton. (J. McDonald).

---

37 Course: Awarded the Flying Badge on 18/11/43:

Abbott FC, 24260; SAC.
Adams JE, 434300; 1ED.
Andrews SC, 429139; 4OTU.
Ball EN, 6888; SAC.
Bartlett BR, 434732; 2ED.
Berthelson ML, 426451; 4OTU; (20), Sgt, 25 Sqn RAAF, Pearce, WA, 28-3-44. A2.
Britton AC, 432746; 2OTU.
Brown RPS, 434615; 2OTU; (20), F/S, 78 Sqn RAAF, New Guinea Area, 10-8-44. Lae Missing Memorial.
Carroll JR, 432751; 2ED.
Cobban AM, 428869; 3WAGS.
Crook BK, 436185; 3WAGS.
Davidson SG, 432676; 4OTU.
Day WE, 34778; 2ED.
Dowling AJ, 429535; 3BAGS.
Ferrier MC, 22392; SAC.
Ferris NS, 430584; 2ED.
Fleming EW, 432634; 2OTU: (20), Sgt, 5 SFTS, Mangoplah, NSW, 24-3-44. A1.
Gordon DP, 432946; 2ED.
Hepburn AG, 432386; 2OTU.
Holland JW, 432197; 3BAGS.
Hopper HA, 424708; 2ED.
Humphreys JD, 422955; SAC.
Joubert PN, 432988; 2OTU.

Lance GC, 433164; 2ED.
Lundie JP, 432831; 2OTU.
Luton HF, 429120; 2OTU.
Macneil HS, 432834; 2OTU.
Martin RB, 430284 ; 4OTU.
McDonald J, 432997; 3BAGS.
Myers DJ, 19505; 4OTU.
Nall BA, 432853; 2ED.
O'Neill JP, 432558; 3BAGS.
O'Neill KL, 432591; 3WAGS.
O'Reilly EN, 432559; 2OTU; (21), P/O, 77 Sqn RAAF, Admiralty Is, 23-3-44. NG1.
Palme BA, 432562; 2OTU; (20), F/S, 77 Sqn RAAF, New Guinea Area, 23-11-44. NG2.
Pitham HA, 429040; 2ED.
Rowley DH, 434564; 2ED.
Shaw AL, 429133; 3BAGS.
Stevenson EMacL, 432589; 2OTU; (20), F/S, 452 Sqn RAAF, NEI, 14-4-45. NEI1.
Svenson NO, 432631; 3BAGS.
Swinbourne GC, 432593; 2ED; (20), F/S, 73 Sqn RAF, Egypt, 4-11-44. E1.
Taylor CA, 433007; 2ED.
Telfer BW, 432035; SAC.
Vickers BH, 432647; 2OTU.
Warnken RK, 432414; 2ED.

38 Course: Awarded the Flying Badge on 16/12/43:

Angus CP, 429691; EMB; (23), F/S, 2 AFU, Scotland, 6-12-44. UK4.
Barclay JJ, 434769; EMB.
Begg KR, 432985.
Brown FA, 432760; EMB.
Browne SU, 434824; EMB.
Coghlan WH, 436122; EMB,
Conyers JH, 436123; EMB.
Coutts MJM, 434678.
Cox RM, 432487; EMB.
Cox SJ, 433154; 1AD.
Daniel WH, 9344; EMB; (24), F/S, 567 Sqn RAF, United Kingdom, 23-11-44. UK5.
Day RG, 435115; 3ED.
Dowker HAC, 430255; EMB.
Doyle KN, 423450; EMB; (21), W/O, 7 SFTS, United Kingdom, 8-6-45. UK6.
Egert ARM, 434626; 3ED.
Fitzsimons JA, 436191; EMB.
Gibb GK, 430516; EMB; (20), F/S, 215 Sqn RAF, India, 7-6-45. I1.
Harris-Walker GA, 423463; EMB.
Hoey JR, 434124; 3ED.
Jarden SM, 432809; 2ED.
Jones RD, 433113; 2ED.
Lester PJ, 40373; EMB; (26), P/O, 82 Sqn RAAF, Japan, 19-3-47. J1.

Little J, 432959; EMB.
Maher JP, 433323; EMB.
Matis P, 429121; EMB.
Matyear T, 425452; 3ED.
McHenry PW, 430265; EMB.
McMahon MA, 430266; 1ED.
Oswin DMcP, 432860; (19), F/S, 4 Communication Unit, Brisbane, Qld, 22-7-44. A3.
Pardey AW, 432861; EMB.
Paul FGT, 8728; EMB.
Perriman RL, 433133; 2ED.
Phelan WJ, 433173; EMB.
Polain JG, 433392; 2ED.
Richards GL, 436276; EMB.
Robinson CJ, 429043; EMB.
Rowe L, 434520.
Saal VL, 434654.
Savage DI, 435180; 3ED; (19), F/S, 29 OTU, United Kingdom, 5-1-45. UK6.
Sheldrick KEA, 434657; EMB.
Stewart GH, 436278; 5ED.
Walton AGD, 433241; EMB.
Watkins WE, 436218; EMB.
Williams V, 436299; EMB.
Wyga PA, 428945; EMB.
Yeo RJ, 432331.
   46(1005)
EMB = Granted pre-embarkation leave 17-22-12-43

39 Course: Awarded the Flying Badge on 16/ 1/44:

Addison RR, 433558; EMB.
Armitage FW, 433385; 1WAGS.
Bellamy GJ, 432737; 2OTU.
Brims DJ, 434566; EMB.
Brown RJ, 432745.
Chilcott AE, 429172.
Coates VT, 434715; EMB.
Curtis JR, 432762; EMB.
Cusack WH, 432664; EMB.
Davis RE, 15145; 2OTU.
Delaney JW, 432717; 1WAGS.
Ellis KG, 436126; 1WAGS.
Evans WR, 433204.
Gerner CH, 433206; EMB.
Given AS, 434914; EMB.
Goldsworthy CH, 22846.
Griffiths GW, 433641; EMB.
Hammond GF, 434516; 4OTU.
Hefferman LJ, 432797; EMB.
Hennes JR, 433104; EMB.
Heydon IM, 433315; EMB.
Hipe KH, 433160; EMB.
Hunter WK, 434104; EMB; (21), F/S, RAF Station Fayid, 17-3-45. E1.
Johnston DA, 12064.
King JB, 424656.
King LN, 434344; 1WAGS; (21), F/S, 80 Sqn RAAF, NEI, 23-3-45. NEI2.
Knock JH, 432821; 1WAGS.
Lalor RK, 432822; EMB.
Loomes AT, 432829; EMB.
Macdonald IG, 436385; EMB.
Maddock JA, 32206.
Marqis GF, 433121; EMB.

Martin SM, 433120 ; EMB.
McDonald LP, 434529; EMB.
McKenzie AL, 434993; EMB.
McPhee VB, 434161; 2ED.
Messervy PC, 62733; EMB.
Morrison JM, 433388.
Nicholson PJ, 433617.
Normoyle JR, 434997; EMB.
O'Connel JM, 433401.
O'Connor PJ, 423518; 2ED.
Pettet AH, 432867; 2OTU.
Plastow JP, 6734; 4OTU; (22), P/O, 4 OTU, Nelson's Bay, NSW, 7-4-44. A4.
Ross AR, 433226; 2OTU; (19), Sgt, 2 OTU, Mildura, Vic, 26-3-44. A5.
Sargeant FC, 433397; EMB.
Tanner DJ, 435218; EMB.
Thornley NL, 34772; 2OTU; (22), F/S, 80 Sqn RAAF, Halmaheras, 14-1-45. Ambon Missing Memorial.
Tothill CC, 429003; 1WAGS; (26), F/S, 80 Sqn RAAF, NEI, 22-12-44. NEI2.
Walker DJ, 432917; 4OTU.
Wall CB, 434494; EMB.
Wedd CW, 35027; EMB; 1654 Conversion Unit, RAF, UK Coast, 12-4-45. Runnymede Missing Memorial.
White AA, 432912; EMB; (20), F/S, HQ RAF ME, Egypt, 13-1-45. E1.
White AR, 413102; EMB.
Wild B, 432925; EMB.

55/1060

EMB = Granted 6 days pre-embarkation leave 18-1-44 to 23-1-44

40 Course, 5SFTS, 13 February 1944. L-R: Back Row; A. Woollam, R.R. Chapman, L.E. Howell, C.R. Hall, K. Wildman, D.C. Mackenzie, J.M. McCosker, V. Cranmer, R.E. Bussell, G.R. Morris, A.R. Nancarrow, S.G. Blanton, E.H. Lund, K.P.W. Moore, C.R. Henderson, A.J. O'Brien, W.A. Wales: Third Row; R.G. Bettison, H.A. Coulter, R.L. Ferguson, K.W. Strike, G.G. Walker, M.D. Brown, S.C. Morley, K.G. Jeffrey, R.J.M. Byrne, W.J. Dodds, L.R. Crossingham, M.A. Beanland: Second Row; J. Ives, W.H. Pill, R.F. Gordon, B.T. Lynn, H.J. Nicholas, J. Doran, W.A. Burrell, A.J. Atkinson, G.C. Wray, G.W. Curtis, E.G. Carne, T.J. O'Neill, A.H. Nelson, H.N. Basham: Front row; L.L. Peck, B.W. Atkinson, G.J. Hunter, G.W. Eaton, W.G. Liddle, S.G. Hay, L.A. Watson, K.P. Hurley, F.J. Boundy, B.G. Ball, L.B. Irving, M.R. Hardwick, H.McR. Hirst, G.J. Ellis. (V. Cranmer)

40 Course: Awarded the Flying Badge on 13/2/44:

Atkinson AJ, 435409; EMB.
Atkinson BW, 433559; CFS.
Ball BG, 435323; EMB.
Basham HN, 434699; EMB.
Beanland MA, 435459; EMB.
Bettison RG, 433561; 2ED.
Blanton SG, 432743; EMB.
Boundy FJ, 40403; EMB.
Brown MD, 432747; EMB.
Burrell WA, 435324; EMB.
Bussell RE, 433570.
Byrne RJM, 435331; EMB.
Carne EG, 435162; EMB.
Chapman RR, 434321; EMB.
Coulter HA, 433579; EMB.
Cranmer V, 433015; EMB.
Crossingham LR, 433803; EMB.
Curtis GW, 435336; EMB.
Dodds WJ, 433373; EMB.
Doran J, 33369, ; EMB.
Eaton GW, 435015; EMB.
Ellis GJ, 432372; CFS.
Ferguson RL, 433726; EMB.
Gordon RF, 35824; EMB.
Hall CR, 433841; EMB.
Hardwick MR, 433383; EMB.
Hay SG, 434171; EMB.
Henderson CR, 433594; EMB.
Hirst HMcR, 3023; EMB.
Howell LE, 36431; EMB.
Hunter GJ, 433598; EMB.
Hurley KP, 433467; EMB.

Irving LB, 430821; EMB.
Ives J, 435312; EMB.
Jeffery KG, 433384; EMB.
Liddle WG, 428646; EMB.
Lund EH, 433215; EMB.
Lynn BT, 435343 ; EMB.
Mackenzie DC, 433603.
McCosker JM, 433472; EMB.
Moore KPW, 433450; EMB.
Morley SC, 434990; EMB.
Morris GR, 428646; EMB.
Nancarrow AR, 432854; CFS.
Nelson AH, 25183; EMB.
Nicholas HJ, 430918.
O'Brien AJ, 435373; 2ED.
O'Neill TJ, 433618; EMB.
Peck LL, 430849; 2ED.
Pill WH, 265790; EMB.
Spencer AF, 432078.
Stewart IM, 433829; EMB.
Strike KW, 432716; EMB.
Wales WA, 35736; EMB.
Walker GG, 433701: EMB.
Watson LA, 433145; EMB.
Whiting NF, 434758; EMB; (20), F/S, 22 EFTS, United Kingdom, 27-11-44. UK1.
Wildman K, 433365; EMB.
Woollam A, 432024; EMB.
Wray GC, 430296 ; EMB.

60/1120

EMB = Granted pre-embarkation leave 14-2-44 to 19-2-44

41 Course: Awarded the Flying Badge on 9/4/44:

Beasley NH, 433636; 2ED.
Bolton JO, 33060; 2ED.
Cameron I, 428911; 2ED.
Cherry ML, 430914; 3WAGS.
Christian JH, 433800; 2ED.
Dinnison JL, 27301; 3WAGS.
Foster B, 435378; 3WAGS.
Granger RJ, 434950; 3WAGS; (23), F/O, 5 Sqn RAAF, Mareeba, Qld, 5-11-44. A6.
Griffen, 435201; 1ED.
Hainsworth HL, 433723; 2ED.
Hewitt NE, 430915; 1ED.
Holst RG, 434750; 1ED.
Howarth BW, 433550; 2ED.
Howell KF, 433814; 2ED.
Keck JH, 419528; 2ED.
Kett JF, 121338; 1ED.
Krasenstein H, 433600; 5ED.
Larner RA, 428168; 1ED.
Loats HJ, 430964; 1ED.
Luchich JD, 435293; 2ED.
Marshall JT, 428153 ; 1ED.
McFadyen JR, 430766; 1ED.
McKenna GW, 40113; 1ED.
McLean RCW, 433336; 2ED.
McVey G, 435117; 3WAGS.

Meehan TR, 435017; 3WAGS.
Menzies C, 36730; 2ED.
Nesbitt JM, 433616; 2ED.
Nicholls BFS, 432856; 2ED.
O'Connell RJ, 12904; 2ED.
Rabig MG, 8953; 2ED.
Ricketts GAP, 435191; 2ED.
Robinson JS, 430767; 1ED; (21), F/S, 254 Sqn RAF, United Kingdom, 19-1-45. UK1.
Ross GA, 433418; 2ED.
Seale DA, 432273;2ED.
Skinner RJ, 430883; 1ED.
Smith RJ, 428169; 3WAGS.
Smith RT, 435031; 1ED.
Sole AB, 433426; 2ED.
Stanbury BT, 430710; 1ED.
Stevenson JA, 433628; 2ED.
Stuart B, 433429; 2ED.
Taylor JR, 433630; 2ED.
Tilbrook MJ, 5747; 2ED.
Wearne F, 432464; 2ED.
Wharton JCF, 428941; 2ED.
Wilks JC, 205831.
Wilkens DR, 430567; 2ED.
Witford JL, 26931; 3WAGS.

49/1169

42 Course: Awarded the Flying Badge on 7/5/44:
On 21/11/43 51 LACs Aircrew 11 were posted in from 5, 8 and 10 EFTSs.
Wastage – Scrub rate = 9/51 = 18%.

Baker LEI, 433765; 1WAGS.
Barker RL, 23158; 3WAGS.
Barnes FM, 431083; 2OTU.
Beard AB, 433309; 2PD.
Bell HA, 430321; AGS.
Brearley M, 439349; 2OTU.
Brown GT, 428904; AGS.
Brown WH, 6787; 1WAGS.
Buchan EJ, 433434; AGS.
Coghill AD, 433280; AGS.
Cooney K, 433529; 2PD.
Cox RA, 422435; 3WAGS.
Cutler SH, 435566; 3WAGS.
Fahey MJ, 430903; AGS; (21), Sgt, AGS, Seaspray, Vic, 17-8-44. A7.
Furlong RM, 435805; AGS.
Harris RW, 430829; 1AOS.
Heagney JB, 439344; 1WAGS.
Hurst CE, 430775; 2OTU.
Jones FO, 68446; 2OTU.
Kemm RM, 433916; 3WAGS.
Lee RD, 431077; 1PD.
MacIver MIL, 435243; 3WAGS; (20), F/O, 8 OTU, Parkes, NSW, 6-6-45. A8.

Manie RJ, 431070; 1WAGS.
McKean AM, 435575; 2PD.
McLean RK, 15883; 2OTU.
Melchert CJ, 435511; 3WAGS.
Moore JC, 439373; 2PD.
Murphy CD, 430727; 1AOS.
Moss JR, 431325; 1WAGS.
Mulray KD, 436207; 2OTU.
Munsie RJ, 433935; 1WAGS.
Perriman RJ, 433951; 2PD.
Perry HG, 64639; 2PD.
Rees FF, 433859; 2OTU; (21), Sgt, 2 OTU, Mildura, Vic, 19-6-44. A5.
Reilly WJ, 435445; 2OTU.
Rowe WJ, 48575; 3WAGS.
Sharp WJ, 431072; 3WAGS.
Tate GC, 52035; 2OTU.
Uniacke CJ, 431073; 2OTU.
Watmuff BI, 437604; 3WAGS.
Wheatley CG, 433968; 2PD.
Wilson IA, 435189; 1WAGS.

42/1211

Course 43: Awarded the Flying Badge on 4/6/44:

Aboud S, 433834; 2PD.
Adams DC, 5510; 2AOBS.
Ash ER, 433883; 1PD.
Beard GK, 403852; 2AOBS.
Botterill WJ, 15137; 2PD.
Boyle FW, 439448; 1PD.
Brown DM, 433698; 2OTU.
Brown FR, 12802; 2OTU.
Chambers CS, 439350; 2PD.
Crawford CG, 433897; 2PD.
Crooks DG, 439292; 2OTU.
Ellerston-Jones EK, 433293; AGS.
Farqharson JA, 431275; 2OTU.
Forbes DS, 439694; 2OTU.
Garroway WM, 439356; 1PD.
Graham M, 433812; 2PD.
Grimm NL, 433905; 2PD.
Gunther FA, 435753; AGS.
Harding KR, 439362; 1PD.
Healey W, 439260; 2OTU.
Johns MW, 433914; 1PD.
Jones DH, 435318; 1PD.
Kalinowski JJ, 439695; 2OTU.
Kidney WC, 433003; 2PD; Sgt, 4 S of Tech Training, United Kingdom, 24- 6-45. UK7.

Lloyd DG, 433787; 2OTU.
Lucas HA, 18430; 2AOBS.
Lyon TH, 435562; 1PD.
Marsland EH, 78623; 2PD.
Mason EL, 14336; 2AOBS.
Miskell EW, 439338; 2PD.
Macgibbon JA, 439487; 2PD.
McCormack FR, 42266; AGS.
McNabb F, 433940; 2OTU.
Munro TW, 435725; 2OTU.
Newton MJ, 59500; 1PD.
Neil OK, 439660; 2PD.
Payten TW, 439666; 2PD.
Platt L, 439491; 2PD.
Ray RW, 428881; 2PD.
Rivers WB, 433063; 2PD.
Rogers K, 433956; 2PD.
Salmon JA, 431114; 1PD.
Smyth SD, 435491; 2PD.
Swan HG, 15417; 2PD.
Thomas W, 431340; 2OTU.
Thornton G, 431341; AGS.
Vautin CD, 439382; 2PD.
Walsh DE, 43913; 2PD.
Wilson BC, 433959, 2PD.

49/1260

Course 44: Awarded the Flying Badge on 1/7/44:
On 14/2/44 76 LACs Aircrew 11 were posted in from 1, 5, 7, 8, and 10 EFTSs.
Wastage – Scrub rate = 38/76 = 50%.
Posted to 8OTU to undergo No. 34 Fighter O/T Course; High Altitude Course and then 8OTU.

Allan MA, 439736; 2PD.
Badgery P, 439689; 8OTU.
Baldie DW, 439731; HAC.
Bellew JT, 439739; 2PD
Brown DW, 75770; 8OTU.
Brown LE, 435439; HAC; (24), Sgt, 77Sqn, Dutch New Guinea, 6-12-44. Lae Missing Memorial.
Byrnes JW, 63856; 2PD.
Clarke AT, 423663; 2PD.
Clifford KMcR, 435628; HAC.
Dray WJ, 433780; HAC.
Eddy LL, 36616; 8OTU.
Edwards EF, 439708; HAC.
Edwards WN, 65053; 2PD.
Gadsby T, 65277; 2PD.
Goldston JR, 431222; HAC.
Goodsell KG, 439372; 2PD.
Gray KT, 439651; 2PD.
Gurney BF, 439285; 8OTU.
Hawdon CM, 439761; HAC.

Helsham DH, 439418; HAC.
Kearney KH, 439836; HAC; (24), F/O, 84Sqn, Ross River, Qld, 6- 4-45. A9.
Keavney JT, 439655; 2PD.
Macaway JD, 75459; HAC.
McKenzie WJ, 120020; 2PD.
Nelson KJ, 430665; 2PD.
Phillips FV, 435553; HAC.
Ralph KA, 439713; 2PD.
Rudder RR, 73123; 2PD.
Scott JC, 439728; HAC.
Skelton WD, 424686; HAC.
Smith FN, 441260; 8OTU.
Smith JW, 23913; 8OTU.
Soutar AF, 433364; 2PD.
Stewardson JF, 15119; 2PD.
Stewart R, 439679; HAC.
Walker RE, 14479; HAC.
Waters LV, 78144; HAC.
Weger JA, 7141; HAC.

38/1298

Course 45: Awarded the Flying Badge on 26/8/44:
Postings on High Altitude Courses were to 1, 2, 3 and 5
ITSs to undergo the respective High Altitude Courses and further to Aircrew School;

Allan JP, 439859; 2A19.
Blaxell KJ, 439862; 2A19.
Breen JR, 439846; 2A19.
Brewster RT, 120395; 2A18.
Bumpstead L, 18953; 1A28.
Collins AR, 439746; 2A18; (19), Sgt, 8OTU Narromine, 20- 9-44. A10.
Cumming SG, 433658; 2A19.
Dalrymple JH, 481531; 1A28.
Davies DL, 431532; 1A28.
Flannery JF, 53078; 2A19.
Fox RF, 431225; 1A28.
Fraser J, 439754; 2A19.
Fry DL, 431409; 1A28.
Gosden BN, 43114; 5A4.
Guthrie RD, 439513; 2A19.

Haseler WH, 435699; 3A7.
Jones RT, 439769; 2A19.
Jorgensen MN, 439805; 3A7.
Matthews AW, 439897; 2A19.
Middlemiss W, 436633; 1A28.
McKimm WR, 431327; 2A18.
Mackinnon AW, 439371; 2A19.
Potter WJ, 433953; 2A19.
Ryan DR, 431304; 1A28.
Simmonds EM, 439791; 2A18.
Swifte EF, 431519; 1A28.
Thornley CH, 439672; 2A19.
Waddell AJ, 439924; 2A18.
Wakley RC, 439505; 2A19.
Wiesener BW, 439928; 2A19.

30/1328

Course 46: Awarded the Flying Badge on 21/10/44:
On 8/4/44 53 LACs Aircrew 11 were posted in from 5, 8 and 10 EFTSs.
Wastage – Scrub rate = 20/53 = 38%.

Baldwin H, 72213.
Barnett RW, 440049.
Belyea HD, 430921.
Bennett JR, 440051.
Bird RR, 440053.
Bushell GL, 440036.
Campbell AM, 431552.
Clancy DJ, 440057.
Craddock FW, 64998.
Ehsman RN, 440118.
Fairfax JW, 440066.
Frizell HL, 439755; (20), F/S, 2OTU Mildura, 25- 7-45. A5.
Gillies R, 439885.
Guy RV, 435831.
Hartridge GH, 440072.
Madill RM, 35445.
Milledge RW, 438258; (20), F/S, 2OTU Mildura, 13-9-45. A5.

Morrow J, 440119.
Roberts J, 42951.
Sands DF, 440014.
Shuter JC, 438270.
Snell SR, 36701.
Thomson RG, 435835.
Trethewey SG, 440107.
Trimble JW, 63683.
Velnagel J, 435823.
Walpole RW, 435384.
Watkins WE, 431541.
Watts LG, 439927.
Webb JH, 439955.
Willcocks R, 440112.
Williams RW, 440102.
Wrench CE, 123924.

33/1361

Course 47: Awarded the Flying Badge on 18/11/44:

Baker DR, 15121.
Banks AN, 431948.
Barnett RW, 443295.
Brown GW, 425827.
Bryan JW, 443546.
Campbell FA, 435826.
Colclough JC, 443300.
Cuthbert RH, 438415.
Cuncliffe JH, 440141.
Drosten JW, 205907.
Evans RVJW, 69582.
Field MR, 440125.
Flanagan KStC, 435935.
Freeman RG, 435812.
Goodall AJ, 438620.
Hardman MC, 432929.
Harrison KV, 438391.
Hepburn LM, 23873.
Howard VS, 130007.
Hearne BG, 438392.
Ingleden GT, 442574.
Jones RA, 68733.
Kaye LP, 62418; (21), F/S, 2OTU Mildura, 25- 4-45. A5.

Kerr SA, 443410.
Lloyd MJ, 433663.
Loneragon BB, 443412.
Lynch EJ, 35636.
Mullins FA, 66780.
Mackey G, 440079.
Midgley EHC, 65008.
McArthur HA, 435922.
Oliver AG, 443453.
Peter FC, 443517.
Poll C R, 61152.
Poole TEE, 435879.
Preston JB, 64642.
Rosen L, 443472.
Ruck JN, 49527.
Schurr L, 21076.
Steele JMcD, 11937.
Thorn GB, 431981.
Whitty AL, 443291.

42/1403

48 Course, 5SFTS, 16 December 1944. L-R: Back Row; K.J. Hall, K.C. Fisher, D.P. Lapidge, R.D. Reuter, R.B. Butters, N.J. Wilson, R.J. Davies, M.C. Morrison, W.J. Pryor, L.J. Skinner, D.W. Evans: Middle Row; G. Forbes, R.J. Zahnleiter, S.E. Lang, A.J. Saunders, R.S. Young, P.D. Cogan, J.C. Read, K.A. Hollands, F.M. Bower, P.J. Tresize, D.P. Kenny: In front; N.D. Fulton, L.E. Montgomery, W.M. Williams, M.H. Payne, E.L. Wills, G/C Curnow, W/C Honey, W.E. Foster, W.E. Anderson, J. Fullerton-Smith, H.G. Bryans, R.S. Hampshire. (R.J. Davies).

Course 48: Awarded the Flying Badge on 16/12/44:[3]

On 14/2/44 46 LACs Aircrew 11 were posted in from 1, 5, 8, and 10 EFTSs.
Wastage – Scrub rate = 14/46 = 30%.

Anderson WE, 72167.
Bower FM, 35613.
Bryant HG, 443604.
Butters RB, 443388.
Cogan PD, 443393.
Davies RJ, 443666.
Evans DW, 443530.
Fisher KC, 431868.
Foster WE, 443813; (28), P/O, 8OTU Parkes, 29- 5-45. A8.
Fullerton-Smith J, 443669.
Fulton ND, 70798.
Hall KJ, 435971.
Hampshire RS, 443817.
Hollands KA, 4358732.
Kenny DP, 442551.
Lane RR, 435961.
Lang SE, 435973.

Lapidge DP, 440371.
Montgomery LE, 443787.
Morison MC, 443819.
Payne MH, 10545.
Pryor WJ, 443689.
Reuter RD, 442661.
Read JC, 443570.
Saunders AJ, 443620; (21), Sgt, 2OTU Mildura, 30-3-45. A5.
Skinner LJ, 438794.
Trezise PJ, 421139.
Williams WM, 438798.
Wills EL, 75492.
Wilson NJ, 443811.
Young RS, 443716; (24), Sgt, 2OTU Mildura, 13- 2-45. A5.
Zahnleiter RJ, 440312.

32/1435

Course 50: Awarded the Flying Badge on 13- 1-45:[3]

Ashton CO, 8574.
Baird T, 119431.
Barkell VG, 443752.
Berry NB, 443652.
Brazel KC, 443656.
Christopherson L, 442673.
Crowe T, 443737.
Dunn RJ, 14783.
Forbes G, 438775.
Graham KL, 79237.
Hankinson A, 443672.
Hartman AC, 438704.
Howard PF, 442721.
Kirkby DR, 443705.
Johnston HF, 435986.
Law GM, 438552.
Littlewood EJ, 49069.
Lockwood TW, 13489.
Johnson AW, 443483.
Martin PR, 442607.
Martin RH, 443785.
Munro EG, 443680.

Macpherson JD, 442688.
McCrohan TE, 54717.
McFarlane JW, 442646.
McNaughton L, 443790.
Nelson GE, 443791.
Patterson WB, 439000.
Prescott RC, 47206.
Robertson WS, 442730.
Smith AO, 443828.
Stickley W, 443736.
Walsh LJ, 443732.
Ward R, 35330.
Way HJ, 442663.
Wensor RE, 438797.
Westman AE, 126337.
Wilde GS, 438566.
Willis ES, 444068; (20), F/S, 84 Operational Base Unit RAAF Labuan Is, 31- 1-46. Bo1.

39 /1474

Course 57: Awarded the Flying Badge on 29- 6-45:[3]

Bawden RA, 441636.
Bax NJ, 50971.
Beilby WE, 442700.
Bickett IM, 443855.
Braithwaite R, 438978.
Bird KC, 443654.
Brown RW, 443994.
Buckley IK, 439020.
Campbell PM, 443868; (19), F/S, Crew Conversion Unit Wollar, 6-11-44. A4.
Cornish RH, 438830.
Dunne J, 438987.
Eagle JC, 438988.
Fisher G, 443848.
Flockart RK, 438991.
Gibson JP, 441685.
Grassel CJ, 443884.
Hart SW, 439045.
Holt HJ, 45962.
Hopkins PW, 438993.
Howell DF, 440347.
Jackman T, 442706.

Jenkins WD, 444066.
Jones NF, 443893.
Layton GP, 444019.
Logue L, 442794.
Miller AW, 438846.
McGinnis GS, 438999.
Mulkearns NG, 439170.
O'Halloran LI, 441728.
Parrington DB, 439031.
Robin DR, 442731.
Schrauf RE, 441712.
Schwarz SF, 27111.
Short PJ, 443846.
Sillitoe KF, 439969.
Springall JM, 73528.
Walden NH, 444051.
Wearne ME, 441831.
Webb AA, 444190.
Witt KS, 439014.
Wymer WS, 443950.

41 /1515

The places of burial, and the missing memorial for those who have no known grave, have been abstracted from the registers of those who "Died on Service" held at the RAAF Historical Unit, Canberra. The Unit also holds a list compiled by the late Jock Ross of RAAF Historical Records showing the location of the cemeteries:

Cemeteries where 5 SFTS airmen are buried:

Australia
A1	Wagga War Cemetery, NSW
A2	Karrakatta War Cemetery, WA
A3	Lutwyche War Cemetery, Qld
A4	Sandgate War Cemetery, NSW
A5	Mildura War Cemetery, Vic
A6	Atherton War Cemetery, Qld
A7	Sale War Cemetery, Vic
A8	Parkes War Cemetery, NSW
A9	Townsville War Cemetery, Qld
A10	Narromine War Cemetery, NSW
A11	Church of England Civilian Cemetery, Temora, NSW
A12	Adelaide River War Cemetery, NT
A13	Woronora Cemetery, NSW
A14	Tocumwal War Cemetery, NSW
A15	Bowral Civil Cemetery, NSW
A16	Port Pirie War Cemetery, SA
A17	War Graves Cemetery Rookwood, NSW
A18	Camden War Cemetery
A19	Temora War Cemetery
A20	Atherton War Cemetery
A21	Deniliquin War Cemetery

Belgium
B1	Hotton War Cemetery, Luxembourg
B2	Geeraardsbergen Communal Cemetery

Borneo
Bo1	Labuan War Cemetery

Burma
Bu1	Tuakkyan War Cemetery

Egypt
E1	Fayid War Cemetery
E2	Moascar War Cemetery

France
F1	St Samson Churchyard, Troarn
F2	Labusiere-sur-Ouche, Veuvey-sur-Ouche, Cote d'Or
F3	Banneville-La-Campagne British War Cemetery
F4	Souvenir Francais Evreux Comm. Cemetery
F5	Roye New British Cemetery
F6	St Pierre Cemetery, Amiens

F7   Mazargues Cemetery Extension, Marseilles
F8   Frenouville Local Churchyard
F9   Bussy-le-Chateau Churchyard
F10   St Marie Military Cemetery, Le Havre
F11   Tilly-sur-Seulles British War Cemetery
F12   Droupt Sainte Marie Churchyard
F13   Hottot-Les-Baques War Cemetery

Germany

G1   Berlin 1939-45 War Cemetery
G2   Reichswald Forest War Cemetery, Cleves, West Phalia
G3   Rheinberg War Cemetery, West Phalia
G4   Durnbach War Cemetery, Bavaria
G5   Becklingen War Cemetery, Soltau
G6   Hamburg Cemetery, Ohlsdorf
G7   Reichswald Forest War Cemetery RAF Extension

Holland

H1   Hellendorn General Cemetery
H2   Heteren General Cemetery
H3   Woensel Cemetery, Eindhoven
H4   Bergen-op-Zoom Canadian War Cemetery
H5   West Terschelling General Cemetery, Dutch Frisian
      Is.

India (Pakistan)

I1   Maynamati War Cemetery, Comilla, Pakistan
I2   Madras War Cemetery

Italy

It1   Florence War Cemetery
It2   Sangro River War Cemetery
It3   Cassino War Cemetery
It4   Rome War Cemetery
It5   Ancona War Cemetery
It6   Ravenna War Cemetery
It7   Minturno War Cemetery

Japan

J1   British Commonwealth War Cemetery, Yokohama

Middle East

ME1   Medjez El Bab War Cemetery
ME2   Moascar War Cemetery

NEI (Indonesia)

NEI1 Macassar War Cemetery
NEI2 Ambon War Cemetery
NEI3 Galala War Cemetery

New Guinea
NG1   Lae War Cemetery.
NG2   Bomana War Cemetery

Tunisia
T1   Tabarka, Ras Rajel War Cemetery

United Kingdom
UK1   RAF Cemetery Cambridge, Cambridgeshire
UK2   RAF Regional Cemetery Harrogate, Yorkshire
UK3   Brookwood Military Cemetery, Surrey
UK4   Newton Stewart Cemetery, Wigtown, Scotland
UK5   Maidstone Cemetery, Kent
UK6   RAF Cemetery Oxford, North Hinksey, Berkshire
UK7   Llantwit Major Cemetery, Glamorgan
UK8   Sleepy Hillock Cemetery, Montrose, Angus
UK9   Bath RAF Cemetery, Englishcombe, Somerset
UK10 Fogo Churchyard, Berwickshire
UK11 North Walsham Cemetery, Norfolk
UK12 Cirencester Cemetery, Gloucester
UK13 Haverigg (St Lukes) Churchyard, Millom, Cumberland
UK14 East Chevington Cemetery, Northumberland
UK15 St John Churchyard, Annan, Dumfrieshire
UK16 Christchurch Cemetery, Hampshire
UK17 Grangemouth (Grandsable), Stirlingshire
UK18 St Peters Churchyard, Stoke-on-Trent, Shropshire
UK19 RAF Cemetery, Chester
UK20 Silloth Cemetery (Causeway Head), Holme Law, Cumberland
UK21 Oswestry General Cemetery, Shropshire
UK22 Costorphine Hill Cemetery, Scotland
UK23 Brookwood Military Cemetery, Surrey
UK24 St Nicholas Churchyard Extension, West Thorney, Sussex
UK25 Reading Municipal Cemetery, Oxford
UK26 North Bournemouth Cemetery
UK27 Finningley Churchyard Ext., Nottinghamshire

Yugoslavia
Y1   Belgrade War Cemetery

Major Casualties by Course among Graduates of 5SFTS, Uranquinty

Major casualties[1] (i.e. casualties that have to be reported to next of kin) from 17 Course to cessation of the EATS (53 missing, 241 killed)

Course	No. of graduates	Killed or missing	% lost	Missing
17	40	12	30	
18	53	20	38	6
19	66	21	32	7
20	68	21	31	7
21	58	9	16	1
22	27	9	33	1
23	25	6	24	2
24	33	9	27	2
25	29	9	31	
26	61	11	18	5
27	58	12	21	3
28	49	8	16	1
29	45	13	29	3
30	51	9	18	1
31	39	3	8	1
32	49	8	16	2
33	41	7	17	3
34	49	6	12	2
35	36	5	14	1
36	44	3	7	1
37	46	7	15	1
38	46	7	15	
39	55	8	15	2
40	60	1	2	
41	48	2	4	
42	42	3	7	
43	49	1	2	
44	38	2	5	1
45	30	1	3	
46	33	2	6	
47	42	1	2	
48	32	3	9	
50	39	1	3	
57	41	1	2	

Fatal Accidents

Fatal Accidents – Killed on war Service - Uranquinty

42-42-42	F/O G Keig and LAC G Monfries WT operator
7- 4-42	LAC R Oppy 412042 and LAC A McClymont A20-79
3- 7-42	LAC B Mc Credie 413010 and LAC C Teys 405945
31- 7-42	LAC R Wallace 409639
1-12-42	LAC RJ Newbigging 421819 Buried in the Presbyterian portion of Wagga Cemetery.
1- 3-43	W/O K Averill 406429 and LAC LW Rayner 426913
8- 1-43	LAC HV Thompson 421946 and LAC RC Walker 418587
8- 1-43	LAC JL McCarthy 421998
2- 5-43	LAC E Dow 418740
14- 7-43	LAC JG Thomson 423564
1- 8-43	LAC JW Barnwell 432300
8- 8-43	LAC RT Cooper 428633, LAC JW Chantler 422931 and W/O FK Smith 407450
19- 8-43	LAC SH Starmer 429410
43-43-43	F/O DT Burrows 408103 and LAC HN Slapp 432979
30-10-43	F/S LD Fuller 409534 and LAC AJ Nilon 432857
23-11-43	LAC F StJ Page, 433129
31- 1-44	LAC PH Penfold 433621
11- 4-44	LAC JG Cameron 64456
13- 4-44	LAC GC Harkness 433422
11- 5-44	F/L GJ O'Sullivan 406406 and LAC WE Marks 438000
27- 9-44	F/S DA Raftery 432264 and LAC AV Quirk 440960
44-44-44	P/O LH Williams 410404 and LAC LD Leysley 443782
26- 3-45	W/O JD Tamlyn 409613 and W/O LM Loftus 409419
4- 4-45	F/S MP McGee 442296
12- 6-45	LAC H O'Rorke 449012
15- 6-45	F/O JV Reed 419833 and P/O RJ Cook 442489
10- 9-45	F/L NB Everett 409791 and Sgt P Maxwell 438265

Appendix 1

MEMORANDUM OF AGREEMENT BETWEEN THE GOVERNMENTS OF THE UNITED KINGDOM, CANADA, AUSTRALIA, AND NEW ZEALAND , RELATING TO TRAINING OF PILOTS AND AIRCRAFT CREWS IN CANADA AND THEIR SUBSEQUENT SERVICE.

1.   It is agreed between the Governments of the United Kingdom, Canada, Australia, and New Zealand that there shall be set up in Canada a co-operative air training scheme as set out in this Agreement, and that the personnel so trained shall be allocated in accordance with Articles 14 and 15.

2.   This Agreement shall become operative at once and shall remain in force until 31st March, 1943; unless, by agreement between the Governments concerned, it be extended or terminated at an earlier date.

3.   The Government of Canada will act as administrator of the scheme for itself and the other Governments concerned, as hereinafter provided, and it is understood that the undertakings given herein by the Government of Canada to the other Governments concerned are respectively subject to the due performance on the part of such Governments of their several undertakings given herein in support of the scheme.

4.   The Government of Canada, acting as administrator as aforesaid, will take the measures it considers necessary for the setting up of an organisation which, when fully developed, will be capable of completing the training of the following numbers every four weeks:-

> Pilots (elementary flying training) 520
> Pilots (service flying training) 544
> Observers 340
> Wireless operator-air gunners 580

The Government of Canada, will, moreover, endeavour to complete the organization it considers necessary to give the above outputs so as to accord as nearly as may be found practicable with the programme of development set out in Appendix I.

5.   (a) The Governments of Australia and New Zealand will endeavour to send from time to time enough pupils for training to Canada to keep filled the following proportions of places in the appropriate training schools as shown in Tables A, B and C of Appendix 1, which proportions will be allotted to them for this purpose:-

Australia

> Pilots (service flying training) 2/16ths
> Observers 1/10th
> Wireless operator-air gunners. 1/10th

New Zealand

> Pilots (service flying training) 1/16th
> Observers 1/10th
> Wireless operator-air gunners. 1/10th

(b) The Government of Canada will endeavour to provide from time to time enough pupils for training in Canada to keep filled the following proportions of places in the appropriate training schools as shown in Tables A,B and C of Appendix 1, less the ten per cent or portion thereof supplied by the Government of the United Kingdom under the provisions of clause (c) hereof:-

       Pilots (elementary flying training) .... The whole
       Pilots (service flying training) 13/16ths
       Observers 8/10ths
       Wireless operator air-gunners 8/10ths

(c) The Government of the United Kingdom may send and the Government of Canada, as administrator of the scheme, undertakes to receive pupils for pilot and observer training in Canada in numbers not exceeding ten per cent of the intake of elementary flying training schools and air observer schools in Canada; and in addition the Government of the United Kingdom will endeavour to send and the Government of Canada, as administrator of the scheme, undertakes to receive pupils for training in Canada in sufficient numbers to keep filled any deficiency in the supply of such pupils from Australia, New Zealand and Canada.. The numbers sent by the Government of the United Kingdom may also include pupils from Newfoundland.

(d) The numbers, and the categories of pupils sent, may be varied from time to time by agreement between the Governments concerned.

(e) It is agreed that if the Governments of Canada, Australia and New Zealand fail to keep filled the training places allotted to them respectively they will nevertheless bear their full respective shares of the costs and expenses as provided for in Article 10.

4.   Pupils sent for training in Canada under the provisions of Article 5 will receive pay, allowances and other emoluments in accordance with the provisions set out in Appendix 11 to this Agreement.

7.   The training to be given shall be in accordance with the syllabus of instruction laid down for each similar course of training in the United Kingdom.

8.   To assist in the carrying out of the training scheme, the Governments of the United Kingdom, Canada, Australia and New Zealand will lend personnel in such ranks and in such numbers as may be agreed upon with the Government of Canada as administrator of the scheme.

9.   The share of the cost of the scheme to be borne by the Government of the United Kingdom will take the form of contributions in kind, to be delivered at such times and in such numbers as may be required for the efficient carrying out of the scheme in accordance with the programme of development set out in Appendix 1 as follows:-

(a) Engines for Moth airframes manufactured in Canada up to a maximum of 50 per cent of the total number of aircraft required for the initial equipment and immediate reserve establishments for the full training capacity, in accordance with Appendix 1, of the elementary flying training schools.

(b) All the Anson aircraft (without wings) that may be required for the initial equipment and immediate reserve establishments for the full training capacity, in accordance with Appendix 1, of the service flying training schools, the air observer schools and the air navigation schools.

(c)   All the Battle aircraft that may be required for the initial equipment and immediate reserve establishments for the full training capacity, in accordance with Appendix 1, of the bombing and gunnery schools and the air armament school.

(d)   The appropriate initial stock of spare parts for the airframes and engines to be supplied under the provision of the clauses (a), (b) and (c).

(e)   Such numbers of airframes and engines as may be required from time to time to replace the wastage resulting from loss or damage beyond economical repair of the airframes and engines to be supplied under the provision of clauses (a), (b) and (c).

(f)   An appropriate stock of spare parts for the running maintenance of the airframes and engines to be supplied under the provisions of clauses (a), (b) and (c).

(g)   533 Harvard airframes, 666 Wasp engines and the appropriate share of the stock of spare parts, which have already been ordered for use in service flying training schools.

In addition, the Government of the United Kingdom will bear the cost of packing, loading and transporting to Canada the airframes, engines and equipment to be supplies under the provision of clauses (a), (b) and (c), (d), (e), (f) and (g) above. The cost of unloading and of transportation in Canada will be borne by the Government of Canada, as administrator of the scheme.

The types of aircraft and aircraft engines and spare parts to be supplies by the United Kingdom Government under the foregoing arrangements may be varied from time to time by agreement between the Governments concerned.

10.   The Governments of Canada, Australia and New Zealand agree the costs and expenses paid or incurred by the Government of Canada as administrator of the scheme (exclusive of the contribution in kind and expenses to be made and borne by the Government of the United Kingdom as provided for in Article 9) shall be apportioned among them as follows:-

(a)   The Government of Canada will bear the whole costs and expenses of the Initial Training and Elementary Flying Training.

(b)   The costs and expenses remaining will be apportioned in the following percentages:-
            Canada 80.64
            Australia 11.28
            New Zealand 8.08

The foregoing percentages are based on the allocations of training places mentioned in Article 5; and it is agreed that if any substantial changes in these allocations are made by mutual agreement between the Governments concerned the percentages will be reviewed.

11.   (a) Except for any advances made by the other Governments concerned, as provided for in clause (b) of this Article, the Government of Canada, as administrator of the scheme, will in the first instance advance all the costs and expenses incurred as such administrator under the provisions of this Agreement, and the Governments of Australia and New Zealand will repay to the Government of Canada, as herein provided for, in Canadian dollars, their share of the amounts advanced, in the proportions specified in Article 10.

      (b) The Governments of the United Kingdom, Australia, and New Zealand will make advance payments necessary for pay and allowances, transportation charges, and other

expenses during the journey to Canada in respect of pupils sent to Canada by such Governments for training, and for such other costs and expenses as may be agreed upon from time to time; and the Governments of the United Kingdom, Australia, and New Zealand will, immediately after the end of each month, notify the Government of Canada, as administrator of the scheme, of the amounts of any advance payments made by them during such month, and will, as soon as possible thereafter, send to the Government of Canada a detailed statement in respect of such advance payments.

(c)   In connection with the repayments to be made by the Governments of Australia and New Zealand, as provided for in clause (a), due allowance will be made for any advance payments made and notified by the Governments of Australia and New Zealand, under the provisions of clause (b).

(d)   The Government of Canada, as administrator of the scheme, will refund to the Government of the United Kingdom any advance payments made by that Government under the provisions of clause (b), and the amount of such refunds shall be included in the costs and expenses of the scheme to be apportioned between the Governments of Canada, Australia, and New Zealand, as provided for in clause (a) and in Article 10.

(e)   In this Agreement the term "costs and expenses" shall mean all expenditures, costs, charges and liabilities made or incurred by the Government of Canada, as administrator of the scheme, and without restricting the generality of the foregoing shall include:- (i)   Pay, allowances, and other expenses of the personnel lent under the provisions of Article 8 and a cash contribution (computed in accordance with recognised practice as between Governments in such cases) towards the future non-effective benefits of such personnel.

(ii)   Pay, allowances, transportation charges, and other expenses connected with the training of Canadian pupils in Canada from the dates of their enlistment to the dates of their embarkation in Canada under the provisions of Article 16; or, in the case of Canadian pupils taken to fill vacancies in the Home Defence Squadrons of the Royal Canadian Air Force, as provided for in Article 14, to the dates of their being so taken.

(iii)   Pay, allowances, transportation charges, and other expenses connected with the training of pupils in Canada from the dates of their leaving the United Kingdom, Australia, New Zealand or Newfoundland for the purpose of taking up training in Canada to the dates of their embarkation in Canada under the provisions of Article 16.

But the term "costs and expenses" shall not include:-
(iv)   The contribution in kind and expenses to be made and borne by the Government of the United Kingdom as provided for in Article 9.
(v)   Costs and expenses of clothing and personal equipment of pupils other than such replacements as may be necessary during the period of training and other than flying clothing and equipment.
(vi)   Pensions or allowances to personnel lent under the provisions of Article 8 and to pupils or their dependents in respect or disability or death. The costs and expenses mentioned in (v) and (vi) above will be borne by the Governments lending the personnel and sending the pupils in respect of whom such costs, expenses, pensions or allowances are incurred.

12. The Governments of Australia and New Zealand will from time to time, within one month after a summarized statement of accounts has been presented them (showing the payments made during the preceding month by the Government of Canada, as administrator of the scheme, and taking account of any receipts, and of any advance payments made and notified, as provided for in Article 11 (b), by the Governments of Australia and New Zealand, and also of any adjustments in respect of previous months) pay or cause to be paid to the Government of Canada their due proportion as agreed upon in Article 10 of the costs and expenses of the scheme as shown by such statement.   These monthly payments will be regarded as advances on account, and the costs and expenses of the scheme as at the end of each financial year will be finally adjusted and paid when the accounts for such year have been audited.

13. (a) The Government of Canada will, in consultation with the other Governments concerned, appoint an officer to act as its Financial Adviser on carrying out its functions as administrator of the scheme. Such proposals for expenditure as the said Financial Adviser may require shall be referred to him for approval and no expenditure on such proposals shall be incurred until his approval has been given. Any proposal disapproved by the Financial Adviser may, at the instance of the officers responsible therefor, be referred to the Minister of National Defence for final decision. Any reports made by the Financial Adviser shall be made available by the Government of Canada to all the other Governments concerned, and these latter shall be entitled to obtain from the Financial Adviser information on all matters affecting the cost of the scheme and their participation in it.

  (b)   Monthly financial statements shall be furnished by the Government of Canada to the Governments of Australia and New Zealand.

  (c)   A record of all expenditure and all sums received in connection with the training of pupils in Canada under this scheme will be maintained by the Comptroller of the Treasury of the Government of Canada, and will be audited by the Auditor General of Canada. This record will be made available after audit for examination by representatives of the Governments concerned.

  (d)   The Government of Canada shall make available to the Governments of Australia and New Zealand, as early as possible after the close of each financial year ending 31st March, a statement, accompanied by a certificate of the Auditor General, of the receipts and payments in connection with the scheme showing the expenditure under appropriate heads.

14. It is agreed that the Government of Canada may, out of the Canadian pupils who complete their training under this scheme, fill vacancies which occur in the Home defence Squadrons of the Royal Canadian Air Force, provided, that the numbers so disposed shall not exceed the following:-

Pilots .... 136 a year
Air observers .... 34 a year
Wireless operator-air gunners .... 58 a year

All the other pupils, on completion of their training, will be placed at the disposal of the Government of the United Kingdom, subject to that Government's making the arrangements indicated in Article 15, and bearing liability as provided for in Articles 16 and 17 of this Agreement.

15.   The United Kingdom Government undertakes that pupils of Canada, Australia and New Zealand shall, after training is completed, be identified with their respective Dominions, either by the method of organizing Dominion units and formations or in some other way, such methods to be agreed upon with the respective Dominion Governments concerned. The United Kingdom Government will initiate inter-governmental discussions to this end.

16.   The Government of the United Kingdom will, subject to the provisions of Article 17, provide the pay, allowances, pensions and other non-effective benefits, maintenance and other expenses of the pilots and aircraft crews who are trained in Canada (other than those made available for service with the Royal Canadian Air Force in accordance with the provisions of Article 14) with effect from the dates of their embarkation in Canada for service with, or in conjunction with , the Royal Air Force. The Government of the United Kingdom also undertakes to arrange for those pupils who are made available for service with, or in conjunction with, the Royal Air Force to be embarked as speedily as possible after the completion of their training, and to defray the cost of their passages to the stations to which they are appointed on leaving Canada.

17.   The pay, allowances, pensions and other non-effective benefits, maintenance and other expenses, for which the Government of the United Kingdom undertakes liability under the provisions of Article 16, will be as laid down in Royal Air Force regulations. If it should be decided by the Government of Canada, the government of Australia, or the Government of New Zealand to supplement the amounts so issued, any such supplement will be borne by the Government concerned.

18.   The Government of Canada, as administrator of the scheme, will have charge of the assets acquired for the purpose of the scheme. On the termination of this Agreement such of the said assets as have been acquired and paid for as part of the cost of the scheme will be disposed of as follows:-

   (a)   Any land, but not buildings, structures or fixtures thereon, acquired or improved for the purpose of the scheme will become the property of the government of Canada.
   (b)   The assets acquired for the purposes of the Initial Training Schools and the Elementary Flying Training Schools, will become the property of the Government of Canada.
   (c)   All other assets, except those contributed in kind by the Government of the United Kingdom, will be shared between the Governments of Canada, Australia and New Zealand in the same proportions as laid down in Article 10 for the apportionment of the costs.
   (d)   Any of the assets contributed by the Government of the United Kingdom which remain will revert to that Government.

The distribution of the assets under the above arrangements may be made in kind or otherwise, as may be agreed upon.

19.   Arrangements will be made between the Governments concerned to facilitate communications between them under this Agreement or otherwise in connection with the scheme, either by means of cable or through representatives in Canada to be named by them.

Done in quadruplicate, at Ottawa, this 17th day of December, 1939

Done in quintuplicate, at Ottawa, this 17th day of December, 1939.

On behalf of the Government of the United Kingdom

On behalf of the Government of Canada

On behalf of the Government of Australia

On behalf of the Government of New Zealand

PROGRAMME OF THE DEVELOPMENT OF THE TRAINING SCHEME IN CANADA

1. To produce the output given in Article 4 above the following schools will be necessary in Canada:

Initial Training Schools 3
Elementary Flying Training Schools 13
Service Flying Training Schools 16
Air Observer Schools 10
Bombing and Gunnery Schools 10
Air Navigation Schools... 2
Wireless Schools.. 4

PILOT TRAINING   Table "A"

Initial Training Weeks (Cumulative)	Elementary Training 4	Service Training 12 28	
	No. 1 E.F.T.S.	No. 1 S.F.T.S. (Canada)	
	No. 2 "	No. 2 " "	
	No. 3 "	No. 3 " "	
	No. 4 "	No. 4 " "	
Initial Training Schools in Canada or United Kingdom	No. 5 "	No. 5 " "	
	No. 6 "	No. 6 " "	
	No. 7 "	No. 7 " "	
	No. 8 "	No. 8 " "	
	No. 9 "	No. 9 " "	
	No. 10 "	No. 10 " "	
	No. 11 "	No. 11 " "	
	No. 12 "	No. 12 " "	
	No. 13 "	No. 13 " "	
The initial training and elementary flying training of pupils for No. 14 S.F.T.S. will be carried out in New Zealand, and that for Nos. 17 and 18 S.F.T.S.s in Australia		No. 14 " "	
		No. 17 " "	
		No. 18 " "	

	Intake	Output	Intake	Output
Per school per four weeks	48	40	40	34
Total all schools in Canada	624	520	640	544

Wastage -------------------------------------- 16 ²/₃%   15%

29% on original elementary school intake

PROGRAMME SHOWING DATES OF OPENING OF PILOT AND AIR CREW TRAINING SCHOOLS

Date	Initial Training School	Elementary Flying Training School	Service Flying Training School	Air Observer School	Bombing and Gunnery School	Wireless School	Air Navigation School
1940							
April							
May	1	1		1		1	
June		1					
July			1	1			
August		1	1		1		
September	1		1	1			
October		1	1		1		1
November				1		1	
December		1	1		1		
1941							
January			1	1			
February		1	1		1		
March		1			1		
April		1	2	1	1	1	
May			1		1		
June		1	1				
July	1				1		1
August		1	1	1			
September							
Octobe		1	1	1			
November					1	1	
December		1	1	1			
1942							
January					1		
February		1	1				
March					1		
April			1				
Totals	3	13	16	10	10	4	2

AIRCRAFT REQUIREMENTS

The airframes and engines required for the initial equipment and immediate reserve of the schools in Canada when the scheme is in full operation are as under.

Type and Purpose	AIRFRAMES (includes 50% immediate reserve)	ENGINES (includes 100% immediate reserve)
CANADA		
Moths and/or Fleets for Elementary Flying Training Schools	.... 702	 936
Harvards for Service Flying Training Schools	.... 720	 960
Ansons for Service Flying Training Schools, Observer Schools, and Air Navigation Schools	.... 1,368	 3,648
Battles for Bombing and Gunnery Schools	.... 750	 1,000

NOTE.-Aircraft required for the Flying Instructors School, the Air Armament School and the instructors sections of the Air Navigation Schools are not included in the above. These schools and sections are disbanded as the scheme approaches completion, and the aircraft used by them in the early stages are absorbed into other units.

PERSONNEL REQUIREMENTS

The personnel required to man the schools, etc. in Canada when the
scheme is in full operation is as under.

	Officers	Airmen	Civilians	Works Maintenance Personnel
Commands and Groups, and extra Head-quarters Organization	288	603	134	....
Initial Training Schools	39	393	....	36
Service Flying Training Schools	752	11,376	64	320
Air Observer Schools	250	2,470	....	100
Bombing and Gunnery Schools	450	6,920	....	150
Elementary Flying Training Schools	351	4,134	....	130
Wireless Schools	96	1,284	....	80
Air Navigation Schools	126	1,278	....	40
Repair Depots	51	141	1,308	36
Equipment Depots	66	228	3,318	60
Technical Training Schools	41	627	....	30
Records Office	14	277	....	....
Recruit depots	28	424	....	40
Recruiting Organization	134	211	105	....
Totals	2,686	30,366	4,929	1,022

(a)   Civilians may replace a proportion of the airmen in certain units.

(b)   The above tables does not include schools, etc. which close as the scheme approaches
completion; the personnel from these schools will be absorbed into other units.

(c)   Some, or all, of the Elementary Flying Training Schools and Air Observer Schools may be
organized on a civilian basis.

CONDITIONS OF SERVICE OF PILOTS AND AIRCRAFT CREWS

(a)   Pupils from Canada.

(b)   Pupils other than those enlisted in the Royal Canadian Air Force, the Royal Australian Air Force and the Royal New Zealand Air Force.
Pupils other then those enlisted in the Royal Canadian Air Force, the Royal Australian Air Force and the Royal New Zealand Air force will be enlisted in the Royal Air Force.

(c)   Pupils sent by Australia and New Zealand. Pupils sent by Australia and New Zealand will be enlisted in the Royal Australian Air Force and in the Royal New Zealand Air Force respectively.

Pay, allowances, etc., during service in Canada.

During service in Canada, airmen of the Royal Australian Air Force and of the Royal New Zealand Air Force will be attached to the Royal Canadian Air Force, and, subject to the conditions laid down in the Financial Regulations and Instructions for the Royal Canadian Air Force on Active Service, they will receive from the appropriate Royal Canadian Air Force paying officer the pay, allowances, etc., of the rank and group in the Royal Canadian Air Force, as appropriate under (a) above, except that the following special arrangements will be made in regard to the issue of allowances to family or other dependents outside Canada.

The allowances and compulsory allotment from pay in respect of family or other dependents, which would be appropriate under Royal Australian Air Force or Royal New Zealand Air Force regulations will, if the family or other dependents reside outside Canada, be issued by the Government of Australia or the Government of New Zealand, who will reclaim from the Government of Canada, as administrator of the scheme, the amount so issued. The Royal Canadian Air Force officer paying the airman will deduct from the airman's pay the amount of assigned pay chargeable under Royal Canadian Air Force regulations.

Airmen will not be insured under Canadian insurance schemes, and any insurance contributions (employers' and employees' shares) necessary to ensure benefits for Australian or New Zealand airmen under Australian or New Zealand schemes will be paid by the Government of Australia or the Government of New Zealand, who will arrange with the Government of Canada, as administrator of the scheme, for the recovery from pay of any employees' shares of such contributions so recoverable.

Pay, allowances, etc., during service with the Royal Air Force.

On embarkation for service with the Royal Air Force, officers and airmen will be attached to that force, and, subject to the conditions laid down in King's Regulations and Air Council Instructions, they will receive from the appropriate Royal Air Force paying authority the pay, allowances, etc., of the rank and branch (or group) in the Royal air Force corresponding to that held in the Royal Australian Air Force or in the Royal New Zealand Air Force, except that the following special arrangements will be made in regard to the issue of allowances to family or other dependents in Australia or New Zealand.

The allowances and compulsory allotment from pay in respect of family or other dependents which may be payable under Royal Air Force regulations will, if the family or other dependents reside in Australia or New Zealand, be credited to the Government of Australia or to the Government of New Zealand, who will issue to the family or other dependents the allowance and compulsory allotment from pay which may be payable under Royal Australian Air Force or Royal New Zealand Air Force regulations.

If the pay and allowances admissible under Royal Australian Air Force or Royal New Zealand Air Force regulations exceed those admissible under Royal Air Force regulations, and the Government of Australia or the Government of New Zealand decide that this difference is to be credited to the officer or airman, the difference (after taking into account the payment made under the preceding paragraph) will be issued by the Government of Australia or the Government of New Zealand as deferred pay, either on termination of service or otherwise in special circumstances.

Personnel will not be insured under United Kingdom insurance schemes, and any insurance contributions (employers' and employees' shares) necessary to ensure benefits under Australian or New Zealand schemes will be paid by the Government of Australia or the Government of New Zealand, who will arrange with the Government of the United Kingdom to recover from pay any employees' shares of such contributions so recoverable.

Reproduced with kind permission of MODUK

Appendix 2

Memorandum of Agreement between H.M. Government in the United Kingdom and H.M. Government in Australia as to the training of pilots and aircraft crews in Australia, and their subsequent service with the Royal Air Force, and as to the provision of pupils from Australia for training in Canada as pilots and aircraft crews.

---

1.   It is agreed between H.M. Government in the United Kingdom and H.M. Government in Australia that arrangements shall be made by the latter, as provided for in this Memorandum, to train pilots and aircraft crews in Australia, and also to provide from Australia other pupils for training in Canada as pilots and aircraft crews, for service with the Royal Air Force, and that the pilots and crews so trained shall serve as provided for in this Memorandum.

2.   This Agreement shall become operative at once and shall remain in force until 31st March, 1943, unless, by agreement between the two Governments, it is extended or is terminated at an earlier date,

3.   The Government of Australia will take the measures necessary for the setting up of an organisation which when fully developed will be capable of accepting for training the following numbers every four weeks :-

            Pilots (elementary flying training) ---------------- 336
            Pilots (advanced flying training) ------------------ 280
            Observers --------------------------------------- 184
            Wireless operator-air gunners -------------------- 320

The Government of Australia will endeavour to complete the organisation necessary to give the above training capacity as speedily as possible.

4.   The organisation will also provide from time to time, for training in Canada, enough pupils to keep filled the following training schools in Canada :-

            Pilots (advanced flying training) ------------------ 2 schools.
            (i.e. 80 pupils every four weeks).
            Observers --------------------------------------- 1 school.
            (i.e. 42 pupils every four weeks).
            Wireless operator air-gunners -------------------- 1 school.
            (i.e. 72 pupils every four weeks).

The initial training and the elementary flying training of the pilots, and the initial training of the observers and the wireless operator-air gunners, will be carried out in Australia.

5.   Pupils trained in Australia under this scheme or sent to Canada to complete their training under this scheme will receive pay, allowances and other emoluments in accordance with the conditions set out in the Appendix to this Memorandum.

6.   The training to be given shall be in accordance with the syllabus of instruction laid down for each similar course of training in the United Kingdom.

7.   To help in the carrying out of the training scheme in Australia, the Government of the United Kingdom will lend to the Government of Australia personnel in such ranks and in such numbers as may be agreed with the Government of Australia.

The Government of Australia will, in accordance with the usual conditions for loans of this nature, bear the pay, allowances and other expenses of the personnel lent and will pay to the Government of the United Kingdom a cash contribution towards the future non-effective benefits of such personnel.

8. The share of the cost of the scheme in Australia to be borne by the Government of the United Kingdom will take the form of contributions as follows:-

(a) Engines for Moth airframes manufactured in Australia up to a maximum of 50% of the total number of aircraft required for the initial equipment and immediate reserve establishments for the full training capacity of the elementary flying schools. (It is agreed, however, that to the extent to which, within the limit of 50% mentioned above, the engines required for these Moth aircraft can be manufactured in Australia, the Government of the United Kingdom will pay to the Government of Australia the sterling price of an equivalent number of similar engines manufactured in the United Kingdom, plus the cost of transportation to Australia).

(b) All the Anson aircraft (without wings) that may be required for the initial equipment and immediate reserve establishments for the full training capacity of the Service Flying Training Schools, the Air Observers Schools and the Air Navigation Schools.

(c) All the Battle aircraft that may be required for the initial equipment and immediate reserve establishments for the full training capacity of the Bombing and Gunnery Schools and the Air Armament School.

(d) The appropriate initial stock of spare parts for the airframes and engines supplied under the provisions of clauses (a), (b), and (c).

(e) Such number of airframes and engines as may be required from time to time to replace the wastage, resulting from loss or damage beyond economical repair, of the airframes and engines supplied under the provisions of clauses (a), (b) and (c).

(f) An appropriate stock of spare parts for the running maintenance of the airframes and engines supplied under the provisions of clauses (a), (b) and (c).

(g) The Government of Australia will endeavour to manufacture all the aircraft including engines and spare parts required for single engine training at the Service Flying Training Schools – these aircraft being of the Wirraway or similar type.

The Government of the United Kingdom will pay to the Government of Australia the value of the first 233 of the airframes and first 291 of the engines, together with an appropriate stock of spare parts, the cash value being reckoned at the price paid by the Government of the United Kingdom for Harvard airframes and Wasp engines and spare parts ordered from North American Aviation Incorporated in November, 1939, for delivery in Canada. Should the Government of Australia be unable to manufacture all such aircraft and engines required for the purposes of this scheme in Australia, the Government of the United Kingdom will supply Harvard airframes, Wasp engines and spare parts in kind.

(h) The Government of Australia will make arrangements as speedily as possible to manufacture wings for Anson aircraft in Australia, but the Government of the United Kingdom undertakes to supply wings for the Anson airframes needed for the purposes of this scheme until wings manufactured in Australia become available. The cost of any wings so supplied and the additional freightage charges incurred as the result of their being supplied from the United Kingdom would be set off against part of the payment due from the Government of the United Kingdom under the provision of clause (g).

In addition, the Government of the United Kingdom will bear the cost of packing, loading and transporting to Australia the airframes, engines and equipment which they provide under the provisions of clauses (a), (b), (c), (d), (e), (f), and (g). The cost of unloading and of transportation in Australia will be borne by the Government of Australia.

The types of aircraft and aircraft engines and spare parts to be supplied by the United Kingdom Government under the foregoing arrangements may be varied from time to time by agreement between the two Governments.

10.   The Government of Australia agrees to bear all the remaining costs and expenses, including transportation charges, connected with the training of pupils in Australia from the dates of their first entry to the dates of their departure from Australia.

11.   On completion of their training in Australia, the pilots and aircraft crews will be placed at the disposal of the government of the United Kingdom, subject to that Government making the arrangements indicated in paragraph 12 and bearing liability as provided in paragraphs 13 and 14.

12.   The United Kingdom Government undertake that pupils trained in accordance with this Agreement shall, after training is completed, be identified with Australia, either by the method of organising Australian units or formations or in some other way, such methods to be agreed upon between the two Governments. The United Kingdom Government agrees to initiate inter-governmental discussions in order to work out agreed proposals to this end.

13.   The Government of the United Kingdom will, subject to the provisions of paragraph 14 of this Memorandum, be liable for the pay allowances, pensions and other non-effective benefits and other expenses of the pilots and aircraft crews who complete their training in Australia, with effect from the dates of their embarkation for service with the Royal Air Force. These expenses will include the costs of their passages to the Royal Air Force stations to which they are appointed on completing their training.

14.   The liability of the Government of the United Kingdom under the provisions of the preceding paragraph will be limited to the issue of pay, allowances, pensions and other non-effective benefits and other expenses at Royal Air Force rates and under Royal Air Force conditions. If it should be decided by the Government of Australia to supplement the amounts so issued, the cost of any such supplement will be borne by them.

15.   Any airframes, engines, or spare parts which have been contributed in kind by the Government of the United Kingdom under paragraph 8 of this Agreement and remain when this Agreement terminates, will then become the property of the United Kingdom Government.

Similarly as regards engines, airframes, and spare parts manufactured in Australia but paid for by the Government of the United Kingdom, that Government will be entitled to a share of the residual value of any which remain on termination of this Agreement. This share will bear the same ratio to the full residual value as the prices originally bore to the actual cost of manufacture.

Riverdale   **JV Fairbairn**

27th November 1939.
Ottawa

Appendix 3

SECRET

MEMORANDUM OF AGREEMENT

between the Governments of the United Kingdom and the Commonwealth of Australia as to the arrangements to be made for the identification with the Commonwealth of Australia of Australian personnel trained under the Empire Air Training Scheme in Canada and Australia.

It is agreed that the arrangements, referred to in Article 12 of the Agreement between the Governments of the United Kingdom and the Commonwealth of Australia, and in Article 15 of the Agreement between the Governments of the United Kingdom, Canada, the Commonwealth of Australia and New Zealand, shall be on the following lines:-

1.   Eighteen Royal Australian Air Force squadrons will be formed for service outside Australia, in addition to those already serving in the United Kingdom, the Middle East and the Far East.

2.   The rate of formation cannot be guaranteed since it is dependent on the rate at which the projected Air Force expansion can be achieved; nevertheless the aim will be to form these eighteen squadrons within the next eighteen months in accordance with the following schedule:-

By March, 1941 -- 2 squadrons to be formed.
By June, 1941 -- 6 squadrons to be formed.
By September, 1941 ---------------------------------- 9 squadrons to be formed.
By December, 1941 ---------------------------------- 12 squadrons to be formed.
By March, 1942 ----------------------------------- 15 squadrons to be formed.
By April or May, 1942 --------------------------------- 18 squadrons to be formed.

3.   To facilitate arrangements for posting Australian air crews, there will be established a Central Posting Organisation and a Central Record Office, the staff of which will include Royal Australian Air Force personnel.

4.   All Australian air crews trained under the above-mentioned agreements, whether serving in Royal Air Force formations or in Royal Australian Air Force formations, will wear Royal Australian Air Force uniform. They will thus retain their Australian identity in either event.

5.   The working of the foregoing arrangements will be reviewed in September, 1941, in order to determine whether the schedule in paragraph 2 can be maintained or accelerated and to consider the position and organisation of Australian air crews whom under these arrangements it may not be practicable to absorb in Royal Australian Air Force squadrons.

6.   At the request of the United Kingdom Government, the Royal Australian Air Force is concentrating largely on the Empire Air Training Scheme in Australia. This has necessitated the provision and employment in Australia of ground personnel who would otherwise have been available for service with the Royal Australian Air Force squadrons overseas and has rendered it impracticable for the Commonwealth of Australia to supply the ground personnel overseas for the squadrons referred to in paragraph 1 as they are formed. It is recognised, however, as desirable, so far as it may mutually be considered practicable, that this United Kingdom ground personnel should gradually be exchanged for Royal Australian Air Force personnel, with a view to achieving homogeneity of personnel in these squadrons.

7.   The concentration of the Royal Australian Air Force upon aircrew training may also, at the outset, result in a shortage of Royal Australian Air Force officers with the necessary qualifications to fill posts as Squadron Commanders, Station Commanders, etc. It is recognised that, if enough Royal Australian Air Force officers with these qualifications are not immediately available, some of these posts may have to be filled by Royal Air Force officers. The replacement of these Royal Air Force officers will be effected progressively as soon as qualified Royal Australian Air Force officers become available for that purpose.

8.   Nothing in these arrangements affects the financial responsibilities of the two Governments under the above-mentioned Agreements.

9.   The cost of the eighteen squadrons referred to in paragraph 1 above will be borne by the United Kingdom Government, except that the pay, allowances, and non-effective benefits of Royal Australian Air Force personnel who serve in the new squadrons will be borne by the United Kingdom Government only to the extent provided for in Article 14 of the Agreement between the Governments of the United Kingdom and the Commonwealth of Australia, and in Article 17 of the Agreement between the Governments of the United Kingdom, Canada, the Commonwealth of Australia and New Zealand. The Commonwealth Government for their part will continue to bear the cost of the five Royal Australian Air Force squadrons already serving in the United Kingdom, the Middle East and the Far East.

10.   If the commonwealth Government so desire, a senior officer designated by them will be given access at all times to Commanders of Stations and Groups and to Commanders-in-Chief of Commands in which Royal Australian Air Force personnel are serving, and will be furnished by them with such information as he may desire. He will also have access to the Chief of the Air Staff. He will be furnished with advance information about any major questions which arise from time to time affecting the employment of Royal Australian Air Force personnel and squadrons. He will be at liberty to make representations to the Air Ministry on any of the above matters.

11.   The arrangements in paragraph 10 will not affect the existing procedure for consultation between the two Governments on major questions affecting the employment of the Royal Australian Air Force personnel and squadrons overseas.

Done in duplicate, at London, England, this 17th day of April, 1941.

On behalf of the Government of the United Kingdom
                    (Signed) Archibald Sinclair

On behalf of the Government of the Commonwealth of Australia.
                    (Signed) S. M. Bruce.

(10784 (2))   Wt.   -   250   4/41   D.L.   G. 344

Endnotes
Dedication

1. RAF slang for aircraft during World War II. In World War I, and between the wars, an aircraft was a "bus" or often, as often it still is, a "crate". The first and third of these terms constitute excellent examples of British meiosis or understatement. Partridge, E. 1945 A Dictionary of RAF slang: with an Introductory Essay, Michael Joseph, London, p. 9.

Introduction

1. **Empire Air Force, Australia Plays Her Part.** Statement and Broadcast by the Rt Hon. R.G. Menzies, K.C., M.P., 11 October, 1939, issued by the Department of Information, Melbourne, 11 October, 1939.
2. MEMORANDUM OF AGREEMENT BETWEEN THE GOVERNMENTS OF THE UNITED KINGDOM, CANADA, AUSTRALIA, AND NEW ZEALAND , RELATING TO TRAINING OF PILOTS AND AIRCRAFT CREWS IN CANADA AND THEIR SUBSEQUENT SERVICE. Ottawa, 17th December, 1939. Air Historical Branch, MOD reference IIIC/5/4. Public Record Office reference AIR20/6305. Appendix 1.
3. **The Battle of Britain.** An Air Ministry Account of the Great Days from 8th August – 31st October 1940, His Majesty's Stationery Office, London. NLA YYp 940 544941 B336.
4. Garrisson A.D. **Australian Fighter Aces** Air Power Study Centre in conjunction with the Australian War Memorial, Canberra. In preparation.
5. Newton D. 1990 **A Few of the Few, Australians in the Battle of Britain,** AWM, Canberra. There were 21 Australians listed on the Roll of Honour; and 53 in Fighter Command 1939-40.
6. RAAF Directorate of Works and Buildings. Plans 40/41/1050 and 40/41/1051, 7 April 1941.

Chapter 1. The Empire Air Training Scheme

1. Interview 29- 9-98 Air Commodore ADJ Garrisson, Canberra.
2. Letter 15- 1-99 VH Polley, 33 Hamlyn Drive, Port Macquarie 2444.
3. Mr Fairbairn and his secretary, RE Elford, were killed in the Lockheed Hudson crash, now the site of the Air Disaster Memorial, at RAAF Base Canberra later RAAF Fairbairn. It was truly a disaster for also killed were the Minister for the Army (Mr GA Street) and the Chief of the General Staff (General Sir Brudenell White).
4. MEMORANDUM OF AGREEMENT BETWEEN H.M. GOVERNMENT IN THE UNITED KINGDOM AND H.M. GOVERNMENT IN AUSTRALIA AS TO THE TRAINING OF PILOTS AND AIRCRAFT CREWS IN AUSTRALIA, AND THEIR SUBSEQUENT SERVICE WITH THE ROYAL AIR FORCE, AND AS TO THE PROVISION OF PUPILS FROM AUSTRALIA FOR TRAINING IN CANADA AS PILOTS AND AIRCRAFT CREWS. 27 November 1939. Air Historical Branch, Ministry of Defence reference IIIC/5/2. PRO reference AIR 20/6303. (Appendix 2).
5. MEMORANDUM OF AGREEMENT BETWEEN H.M. GOVERNMENT IN THE UNITED KINGDOM AND H.M. GOVERNMENT IN NEW ZEALAND AS TO THE TRAINING OF PILOTS IN NEW ZEALAND AND THEIR SUBSEQUENT SERVICE WITH THE ROYAL AIR FORCE AND AS TO THE PROVISION OF PUPILS FROM NEW ZEALAND FOR TRAINING IN CANADA AS PILOTS AND AIRCRAFT CREWS. Air Historical Branch, MOD reference IIIC/5/1; PRO reference Air 20/6302.
6. MEMORANDUM OF AGREEMENT BETWEEN THE GOVERNMENTS OF THE UNITED KINGDOM, CANADA, AUSTRALIA, AND NEW ZEALAND , RELATING TO TRAINING OF PILOTS AND AIRCRAFT CREWS IN CANADA AND THEIR SUBSEQUENT SERVICE.

(Ottawa, 17th December, 1939). Air Historical Branch, MOD reference IIIC/5/4. Public Record Office reference AIR20/6305. (Appendix 1).

7.   Vincent, A.W. **Noble Six Hundred.**

8.   Appendix 1, Table "A".

9.   **Flying Training,** Vol. II, Part 2, Basic Training Overseas, p, 514.

10. **Flying Training,** Vol. 1, Policy and Planning, Air Ministry, 1952, p. 79.

11. See Appendix 2, Article 11.

12. See Air Board Agenda 3233/1941. Memorandum of the organisation and control of the RAAF serving overseas, p. 21 – "5. Summary 1. Personnel sent overseas under the EATS remain members of the RAAF throughout their service."

13. Air Board Agenda 3223/1941, A Memorandum of the Organisation and Control of Personnel of the Royal Australian Air Force Serving Overseas, p. 21. Appendix V (1). (See also Appendix 3, Article 1).

14. Ibid., Appendix V (2). (See also Appendix 3, Article 2).

15. Ibid., p. 21 – "5. Summary 2. New squadrons formed under the EATS from this personnel are by the agreement of 23-12-40 (Appendix V), squadrons of the RAAF. (See also Appendix 3, Article 1).

16. See Appendix 3, Article 9.

17. Ibid., Article 6.

18. **War Report of the Chief of Air Staff Royal Australian Air Force 3rd September, 1939 to 31st Deceamber, 1945 to the Minister for Air.** RAAF Printing and Publishing Unit, Melbourne, 1946, p.21.

19. Department of Public Relations Publication No. 4937.

20. DPR Publication, "Victory Roll".

21. Herington J. 1962 **Air War Against Germany and Italy,** RAAF History in the War of 1939-1945, Vol. III, AWM, Canberra, p. 510.

22. Mordike J. 1995 **Australia's Contribution to the War in Europe: A Dim Memory of a Distant War?** Air Power Studies Centre, Fairbairn, Paper No. 37, p.1, quoting Long G. Some statistics, Battle Casualties-War Against Germany, **The Final Campaigns,** p. 633. NLA 940,5394 AUS.

23. The following are the fatal casualties given for the RAAF 1939-45 from Sir Charles Webster and Noble Frankland, **The Strategic Air Offensive Against Germany,** 1939-1945, Vol. III, **Victory,** 1961, p. 287. Of the total fatal casualties in the European theatre 3,486 were suffered in Bomber Command; 408 in Coastal Command; 191 in Fighter Command; 478 in other units; and 834 in training units.

24. 2EFTS Archerfield, 3EFTS Essendon, 4EFTS Mascot, 5EFTS Tamworth, 8EFTS Narrandera, 10EFTS Temora, 11EFTS Benalla, 12EFTS Lowood.

25. 1SFTS Point Cook, 2SFTS Wagga, 3SFTS Amberley, 4SFTS Geraldton, 5SFTS Uranquinty, 7SFTS Deniliquin, 8SFTS Bundaberg.

26. Directorate of Public Relations Bulletin No. 5133, 11 May 1945.

Chapter 2

1.   MEMORANDUM OF AGREEMENT BETWEEN H.M. GOVERNMENT IN THE UNITED KINGDOM AND H.M. GOVERNMENT IN AUSTRALIA AS TO THE TRAINING OF PILOTS AND AIRCRAFT CREWS IN AUSTRALIA, AND THEIR SUBSEQUENT SERVICE WITH THE ROYAL AIR FORCE, AND AS TO THE PROVISION OF PUPILS FROM AUSTRALIA FOR TRAINING IN CANADA AS PILOTS AND AIRCRAFT CREWS.
     Article 8(a) to (h). (see Appendix 2).

2.   Ibid., Article 8 (h).

3. Air Board Agenda 2643/1939.
4. Appendix 2, Article 8(h).
5. Air Board Agenda 2747/1940.
6. Wilson S. **The Wirraway, Boomerang & CA-15 in Australian Service,** p. 13.
7. Ibid., p. 12.
8. Ibid., p. 46.
9. RELAWM 31891.001.

Chapter 3

1. DPR Bulletin No. 481, 26 February 1941.
2. RAAF Reference 151/1/648, Organisation Memorandum No. 31, Enclosure 13A. Australian Archives.
3. Ibid., Enclosure 18A. (Deniliquin was to be 7SFTS and Bundaberg to be 8SFTS). Australian Archives.
4. Morris S. and Winterbottom J. 1995 'Hey days of the RAAF flying training school, Uranquinty', **The Daily Advertiser,** 30 September, p. 20. The property was "Texas" owned by A. Lewington and well known for its prize-winning wheat crops.
5. Air Board Agenda 3454/1941. Department of Air, File No. 171/57/1, 11 February 1941, Enclosure 5A.
6. Air Board Agenda 3251/1941.
7. Commonwealth of Australia Gazette, No. 70, 5 March 1942. The Lands Acquisition Act 1906-1936.
8. Air Board Agenda 3738/1941.
9. RAAF Directorate of Works and Buildings. Plans 40/41/1050 and 40/41/1051, 7 April 1941.
10. PORs Reels 370 & 371.
11. He was replaced in April 1942 by S/L F.I. Wootten who later went to 21Sqn equipped with Liberators on Morotai.
12. Letter 7- 4-98 R Marriott, 18 Illawarra Road, Flemington 3031.
13. Letter 18- 2-99 AM Day, 4 Pleasurelea Drive, Batehaven 2536.
14. Letter 10- 2-99 AW Boorn, "Quinty", 1 Northcott St., Nth Ryde 2113.
15. Letter 13- 3-98 V Polley, 33 Hamlyn Drive, Port Macquarie 2444.
16. MEMORANDUM OF AGREEMENT BETWEEN H.M. GOVERNMENT IN THE UNITED KINGDOM AND H.M. GOVERNMENT IN AUSTRALIA AS TO THE TRAINING OF PILOTS AND AIRCRAFT CREWS IN AUSTRALIA, AND THEIR SUBSEQUENT SERVICE WITH THE ROYAL AIR FORCE, AND AS TO THE PROVISION OF PUPILS FROM AUSTRALIA FOR TRAINING IN CANADA AS PILOTS AND AIRCRAFT CREWS.
    Article 6. (see Appendix 2).
17. POR Reel 370.
18. Ibid.
19. Letter 15- 1-99 RA Leek, 1 Melanie Court, Buderim, 4556.
20. Ibid.
21. Letter 15- 1-99 D Beaurepaire, PO Box 56, Torquay, 3228.
22. Letter 10- 2-99 AW Boorn.
23. PORs Reels 370 and 371.
24. Letter 15- 1-99 RA Leek.
5. POR 370.
26. Ibid.
27. Ibid.

Chapter 4

1. POR Reel 371.
2. POR Reel 370.
3. Brook, W.H. 1986 **Demon to Vampire** H. Kynoch & Co. Pty Ltd, Melbourne, p. 133. Having nursed a badly damaged Boston back to Nadzab from the target at Salamau on 16 March 1943, F/L Newton returned two days later to the same target and was shot down into the sea. Sgt Eastwood did not escape as the aircraft rapidly sank but Newton and F/S Lyon were captured by the Japanese. After interrogation Lyon was bayoneted to death and Newton was beheaded.
4. Letter 30- 1-99 M Susans, Murrumbateman 2582.
5. Letter 15- 1-99 VH Polley.
6. POR Reel 370.
7. Interview 2-11-98 WK Merrett, 17 Reservoir Road, Pymble 2073.
8. Air Board Agenda 3626/1941.
9. Interview 15- 9-97 D Kingsbury.
10. PORs Reels 370 and 371.
11. Letter 5- 2-99 J Dive, 7 Ormond Road, Roseville, 2069.
12. Letter 6- 3-99 KR Doyle, "Edenderry", Hallidays Point 2430.
13. Letter 8- 2-99 G Clissold.
14. POR Reel 370.
15. Letter 30- 1-99 Olive Jardine, 91 Cox's Road, North Ryde, 2113.
16. Trademark for portable signalling lamp.
17. **WAAAF At War** 1974 E.M. Robertson, Mullaya Publications.
18. The longest serving CO at Uranquinty from July 1943 to June 1945.
19. Letter 28- 2-99 Sheila Van Emden.
20. Interview 22- 2-99 Joan Sullivan.
21. Letter 28- 2-99 Edna Hillier.
22. Robertson E. **WAAAF at War** Illustration p. 96.

Chapter 5

1. The recruitment centre in Sydney was in Woolloomooloo at the corner of Plunkett and Palmer Streets.
2. Commencing with 1 Course EATS, the aircrew numbers started at 400,000. By 17 Course, the first course at Uranquinty, the numbers allocated to trainees were in the 410,000s.
3. Interview 15- 9-97 RJ Davies, 1 Coburn Place, Isaacs 2607.
4. According to Partridge, E. 1945 **A Dictionary of RAF slang: with an Introductory Essay** at p. 8, "erk" derives from air mechanic down the chain through air mech (mek) to air mch to airch to erk.
5. Letter 15- 1-99 DBL Beaurepaire. The working clothes were one piece blue overalls and known as goons or goon skins.
6. Interview 8- 2-99 SB Robertson, 18 Carrington Avenue, Mosman 2088.
7. **Memorandum of Agreement between H.M. Government in the United Kingdom and H.M. Government in Australia....... as to the provision of pupils from Australia for training in Canada as pilots and aircraft crews.** Article 4. Air Historical Branch, Ministry of Defence reference IIIC/5/2. PRO reference AIR 20/6303. (Appendix 2).
8. **Memorandum of Agreement between the Governments of the United Kingdom, Canada, Australia, and New Zealand, relating to training of pilots and aircraft crews in Canada and their subsequent service.** Article 5(a). (Appendix 1).
9. Interview 5- 9-98 JB Wood, 111/11 Yarranabbe Road, Darling Point 2027.

10. The courses at Edmonton ran every two weeks from the commencement of the EATS in April 1940.

11. *Wood JB.* **Conquering Unchartered Skies.**

12. Conversation 13- 1-99 IS Bensley, 48 Martin St, Harbord 2096.

13. Interview 2-10-98 JR Banyard, Canberra.

14. Interview 8-10-98 S Aboud, 1Abbott, Yarralumla 2600.

15. Letter 14- 2-99 G Clissold, 38 Victoria St, Epping 2121.

16. Interview 2-11-98 DE Yates, 3Crane Pl. Lodge, Palm Beach 2108.

17. Interview 23- 2-99 KG Pollard, 26 White Avenue, Queanbeyan 2620.

18. Letter 27- 8-98 D Kingsbury, 66 Noble Pde, Dalmeny 2546. Within the RAAF 1,070 were killed in EATS Schools compared to 8,884 on operational squadrons; Herington J **Air Power Over Europe**, p.508.

19. Article 4 at Appendix 2.

20. Article 5(a) at Appendix 1.

Chapter 6

1. TEE EMM, 1943, Vol. 2, p. 273.

2. **MEMORANDUM OF AGREEMENT BETWEEN THE GOVERNMENTS OF THE UNITED KINGDOM, CANADA, AUSTRALIA, AND NEW ZEALAND , RELATING TO TRAINING OF PILOTS AND AIRCRAFT CREWS IN CANADA AND THEIR SUBSEQUENT SERVICE.** Article 7 (Appendix 1).

3. **Flying Training**, Vol. II, Part 2, Basic Training in Australia, Chapter 8, p. 509.

4. **Memorandum of Agreement between H.M. Government in the United Kingdom and H.M. Government in Australia....... as to the provision of pupils from Australia for training in Canada as pilots and aircraft crews.** Article 3. Air Historical Branch, Ministry of Defence reference IIIC/5/2. PRO reference AIR 20/6303. (Appendix 2).

5. **Air Board Agenda** 2627/1939.

6. **Air Board Agenda** 2610/1939.

7. Interview 27-11-98 E Vonarx, 23 Wooden St, Wagga 2650.

8. The Central Flying School formed at Camden later moved to Tamworth before going to Parkes and back to Point Cook.

9. POR Reel 370.

10. Letter 25- 2-99 AM Day "I had a few trips to and fro in the Wirraways when they were fitted with armour plate around the cockpits and dive brakes at De Havilland at Mascot and Clyde Engineering at Bankstown."

11. POR Reel 370.

12. Letter 16- 1-99 M Susans, 2 Euroka Ave, Murrumbateman 2582.

13. Letter 13-10-99 IS Bentley, 48 Martin St, Harbord 2096.

14. Interview 27-11-98 E Vonarx.

15. Letter 15- 1-99 D Beaurepaire.

16. POR Reel 371.

17. Interview 8-10-98 S Aboud.

18. Interview 27-11-98 E Vonarx.

19. Letter 2-11-98 WK Merrett.

20. Letter 15- 1-99 D Beaurepaire.

21. Interview 2-11-98 DE Yates.

22. Interview 23- 2-99 KG Pollard.

Chapter 7

1. Air Board Agenda 3449/1941.
2. Letter 5- 2-99 JL Dive, 7 Ormonde Road, Roseville, 2069.
3. TM Vols I and II, 1941-1946. HMSO.
4. Other characters were F/O Fixe, the navigator; Sergeant Winde, the air gunner; WAAF Winsome; and Binder, the dog.
5. Corrupted no doubt by WWI diggers from paillasse, French for a straw mattress.
6. Interview 15- 9-97 RJ Davies.
7. PORs 370 and 371.
8. Interview 12- 3-99 FE Taylor, Bungendore 2621.
9. Letter 6- 3-99 KR Doyle
10. Interview 2-11-98 WK Merrett.
11. Letter 15- 3-99 HTB Taylor.
12. Letter 15- 3-99 FE Taylor.
13. Log book CJ Schmitzer.
14. Interview 27-11-98 WN Howard.
15. RAF slang for landings and take-offs.
16. Interview 8-10-98 S Aboud.
17. POR Reel 370.
18. Interview 27-11-98 E Vonarx.
19. Wirraway Ways in a newsheet of the Mosquito Aircraft Association of Australia. F/L Lundberg later flew with 87Sqn.
20. POR Reel 370.
21. Letter 22- 2-99 HK Hansen. In April-May 1942 he recalled B17s landing with little to spare for refuelling on their way to Moresby (Coral Sea).
22. POR Reel 370.
23. Ibid.
24. Interview 2-11-98 WK Merrett.
25. POR Reel 370.
26. Letter 15- 9-98 J Dive.
27. Letter 15- 2-99 R McKenzie, 34 Allambie Avenue, East Lindfield, 2070.

Chapter 8

1. PORs Reels 370 & 371.
2. Ibid.
3. Ibid.

Chapter 9

1. PRO Reel 370.
2. Letter 18-12-98 JA Fitzsimons, 33 The Rampart, Castlecrag 2068.
3. Letter 11- 9-98 R Willcocks, 14 Frenchs Road, Willoughby 2068.
4. Letter 12-12-98 N Lamont,9/26 Adam St, Wentworth 2648.
5. Horrific Injuries are Described in Dullon's **'Flying Low'**
6. PROs Reels 370 & 371.
7. Ibid.
8. Interview 10-9-98 KB Sly, 33 Gotha St, Cleveland 4163.
9. Died on Service Book. RAAF Historical Section.
10. Interview 3- 2-99 V Cranmer.

11. Letter 28- 2-99 Alma Stump (formerly Glasson), Largs Nth 5016.
12. The bombs were filled with stannous chloride.
13. Letter 25- 2-99 AM Day referring to the CO, G/C Ewart.
14. POR Reel 370.
15. Interview.15- 9-97 RJ Davies.
16. Interview 2-10-98 JR Banyard.
17. From 1958 all pilots and navigators on graduation were commissioned.
18. Letter 15- 1-99 D Beaurepaire.
19. Interview 17- 2-99 K Pollard.

Chapter 10

1. Interview 12- 3-99 FE Taylor.
2. Fax 15- 3-99 FE Taylor.
3 Ibid.
4. Interview 2-10-98 JR Banyard.
5. Interview 2-11-98 WK Merrett.
6. Letter 15- 3-99 HTB Taylor.
7. Interview 17- 2-99 K Pollard.
8. Interview 7- 9-98 KB Sly.
9. Letter 31- 1-99 WN Howard.
10. Letter 18-12-98 JA Fitzsimons.
11. Interview 3- 2-99 V Cranmer.
12. Interview 29- 8-98 JB Wood.
13. Subsequently known as No. 45 (Atlantic Transport) Group, RAF Transport Command.
14. Wood JB. **Conquering Unchartered Skies.** In preparation.
15. More Liberators, just about 1,750, were ferried across, more than any other aircraft. 393 Lancasters made in Canada were delivered without any losses.
16. Wood JB. **Conquering Unchartered Skies.** In preparation.

Chapter 11

1. Ilbery P. 1998 **From Uranquinty to Britain with the Empire Air Trainees**, The Daily Advertiser, Weekender, Dec. 27, pp. 23-4.
2. Partridge E. 1945 **A dictionary of RAF slang**, Michael Joseph, London. NLA N427 PAR.
3. Hamilton T. 1991 **The Life & Times of Pilot Officer Prune Being the Official Story of TEE EMM**, HMSO, London.
4. This theatrical show referred to any engagement with the enemy.
5. Fax 15- 3-99 FE Taylor.
6. The group included Geoff Northcott RCAF, Paul Brennan RAAF, and Johnny Plagis of the Royal Rhodesian Air Force.
7. Interview 2-10-98 JR Banyard.
8. Letter 8- 2-99 G Clissold.
9. Letter 1-11-98 WK Merrett.
10. Letter 15- 3-99 HTB Taylor.
11. Letter 26-11-98 RJ Chivers, 10/44 Munn St, Merimbula 2548.
12. 49 Course was held up for six months due to the surplus of pilots which had been built up by the EATS and became 57 Course, the last course at 5SFTS. Ken Witt has described how the interval was impatiently passed in Graham Menzies' book before getting back on course, graduating, only to be surplus to requirements. In this interval several refresher courses were run including Jack Chiver's.

13. 33 Course.
14. Wing Commander JN Davenport DSO DFC and bar GM MID who completed two tours on 455Sqn; the first on Hampdens and the second on Beaufighters.
15. The TFX Beaufighter powered by two Hercules (each of 1,770hp) was armed with four 20mm cannons and eight 3-inch rockets. 455Sqn, originally the first Australian bomber squadron in the UK, converted to the Beaufighter X in December 1943.
16. Using the cathode ray picture of G-Box and the sextant to 'shoot' the star Polaris.
17. Navigator wireless operators. NavWs were a relatively new breed of observer, with skills in wireless as well as navigation, for operations in two-man crews.
18. Letter 27- 9-98 D Kingsbury.
19. Letter 15- 2-99 R McKenzie.
20. Letter 16- 2-99 K Pollard.
21. Interview 7- 9-98 KB Sly.
22. Interview 27-11-98 WN Howard.
23. Letter 31- 1-99 WN Howard.
24. The GH blind bombing system was a more sophisticated form of GEE, the location system provided by fixes from two or more radio beams. The navigator instructed the pilot on course alterations and when pre-arranged co-ordinates appeared on his cathode ray tube released the bombs.
25. Letter 18- 3-99 J McDonald.
26. Interview 8-10-98 S Aboud.

Chapter 12

1. **TEE EMM**, Vol. 1.
2. Bennett J. 1995 **Fighter Nights** Banner Books, Belconnen, ACT 2617.
3. Trained as fighter pilots.
4. Herington J. **Air War Against Germany and Italy**, p.337.
5. MEMORANDUM OF AGREEMENT BETWEEN THE GOVERNMENTS OF THE UNITED KINGDOM, CANADA, AUSTRALIA, AND NEW ZEALAND , RELATING TO TRAINING OF PILOTS AND AIRCRAFT CREWS IN CANADA AND THEIR SUBSEQUENT SERVICE Article 15. ....pupils of Canada, Australia and New Zealand shall, after training is completed, be identified with their respective Dominions, either by the method of organizing Dominion units and formations or in some other way.... (Appendix 1).
6. Memorandum of Agreement between H.M. Government in the United Kingdom and H.M. Government in Australia as to the training of pilots and aircraft crews in Australia, and their subsequent service with the Royal Air Force, and as to the provision of pupils from Australia for training in Canada as pilots and aircraft crews. Article 11. ....On completion of their training in Australia, the pilots and aircraft crews will be placed at the disposal of the government of the United Kingdom....(Appendix 2).
7. McCarthy J. 1994 'Two faces of the Empire Air Training Scheme: the European experience' **The RAAF in Europe and North Africa 1939-1945**, pp. 9-10.
8. Fax 15- 3-99 FE Taylor.
9. F/L R.M. MacKenzie MBE DFC had graduated in June 1942 from Uranquinty – see Uranquinty Graduates Roll.
10. RAAF Historical Records, Microfilm 610, Item 101.
11. Caldwell D 1998 **JG26 War Diary**, Grub St UK, p. 152: Leutnant Kehl claimed this Mustang as his 3rd victory. No mention of strafing by the JG26 pilots.
12. Interview 2-10-98 JR Banyard.

13. RAF slang for the life saving flotation jacket that 'bulges in the right places.' Pilots preferred to fly in their ordinary uniforms plus this inflatable vest called after the celebrated buxom figure of Mae West, Deighton L 1977 **Fighter**, p. 126.
14. RAAF Historical Records, Microfilm 610, Item 139.
15. Fax 15- 3-99 FE Taylor.
16. Thunderbolt fighter aircraft fitted with bombs.
17. Letter 15- 3-99 HTB Taylor.
18. Interview 2-11-98 WK Merrett. Several of 164Sqn's pilots were Belgians, Canadians, New Zealanders and Australians.
19. Ibid. The rockets could be double hung to give 16.
20. Thomas C and Shores C. **The Typhoon & Tempest Story**, p.73.
    These landing strips were designated B (British) or A (American) according to their location within the nation's area of operations.
21. Wilmot C. 1952 **The Struggle for Europe**, Collins, London, pp. 402-4.
22. Thomas C and Shores C. **The Typhoon & Tempest Story**, p.79.
23. Wilmot C. **The Struggle for Europe**, p. 402.
24. Purnell H, **History of Second World War**, Vol. 5, p. 2033-2044.
25. Thomas C, and Shores C. **The Typhoon & Tempest Story**, p. 94.
26. Interview 2-11-98 WK Merrett.
27. Letter 27- 8-98 D Kingsbury.
28. Heavily camouflaged anti-aircraft positions beside a tempting target.
    Price A. **Spitfire**, p. 114.
29. Interview 2-11-98 WK Merrett.
30. Ibid.
31. Letter 8- 2-99 G Clissold.
32. Ibid.
33. Ibid.
34. Letter 27- 9-98 D Kingsbury.
35. Uranquinty Graduates Roll.
36. RAAF Historical Unit, Microfile 610, Item 12.
37. Letter 24- 1-99 J Curtis, Dakota National Air, Bankstown 2200.
38. Letter 15- 3-99 HTB Taylor.
39. Letter 7- 3-99 Mrs M Cousens, Yamba 2464.

Chapter 13

1. Multis refers to aircraft with two or more engines.
2. Ilbery P. 1997 'From Uranquinty to Britain with the Empire Air Trainees', **The Daily Advertiser**, 27 December, pp. 23-4.
3. 467-463 (RAAF) Lancaster Squadrons Association and Airfield Trail, Lincolnshire County Council. Major casualties (i.e. casualties that have to be reported to the next of kin) in the European theatre were 5,397; from Herington J **Air Power Over Europe**, p. 509.
4. Jefford CG. 1988 **A Comprehensive Record of the Movement and Equipment of all RAF Squadrons and their Antecedents since 1912**, Airlife, Shrewsbury, p. 93. ISBN 1 85310 053 6.
5. Ibid.
6. Wilmot C. 1952 **The Struggle for Europe**, Collins, London, p. 351, quoting in part Air Chief Marshal Sir Arthur Harris.
7. SE refers to pilots of single engine aircraft and ME to pilots of aircraft with two or more engines.
8. Lancaster N4783, AR-G of 460Sqn which flew 90 operational sorties.

9.   RAAF Historical Records, AWM, 81/4/135 and 779/3/135.

10.   Ibid.

11.   RAAF Historical Records, Microfile 610 Account of Dulag Luft given by S/L Simpson. Situated at Frankfurt it was the central Interrogation and Transit camp for all Allied Air Force POW.

12.   Ibid. Stalag Luft III consisted of five compounds and a compound a few miles away at Bellaria. Bellaria and East were all RAF and Dominion aircrews, North was mixed Allied and the remainder were American.

13.   **RAF Records in the PRO**. Section Three, R.C. Nesbit, London, 1994. ISBN 1 873162 14 6.

14.   Letter 15- 2-99 R McKenzie.

15.   Letter 31- 1-99 WN Howard.

16.   Interview 15- 2-99 Air Commodore Pickerd OBE DFC, 3 Tubb Place, Pearce 2607. He commented it was reassuring to be in disturbed air, indicating you were in the bomber stream. It was also reassuring to receive signals from the radio detection envelope, Monica, surrounding the aircraft, of the presence of accompanying friendly aircraft.

17.   They were parachute flares fired by the enemy which burned for a few minutes or so.

18.   RAF slang for death.

19.   TIs in the jargon were flares dropped by the pathfinders ahead of the   main bomber force and then assessed as to their position in the target area. If these flares were off target, flares of a different colour were placed and again assessed. From the air they appeared as blobs of red, green or yellow.

20.   A direct hit might result in a catastrophic explosion or follow a sequence of engines on fire – petrol tanks on fire – aircraft in flames – explosion. Little might remain – a badly burnt body, scattered burnt fingers and hands, a foot in socks, pieces of battle dress, scraps of clothing and equipment….

21.   Letter 31- 1-99 WN Howard.

22.   Shore War Service Project. In print.

23.   TEE EMM, 1942, Vol. 2, p. 205.

24.   Letter 27- 9-98 D Kingsbury.

25.   Strips of aluminium foil to obscure themselves as radar targets.

26.   Beaufighters equipped with four 20mm cannon and eight 25lb armour piercing rockets with "J" heads.

27.   Beaufighters equipped with torpedoes.

28.   The "long" runway at Sumburgh was 1300yds with the village at one end and the sea at the other. The "short" runway had cliffs into the sea at either end but with an emergency man-heightened hillock at the eastern end on which a Liberator had teetered and then perched.

29.   RAAF Historical Records, Microfilm Roll 84, 455Sqn.

30.   Gordon I. 1995 **Strike and Strike Again**, Banner Books, Belconnen, p. 159.

31.   Probably shot down by a FW190 from JG5 at Herdla (Norwegian Luftwaffe Units supplied by Alan Scheckenbach).

32.   To be required to ditch meant only minutes' survival in the freezing water.

33.   Interview 17- 2-99 K Pollard.

34.   Letter 31- 1-99 WN Howard.

35.   Letter 24-10-98 D Kingsbury.

Chapter 14

1. Air Board Agenda 3233/1941. Memorandum on the organisation and control of the RAAF serving overseas, p. 12.
2. Interview 31- 1-99 Heather Schmitzer, Pearce 2607.
3. **Units of the Royal Australian Air Force** vol. 2, p. 70.
4. Letter 28- 1-99 D Beaurepaire.
5. Interview 16-12-98 DE Yates.
6. Interview 6- 2-99 KE Goldring.
7. **Units of the Royal Australian Air Force** vol. 2, p. 76.
8. Letter 26- 2-99 KE Goldring.
9. Interview JD Humphreys, 70/381 Bobbin Head Road, Turramurra 2074.
10. **Units of the Royal Australian Air Force** vol. 2, p. 9.
11. **Ibid**.
12. Letter 5- 1-99 JD Humphreys.
13. Interview 8- 2-99 SB Robertson.
14. **Units of the Royal Australian Air Force** vol. 2, p. 15.
15. Interview 15- 9-97 RJ Davies.

Chapter 15

1. Herington J. 1962 **Air War Against Germany and Italy**, RAAF History in the War of 1939-1945, Vol. III, AWM, Canberra, p. 509.
2. Conversation 29- 3-99 Joan Tourle, Macquarie Street, Dubbo 2830.
3. **THE WAR DEAD OF THE BRITISH COMMONWEALTH AND EMPIRE. The Register of the names of those who fell in the 1939-1945 War and have no known Grave**. The Imperial War Graves Commission, London, 1958.
    THE WAR DEAD OF THE COMMONWEALTH. The Register of the names of those who fell in the 1939-1945 War and have no known Grave. The Commonwealth War Graves Commission, London, 1972.   Office of Australian War Graves.
5. Lindsay WR, Tynet Cottage, Spey Bay, Moray, Scotland.
6. Church of St Peter and St Paul, Langham, Norfolk, England.
7. **Airfield Trail**. Lincolnshire County Council.
8. Blundell H.M. 1995 **467-463 Squadrons, R.A.A.F.** (memento for the 50th Anniversary of VE Day), Sovereign Publishing P/L Cairns. ISBN 0 646 14991 1 and **463-Squadron R.A.A.F.**
9. 466/462 Squadrons' Memorial. Wings, 1994
10. Ilbery P. **Spirit of Wartime Camaraderie Preserved in Cairn**, Canberra Times, (1992), 22 August, and **How the Empire's airmen struck back**, Canberra Times (1998), 12 September, Panorama, pp 9,10.
11. The Beaus of the RAF Dallachy Strike Wing have been replaced by the current strike wing based at the neighbouring aerodrome of Lossiemouth. In the minds of those who flew wartime aircraft the Buccaneer might have been a stretched jet version of the Beaufighter but it is no longer possible to make comparison with the sophisticated Tornado.
12. Mordike J. 1995 **Australia's Contribution to the War in Europe: A Dim Memory of a Distant War ?**, Air Power Studies Centre, Paper No. 37, p.1.
13. **The Torchbearers of Shore Old Boys 1939-1999**. Shore War Service Project. Eds J. Gorham & C.J.L. Hewett, 1999 (in press). Out of 2,166 old boys who served in the forces, 629 (29%) served in the RAAF. Of the 227 killed, 118 (52%) were in the RAAF.
14. Friday 9 February 1945 known as 'Black Friday' by the RAF Dallachy Strike Wing when nine of its Beaufighters were lost to Flak and fighters in the anti-shipping strike in Forde Fjord, Norway.

Return and Epilogue

1. **Commonwealth Reconstruction Training Scheme**. Australian Army Education Service Information Booklet. NLA N355 115 0994 AUS.
2. **Return Journey. The Story of the Commonwealth Reconstruction Training Scheme**. Ministry of Post-War Reconstruction, Canberra, 1949. NLA, Np 355.1150994 AVS.
3. **Re-establishment Pamphlet, No.1 Training Scheme**. Issued by the Ministry of Post-War Reconstruction. NLA, Ferg/4367. There was a living allowance of three pounds five shillings per week and a book allowance of ten pounds per annum and an instruments and equipment allowance of 20 pounds pa for the first three years of study.
4. Department of Immigration, File 220/32/26, Uranquinty – Closure of centre. Australian Archives.
5. Ibid.
6. Ibid.
7. Department of Air, File 17-57-1, RAAF Uranquinty, 104A. Australian Archives.
8. Ibid., 79A.
9. Ibid., 97A.
10. Department of Air, File 17-57-1, RAAF Uranquinty, 121A.
11. Air Board Agendum No. 12442.
12. Department of Air, File 17-57-1, RAAF Uranquinty, 130A.
13. Letter 15-3 99 HTB Taylor.
14. RAAF File 3/19/Air, 14A.
15. Ibid. 12B.
16. Ibid. 22A.
17. Letter 15- 3-99 Jenny Lewington, Churchill Square, Uranquinty 2652 and Morris S. and Winterbottom J. 1995 'Hey days of the RAAF flying training school, Uranquinty', The Daily Advertiser, 30 September, p. 20.
18. Wilson S. **Wirraway, Boomerang & CA-15**, p. 76.
19. Letter 24- 1-99 J Curtis.
20. ULI is a small village on the main road (bitumen) from Port Harcourt to Benin City and Lagos. The road which ran through jungle was strengthened for a mile to make a landing strip.
21. Letter 30- 1-99 M Susans, Murrumbateman 2582.

Uranquinty Graduates Roll

1. The researcher of PORs in relation to the abstraction of lists of graduates would be puzzled by the following anomalies but which are explained in Chapter 4:
    Course 48: Awarded the Flying Badge on 16/12/44.
    Course 50: Awarded the Flying Badge on 13- 1-45.
    Course 57: Awarded the Flying Badge on 29- 6-45.
2. "Acknowledgment: RAAF Records". Filmed by HPA for Department of Defence (Air Force Office). This document is disclosed for the exclusive use of the person to whom access has been granted by the Department of Defence. The Commonwealth retains the copyright for this document.
3. **Died on Service** -   Deceased Officers 3,864
                             Deceased Airmen   7,089
                                               10,953.

Major Casualties among Graduates of 5SFTS

1. Herington J. 1962 Air War Against Germany and Italy, RAAF History in the War of 1939-1945, Vol. III, AWM, Canberra, p. 508.

References

Bean C.E.W. 1946 **Anzac to Amiens**, Australian War Memorial, Canberra.

Bennett J. 1995 **Fighter Nights**, Banner Books, Belconnen, ACT. ISBN 1 875593 10 1.

Blundell H.M. 1995 **467-463 Squadrons, R.A.A.F.** (memento for the 50th Anniversary of VE Day), Sovereign Publishing P/L Cairns. ISBN 0 646 14991 1 and **463-Squadron R.A.A.F.**

Bowyer Chaz 1981 **Air War Over Europe**, 1939-1945, William Kimber, London. ISBN 07183 02389.

Brook W.H. 1986 **Demon to Vampire, The Story of No. 21 (City of Melbourne) Squadron**, H. Kynoch & Co. Pty Ltd, Melbourne.
ISBN 1 86252 206 5.

Caldwell D. 1996 **The JG 26 War Diary**, vol. 1 1938-1942, Grub Street, London.

Commonwealth Reconstruction Training Scheme. Australian Army Education Service. AAES Information Booklet No.1 Arbuckle Wardell P/L, Melbourne, 1945. NLA N355.1150994 Aus.

Deighton L 1977 **Fighter, The True Story of the Battle of Britain**, Panther, St Albans, Herts. ISBN 0 586 04611 9.

Dutton G. **Flying Low**, University of Queensland Press. ISBN 07 0222 3662

Easton A. 1997 **We Flew Old Fred the Fox**, Lancaster PO-F (DV372), Hudson, Hawthorn.

Flying Training, vol. I Policy and Planning, Air Ministry, 1952.

Flying Training, vol. II Basic Training Overseas, Air Ministry, 1952.

Gordon I. 1995 **Strike and Strike Again**, Banner Books, Belconnen, ACT. ISBN 1 875593098.

Grey, CG and Bridgman L. 1941 **Jane's All The World's Aircraft**, The British Commonwealth Joint Air Training Plan, Sampson Low, Marston, London.

Hamilton T. 1991 **The Life & Times of Pilot Officer Prune Being the Official Story of TEE EMM**, HMSO, London. ISBN 0 11 772629 X.

Herington J. 1962 **Air War Against Germany and Italy**, RAAF History in the War of 1939-1945, Vol. III, AWM, Canberra.

Howard PF. 1999 **86 Squadran 1943-45 Men, Kittyhawks and Mustangs**, ISBN 06 46370294

Ilbery P. 1998 **How the Empire's Airmen Struck Back**, The Canberra Times, Panorama, Sept. 12, pp. 9-10.

Jefford, C.G. 1988 **RAF Squadrons, A Comprehensive Record of the Movement and Equipment of all RAF Squadrons and their Antecedents since 1912**, Airlife, Shrewsbury. ISBN 1 85310 0536.

Long G. 1963 **Australia in the War of 1939-1945**, Vol. VII, The Final Campaigns, AWM, Canberra. NLA 940 5394 AUS.

Long G. 1973 The Six Years War. A Concise History of Australia in the 1939-45 War, AWM & AGPS, Canberra. ISBN 0 642 993750.

Manual for Air Crew Reservists. RAAF Publication No. 93 (June 1940). NLA N 629.13 AUS.

McCarthy J. 1988 **A Last Call of Empire**, AWM, Canberra. ISBN 0 642 99503 6.

Menzies G.C. **The Royal Australian Air Force at Temora, Uranquinty & Deniliquin During World War Two**. ISBN 0 7316 8723 X.

Menzies R.G. 1939 **Empire Air force, Australia Plays Her Part**, Statement and Broadcast, Department of Information, Parliamentary Library, Canberra.

Mordike, J. 1995 **Australia's Contribution to the War in Europe: A Dim Memory of a Distant War ?**, Air Power Studies Centre, Fairbairn, Paper No. 37. ISBN 0 642 23472 8.

Newton D. 1990 **A Few of the Few, Australians in the Battle of Britain**, AWM, Canberra. NLA, NLq 541294 N562.

Partridge, E. 1945 **A Dictionary of RAF slang: With an Introductory Essay**, Michael Joseph, London. NLA N427 PAR.

Pentland, G. 1970 **Aircraft and Markings of the R.A.A.F. 1939-1945**, Lansdowne Press, Melbourne.

Price, A, 1997 **Spitfire A Complete Fighting History**, The Promotional Reprint Company Ltd, London. ISBN 1 85648 015 1.

Return Journey : The Story of the Commonwealth Reconstruction Training Scheme. Department of Post-War Reconstruction, 1949. NLA Np-355.1150994 AUS.

Robertson, E.M. 1974 **WAAAF At War, Life and Work in the Women's Auxiliary Austraian Air Force**, Mullaya Publications, Canterbury. ISBN 0 859140105. NLA N+ 358 412480994 R649.

Slack, F. and Glynne-Owen, R. **Roll of Honour 467 and 463 Squadrons R.A.A.F.**

Stephens, A. 1995 **Going Solo. The Royal Australian Air Force**, 1946-1971. AGPS, Canberra.

TEE EMM, Vols 2-4, 1942-45, Air Ministry, London.

The Torchbearers of Shore Old Boys 1939-1999. Shore War Service Project. Eds J. Gorham & C.J.L. Hewett, 1999 (in press).

The RAAF in Europe and North Africa. The Proceedings of the 1994 RAAF History Conference. RAAF Air Power Studies Centre, 1994.

Thomas, C and Shores, C 1988 **The Typhoon & Tempest Story**, Arms and Armour Press, London. ISBN 0-85368-878-6.

Units of the Royal Australian Air Force. A Concise History. Compiled by the RAAF Historical Section. AGPS, 1995. ISBN 0 644 42793 0.

Vincent, A.W. 1982 **Noble Six Hundred. The Story of the Empire Air Training Scheme with particular reference to 674 Australians who trained in Southern Rhodesia.** James Yeates & Sons P/L, Bairnsdale, Victoria. ISBN 0-9592069 2 2.

Ward-Jackson, C.H. 1945 **It's a piece of cake, or R.A.F. slang made easy; a light-hearted glossary of colloquialisms of the Royal Air Force, with some account of their derivations**. Sylvan, London. AWM 427.09 W2651.

Webster Sir Charles and Noble Frankland 1961 **The Strategic Air Offensive Against Germany**, 1939-1945, Vol. III, **Victory**, p. 287.

Wilson S. **Wirraway, Boomerang and CA-15 in Australian Service**. Aerospace Publications, Weston Creek, ACT, 1991. ISBN 0 9587978 8 9.

Letters and Interviews

S. Aboud, J.R. Banyard, D. Beaurepaire, I.S. Bensley, W. Boorn, H. Butler, R.J. Chivers, G. Clissold, V. Cranmer, J.E. Curtis, R.J. Davies, J. Dive, Marion Douglas, H. Dowker, K.R. Doyle,W. Fenwick, H. Frost, A.D. Garrisson, K.E. Goldring, G. Grace, F. Hall, H. Hansen, Edna Hillier, A. Hooper, W. Howard, J.D. Humphreys, Olive Jardine, D. Kingsbury, M. Lamont, M. Kerr, R.A. Leek, Jenny Lewington, D. Mackenzie, J. McDonald, R. McKenzie, W.K. Merrett, J. Millard, E. Pickerd, R. Piper, K. Pollard, V.H. Polley, S.B. Robertson, Heather Schmitzer, K.B. Sly, Joan Sullivan, M. Susans, F.E. Taylor, H.T.B. Taylor, Joan Tourle, Judie Trotter, Sheila Van Emden, E. Vonarx, R. Willcocks, K. Witt, M. Wootten, D.E. Yates, Pamela Yonge.

Abbreviations

AC2	Aircraftsman Second Class
A/c	Aircraft
A/C	Air Commodore
A/C/M	Air Chief Marshal
AD	Aircraft Depot
ADGB	Air Defence of Great Britain
AFU	Advanced Flying Unit
AGS	Air Gunnery School
A/M	Air Marshal
AOBS	Air Observers School
ASR	Air sea rescue
ATC	Air Training Corps
ATS	Advanced Training Squadron
A/V/M	Air Vice Marshal
BAGS	Bombing & Air Gunnery School
BCOF	British Commonwealth Occupation Forces
CB	Confined to barracks
CAC	Commonwealth Aircraft Corporation
CF	Communication Flight
CFI	Chief Flying Instructor
CFS	Central Flying School
CGI	Chief Ground Instructor
CRT	Commonwealth Reconstruction Training Scheme
D/F	Direction finding
DFC	Distinguished Flying Cross
DSO	Distinguished Service Order
EATS	Empire Air Training Scheme
ED/EMB	Embarkation Depot
EFTS	Elementary Flying Training School
F/L	Flight Lieutenant
F/O	Flying Officer
F/S	Flight Sergeant
FTS	Flying Training School
FW190	Focke Wulf fighter aircraft
GAF	German Air Force
G/C	Group Captain
GRS	General Reconnaissance School
HAC	High Altitude Course
HCU	Heavy Conversion Unit
IAF	Indian Air Force
IF	Instrument flying
ITS	Initial Training School/Squadron
LAC	Leading Aircraftsman
ME	Multi engine
MOD	Ministry of Defence
NAAFI	Navy Army Air Force Institute
Ops	Flying operations
OTU	Operational Training Unit
PDRC	Personnel Dispatch & Reception Centre
P/O	Pilot Officer
POB	Pilot's Order Book
POR	Personal Occurrence Reports
POW	Prisoner of war
RFC	Royal Flying Corps
SAO	Senior administrative officer
SE	Single engine
SFTS	Service Flying Training School
Sgt	Sergeant
Sqn	Squadron
SWPA	South West Pacific Area
TAF	Tactical Air Force
USAF	United States Air Force
U/s	Unserviceable
WAGS	Wireless & Air Gunnery School
W/C	Wing Commander
W/O	Warrant Officer

Squadrons

RAAF
3Sqn
4Sqn
5Sqn
10Sqn
21Sqn
23Sqn
25Sqn
31Sqn
75Sqn
76Sqn
77Sqn
78Sqn
80Sqn
82Sqn
83Sqn
84Sqn
85Sqn
86Sqn
450Sqn
451Sqn
452Sqn
453Sqn
455Sqn
456Sqn
457Sqn
460Sqn
462Sqn
463Sqn
466Sqn
467Sqn
65 Reserve Sqn

RAF
4SqnIAF
16Sqn
19Sqn
21SqnSAAF
30Sqn
42Sqn
43Sqn
50Sqn
51Sqn
63Sqn
73Sqn
80Sqn
81Sqn
82Sqn
88Sqn
100Sqn
101Sqn
102Sqn
103Sqn
106Sqn
110Sqn
111Sqn
114Sqn
126Sqn
129Sqn
130Sqn
131Sqn
136Sqn
137Sqn
146Sqn
154Sqn
164Sqn
166Sqn
168Sqn
174Sqn
175Sqn
181Sqn
184Sqn

185Sqn
186Sqn
193Sqn
197Sqn
198Sqn
199Sqn
207Sqn
214Sqn
215Sqn
222Sqn
229Sqn
231Sqn
232Sqn
242Sqn
245Sqn
247Sqn
250Sqn
254Sqn
260Sqn
261Sqn
268Sqn
274Sqn
295Sqn
332Sqn
514Sqn
550Sqn
567Sqn
575Sqn
577Sqn
587Sqn
609Sqn
614Sqn
615Sqn
620Sqn
622Sqn
630Sqn
635Sqn
650Sqn
553 Reserve Sqn

I ndex

A.B.C. (airborne cigar), 94
Aboud, S, 32,40,48,78
Accidents: beginners, heavy landings, ballooning, holding off too high, fatal, failure to lock tail-wheel, taxying, 49,53,54,57,61
Accra, 70
ADGB, 81,83
Advanced Flying Unit (AFU)
   5AFU Ternhill, 74,90
   15AFU Castlecombe,76
   17AFU Calveley, 68
   20AFU Kidlington, 40, 76
   21AFU Wheaton Aston, 75
Advanced Training Squadron (ATS),
    20, 41,47,57
Australian Imperial Force (AIF)
   5th Division, 104;
   6th Division, 89,104
Air Board, 31,33
Air Observers School, 32
Air raid; mass daylight, night, night & day, siren, 73,91,94
Air Training Corps, 28, 37
Aircraft,
   Anson,9,36,120
   Avro biplane, 30,36
   Battle, 9, 36, 37,52,78,100
   Beaufighter, 41,76,77,79,83,88, 95,98 100,105,109
   Beaufort, 77,100,101,102,105
   Boomerang, 40,63,100,104,106
   Boston, 69,83,102,105
   Catalina,102
   Ceres,119
   Flying Fortress, 80,82
   Halifax, 77,83,88,89,91,92,93,97
   Hampden, 91,96
   Harvard, 10,
   Hudson, 69,100
   Hurricane, xi,75,77,78,89
   Kittyhawk, 41,89,100,101,102,105,   109
   Lightning, 82,89,103
   Mitchell, 83
   Mosquito, 75,79,88,98
   Mustang, 75,81,82,88,89,90,96,98,   109
   Oxford, 10,40,76,100
   Lancaster, 40,61,69,70,78,83,88,9192,93,94

Liberator, 69,80,97,102
Miles Master, 74,78,90
NA16, 10,
NA33, 11
Sea Fury,122
Spitfire, xi,41,63,74,75,77,79,80,82,83,84,
    85,88,90,100,101,102,106,107,123
Stirling, 78
Sunderland, xii
Tempest, 84
Thunderbolt, 90,103
Tiger Moth, 9,11,32,36,46,74
Tomahawk, 75,89
Typhoon, 75,84,87,88
Vengeance,100, 105
Wackett Trainers, 32, 36
Wellington, 40,75,77
Warwick, 96
 Wirraway, 9,12,16,21,37,39,44,46, 49,100,
    104,105,106
Aircraft Depot, 1AD Laverton, 16
Aircraft Park,
    1AP Geelong, 9,
    2AP Bankstown, 9,
Airfield, B7, 84
Aitape, 101
Algiers, 80
Andes, 68,69
Anzac Service, 116
Anzac Wing, 96,116
Anzio, 83
Aquitania, 33,68
Archer, P/O, JS, 55
Armoured train (Jabofalle), 86
Article 1 of the Agreement of 17/4/1941, 4,
   Article 1/15 Sqns, 84
Ascension Island, 70
Athlone Castle, 69
Austerity loan, 37
Australian War Memorial, 11,92
Azores, 70
Bad Oldseloe railway viaduct, 94
Bale out, 75,86,88,92,98
Balikpapan, 107
Banyard, JR, 32,62,66,75,82,120

'Bar 20', iii
Barge sweep, 105,106,107
Battle from Britain, 65,91
Battle of Britain, xi
Beaurepaire, D,30,40,41,63,101,120
Belem, 70
Belly landing, 86
Belly tank bombing, 101
Bensley, IS,37,38,120
Biak Island, 101,102,103,109
Binbrook, 91
Bluie West, 69
Bomber Command, strategic bombing, xii,33,76,91
Bombing & Air Gunnery School,
   1BAGS Evans Head, 52
   2BAGS Port Pirie, 36, 37
   3BAGS, 100
Bombing technique, GH, 78
   target indicators, 94
Boomerang Club, 73
Boorn, W, 16, 19
Bournemouth, 3PRC, 73
Brand, F/L, 36
Bremen, Focke Wulf factory, 94
Brighton, 11PDRC, 73,78
British Intelligence, 88
British 3rd Division, 86,92
Bruce, Sir Stanley, 3
Burnett, AVM Sir Charles, 4
Burroughs, F/O DT, 61
Burroughs, PF, 80
Cabrank, 84
Caen, 83,84,85,92,93
Camp Miles Standish, 68
Canada, centre of EATS, 2
Canadian 3rd Division, 86,92
Cannon, 88,96
Cape Flattery, 69
Cape Town, Simonstown Naval Base, 66
Carey, J, 49
Casualties,RAAF, 7
Centaur, 33
Central Flying School, Camden, 1,22, 36, 39,
Ceramic, 65
Chappell, A, 32
Chapman, F/L L, 44
Christie, A, 100,124
Chivers, RJ, 75,120
Churchill Square, 24
Churchill, Sir Winston, xi
'Churchill's Own', 90
Clark, Alan, 89
Clissold, G, 25,32,75,87,88
Clyde, 68,70,73
Clyde Engineering, 10,55
Coastal Command, 76
Collett, PL, 94
Commission, short term, I,
Commonwealth Aircraft Corporation (CAC),9,
Commonwealth Reconstruction
   Training Scheme (CRTS), 118,124
Conroy, R, 49
Cook, F/L E, 16, 21 , 36

Coulston, Sgt JL, 55
Cousens, WL, 90,120
Cranmer, V, 61,120
Cross country exercises, 51
   unauthorised low level, 59
   forced landings, 49,
Crowley, BR, 49,
Curnow, G/C, 25
Currie, D, 68
Curtis, J, 12,90,120
Daily Express, 27
Daily Mail, 27
Danube, 94
Davenport, W/C J, 76
Davies, RJ, 30,46,62,106,107,111,121
Davidson, J, 100
Day, AM, 16
D-Day, 75,77,82,83,84,85,87,91
De Havilland, 9,11
De Havilland, Geoffrey, 75
Dive, F/O J, 24,37,44,52
Dive bombing, 61
Dominion Monarch, 66
Dunkley, E, 98,121
Douglas, Marion, 24
Dowker, H, 61
Doyle, KR, 24,46,121
Driffield, 92
Dulag Luft, 93
Duprez, David & Jenny, vii
Dusseldorf, 92,93
Dutneall, RA, 84
EE77, 19
Eddison,, F/L E, 24,41
Elementary Flying Training School
   (EFTS): 4,30,32,
   3EFTS Shellingford, 90
   4EFTS Mascot, 36
   5EFTS Narromine, 46
   6EFTS Tamworth, 32
   8EFTS Narrandera, 32,46
   10EFTS Temora, 46
   11 EFTS Benalla, 32,36,46
   22EFTS Cambridge, 75
Emmerson, B, 120
Empire Air Trainees, 7,13,31
Empire Air Training Scheme
   (EATS): xi,xii,1,
   1 Course, 30
   17 Course, iii,19
   air superiority, 2,5,78
   Agreement, 2
   precise implementation, 4
   syllabus, 16,35
England,
   familiarisation with flying conditions, 74
   invasion of, xi
   airfields, installations & communications, xi
Ewart, G/C U, 15,62
Exodus, Operation, 97
Fairbairn, Hon JV, 2
Falaise Gap, 87,93
Ferry Command, 69

Fighter Command, xi,xii,79,92
First TAF RAAF, 100,102
Fitter 2A, 17
Fitter 2E, 17,49
Fitzsimmons, A, 57
Fjords: 96
  Fede, 29
  Midgulen, 96
  Askevold, 96
Flak, 77,81,82,86,88,92,94,95,96
Flare pots, 61
Flight mechanic, 17,26
Flight rigger, 17,26
Flying Training:
  1FTS Point Cook, 1,35
  Civil Air Reserve, 35
  Aero clubs, 35
Flying in England:
  familiarisation schools, RAF Carlisle, Clyffe   Pypard,
Fairoaks & Theale, 74,76
Frost, H, 14
Funston, N, 48
Focke-Wulf FW190, 81,94
  FW200 Condor, 68
Gander, 69
Gardner, F/O Frank, 16,36
Garrisson, A/C ADJ, 1
Gelsenkirchen,
  synthetic oil plant, 94
Georgic, 97
German Air Force, xi
Gestapo HQ, 98
Gibraltar, 80,82
Glasson, T, 61
Gogerly, Bruce, 124
Goldring, KE, 102,121
Goose Bay, 69
Governor-General,
  Lord Gowrie VC, 61
  Sir William Deane AC KBE, 59
  HRH The Duke of Gloucester, 62
Grace, G, 17
Griffin, R, 51
Ground loop, 37
Hall, F, 20
Hansen, F, 124
Hansen, H, 49,
Harris, ACM Sir Arthur, 91
Hartnell, F/O, 49
Harvey, Gordon, 124
Highland Brigade, 66
Hindley, L, 101,124
Hill, C, 49
Hillier, Edna (James), 26
Hitler, Adolf, Panzer Division, 87
HMAS Cerberus, 122
HMAS Sydney, 122
HMS Victorious, 120
Hollandia, 109
Hooper, A, 17
Hopman, R, 77,93
Horn Island, 101,110
Horsa glider, 88

House of Commons, xi
Howard, P, 109
Howard, W, 48,57,77,78,93,94,97,121
Humphreys, JD,104,121
Hutchings, T, 59
Huxley, F/L FG (CGI), 16
Ilbery, PLT, 76,121
India, 90
Initial Training School (ITS)
  2ITS Bradfield Park, 30,65,66
  Somers, Sandgate, Victor Harbour, Clontarf,   30
Inkster, JM, 60,61
Intermediate Training
  Squadron (ITS), 20, 43,47
James, S/L K, 106,111
Japan, 97
  aircraft: Val & Oscar, 101
Jardine, Olive, 25
  (WAAAF Cpl McNeil),
Jet propulsion, 76
Junkers
  Ju52, 80
  Ju88, 80
Jubb, F/S RV, 92
Karachi, 70
Karsik, 101
Kerville, F/O, 36
Kiel, dockyards, 94
King George VI, xii
King, Rt Hon Mackenzie, 3
King, S/L John, (CFI), RAF, 21
Kingsbury, DH, 23,33,77,85,88,95,98,121
Kiriwina Island, Strip, 101
Klipfontein, 31
Lafferty, K, 49
Lamont, M, 59
Langham, 96,116
Lectures:
  airframes, armaments, engines,
  meteorology, navigation, ship &
  aircraft recognition, signals, 29,44
Leek, R, 17
Lewington family, xii,13
  return to former RAAF base, 119
Lewington, Jenny, 15,43,59
Link trainer, 30, 44
Lippiatt, F, 50
Liverpool, 66
Local Commemorative
  Activities Fund (LCAF), iii
Lord Beaverbrook, 69
Luneburg Heath, 98
Lurline, 68
M-Class minesweeper, 96
MacArthur's Headquarters, 105
Macchi Mc202, 80
MacGregor, G/C Alan, vii
MacKenzie, D, 121
MacKenzie, F/O R, 81
Malta, 80
Manna, Operation, 97
Mannheim, 94
Manus Island, 101,102,123

Manual for Aircrew Reservists, 28
Mareth Line, 80
Mariposa, 69
Marriott, Russell, 16
Master bomber, 94
Matsonia, 68
McCulloch, P/O, 36
McAulay, Lex, vii
McCosker, J, 120
McDonald, J, 78,121
McDonald, John, 12
McInerney, F/O G, 44
McKenzie, R, 30,52,77,93,122
McKissick, Sgt, 49,
McRoberts, Sgt B, 74
Memorials to the missing:
    Adelaide R, Ambon, Labuan,
    Lae, Malta, Moresby, Rabaul,
    Runnymede, Singapore,
    Sydney, 112-6
Merrett, WK, 40,47,51,62,67,75,83, 86,87
Mersey, 73
Messerschmitt Bf109, 74,80
Middlemiss, F/L S (CFI), 21
Millard, J, 10
Miller, A, 124
Milne Bay, 101,102
Misdemeanours, 23
Mitchell, WD, 76,96
Monte Cassino, 83
Montgomery, F/M Sir Bernard, 80,83,98
Morotai, 41,100,102,103,107,109,111
Morse, 33,44
Mortain-Falaise, 84
Mount Vernon, 68
Multis, ME pilots, 33,91,92
Munich transformers, 94
Nadzab, 101,104
Nash, M, 48
National Security Regulations, 13
Nathan, LAC, 49
Nav, W, 77
Negligence, 19
New Britain, 103,106
New Guinea, 101
Newman, F/L B, 111
Newton, Bill VC, 21
Nieuw Amsterdam, 68,78
Night flying, 61
    pundits & occults, 74
No known grave, 4
Normandie, 68
Normandy, 83,84
O'Connell, S/L T, 21
Oberg, F/O R, 40,51
Oil plant,
    Gelsenkirchen, 94
    Leipzig, 94
Operational Training unit (OTU)
    1OTU RAF Bagotville, 33
    1OTU RAAF Bairnsdale, 100
    2OTU Mildura, 41,61,101,102,104,111
    4OTU Williamtown, 105

7OTU Hawarden, 75
8OTU Parkes, 106
14OTU Market Herborough, 75
18OTU Finningley, 77
21OTU Moreton-in-Marsh, 77,92
27OTU Church Broughton, 40,77
29OTU Bruntingthorpe, 77
53OTU Llandow, 74
56OTU Tealing, 90
57OTU Eshott, 75,77
58OTU Balado Bridge, 75
59OTU Brunton, 75
78OTU Fayid (Suez Canal), 90
132OTU East Fortune, 77
Operations Room, xi
Ottawa, 3
Orcades, 66
Otranto, 83
Oxygen, use & failure, 70,77
    Mobile Oxygen Unit, 18
P/O Prune, 44,54
Palliasse, 46
Panama Canal, 66
Panzers, 84
Paxton, F/O R, 21,36,49,59
Personal Occurrence Report (POR), 15
Pilcher, S/L N, 37
Pollard, KG, 33,41,63,77,97,122
Polley, F/O VH, 1,16,21,36,59,122
Poona, 90
POW Camp Fallingbostel, 88
Priestly, R, 63
Prestwick, 69
President Munroe, 33
Prime Minister RG Menzies, xi,118
Public Record Office (PRO) Kew, 2,7
Queen Elizabeth, xii
Queen Elizabeth, 68,75
Queen Elizabeth II, 114
Queen Mary, 68
RAAF Base Uranquinty:
    acquisition, 13; advance party, 15
    closed down, 119; construction, 14
    site chosen, 13
RAAF Historical Section,
    Molly Angel, Richard Bain,
    Janet Beck, David Wilson, vii
RAAF Museum, David Gardner, 17
RAAF Memorial Uranquinty, 3,59
    Wirraway Park, iii, 59
RAAF -over-Europe, 91
RAAF Squadrons:
    3Sqn, xii,37,80,82,89; 4Sqn, 11,16, 104,105; 5Sqn, 105;
    6Sqn, 100; 10Sqn, xii; 12Sqn, 21; 21Sqn, 105; 22Sqn,
    105; 23Sqn, 105; 24Sqn, 105; 30Sqn,.41,100,105;
    75Sqn, 101,102, 105; 76Sqn, 101,102; 77Sqn, 102;
    78Sqn, 41,101,105; 79Sqn, 37,101, 102,106,108,109;
    80Sqn, 101,102, 105; 86Sqn, 109; 100Sqn, 105; 450Sqn,
    90; 451Sqn, 82; 452Sqn, xii,79,102,107,111; 453Sqn,
    79,82,84; 455Sqn, xii,76, 91,96; 456Sqn, 79; 457Sqn,
    41,79, 102,106,107; 460Sqn, 91,92; 462Sqn, 91,92;
    463Sqn, 91, 93,116; 464Sqn, 98; 466Sqn, 91; 467Sqn,
    61,91,116; Reserve Sqns, 23, 37

RAF slang, 73
RAF Dallachy Strike Wing, 80,96
Reid, I, 100
Reykjavik, 69
Royal Air Force, xi
Royal Air Force Squadrons,
    54Sqn, 102; 65Sqn, 96; 81Sqn, 80;
101Sqn, 94; 110Sqn, 40; 126Sqn, 77; 88,95; 130Sqn, 83;
136Sqn, 90; 144Sqn, 96; 148Sqn, 97; 154Sqn, 80, 82;
164Sqn, 83,84; 168Sqn, 81,98; 174Sqn, 87; 175Sqn, 87;
185Sqn, 87; 186Sqn, 83,84; 195Sqn, 93; 197Sqn, 84;
198Sqn, 84; 231Sqn, 81; 232Sqn, 80; 242Sqn, 80; 245Sqn,
87,88; 247Sqn, 87; 250Sqn, 90; 279Sqn, 96; 550Sqn, 93;
553 Reserve Sqn, 74; 609Sqn, 84;
Royal Canadian Air Force (RCAF),
    Squadron: 404Sqn, 96
Riverdale, Lord, 2
Robertson, SB, 31,105,121
Royal Navy, 66
Royal New Zealand Air Force:
    SFTS Wigram, 65
RNZAF Squadron: 489Sqn, 96
Ruhr, 85
Salerno, 82
San Francisco, 68
Sandell, RO, 80
Saunders, G/C, 2
Scherger, ACM Sir Frederick, 11, 20
Schmitzer, C, 48,57,100,101,102,107,108,123
Schmitzer, H, 122
School of Army Cooperation, 104
3 School of General Reconnaissance
    Squires Gate, 77
School of Instruction, 15, 20
Scott, J, 51
Scrub rate, 3,46
    pilot wastage, 52
Single engine, SE pilots, 33,76,79,92
Second Tactical Air Force (2ndTAF),84,87
Service Flying Training School (SFTS),4,
    2SFTS Forest Hill, 13,21,36
    5SFTS Uranquinty, iii,5,13,33,39,75
    6SFTS Mallala, 13
    37SFTS Calgary, 33
Shetlands, 96
Sicily, 80
Sissinghurst, 82
Skagerrak, 96
Slapp, HN, 61
Sloan, R, 77,93
Sly, KB, 47,60,77,123
Smith, DG, 93
Smith, ACW EM (Trotter), 62
South Africa, Union of, 3
Southampton, 68,73
Southern Rhodesia, xi,3
Stalag 17, 88
Stalag Luft III, 93
Stevenson, F/S E McLeod, 111
Stirling Castle, 121
Stone, H,
Storepedo flights, 106
Stratocruiser, 71

Sullivan, Joan (Symonds), 25,26
Susans, F/O R, 21,37,49,106,123
Swinderby, xii,91
Tadji, 103,106
TAF, 82,90
Tarakan, 107
Tatler & Bystander, 87
Taylor, FE, 46,47,65,73,80,82,124
Taylor, HTB, 47,68,75,83,90,119
TEE EMM, 44
The Monarch of Bermuda, 80
The Rock, 13
Thomson, B, 44
Thorney Island, 83
Tito; partisans, 89,97
Torokina, 106
Tucker, Sgt C, 49
Tustin, R, 117
U-Boat, 65,68,69,93
United Kingdom,
    Ministry of Defence, vii
    Air Historical Branch, vii
United States 5th Air Force:
    7th & 8th Sqns, 102
Uranquinty Graduates Roll, 125-156
V-1, 84,85
V-2, 84,85
Van Emden, Sheila, 26
Visual Control Posts, 84
VJ Day, 108
Vonarx, F/O Earl, 36,37,40,48
WAAAF: birthday, 25
    musterings, 25
    take place of airmen, 26,
Wackett, Sir Lawrence, 10,20
War cemeteries, list of, 157
Ward, Sgt G, 44
Ward, WB, 80
Watts, H, 51
Western Appproaches, 66
Westralia, 66
Wewak, 104,106
Wileman, WR, 121
Willcocks, R, 57,58,121
Williams, AM Sir Richard, 99
Williams, S/L I, RAF, 16
Williams, WM, 124
Wilmot, Chester, 92
Wilson, K, 82
Windmills; 88mm guns hidden in, 86
Window, 95
Wings Parade, 24,61
Wireless & Air Gunnery Schools
    2WAGS Parkes, 37
    3WAGS Maryborough, 22,32
Witt, K, 124
Wood, JB, 31,69
Yarragundry, iii,14
Yates, DE, 32,41,102
Yonge, Pamela, 24
Zebra markings, 6

Memorabilia

(David Duprez)